MAKING WAVES

MAKING WAVES
DAVID HASSELHOFF

THE AUTOBIOGRAPHY

WITH PETER THOMPSON

HODDER &
STOUGHTON

For my wonderful family, especially Mom and Dad

Picture credits

Front cover: Roman Saliki.

Back cover: Debra Hurford Brown.

First colour section: p. 1 – all photographs DHPC; p. 2–3 – all photographs DHPC; p. 4 (clockwise from top left) Universal City Studios, Glen Larson, Universal, Courtesy of V. Canakiah (www.Voodooknight.co.uk); p. 5 (clockwise from top left) MCA TV, MCA TV, *This Is Your Life*, Universal, DHPC; p. 6 – all DHPC; p. 7 – all DHPC; p. 8 (top) DHPC, (bottom) *This Is Your Life*.

Second colour section: p. 1 – Fremantle; p. 2 (top) DHPC; (bottom) Fremantle; p. 3 (clockwise from left) Fremantle, Fremantle, Fremantle, DHPC; p. 4 – all DHPC; p. 5 (top) DHPC, (bottom left) DHPC; (bottom right) Tonino Guzzo; p. 6–7 – all DHPC except Muhammad Ali (Howard L. Bingham); p. 8 (clockwise from top) Broadway TV Network, Billy Chicago Ltd, Eddie Sanderson, Nickelodeon, Colombia Pictures, DHPC.

Black and white photographs: p. 2 – Hirschfeld; p. 9 – Gary Smith; p. 10 – DHPC; p. 24 – DHPC; p. 40 – DHPC; p. 55 – Peter Thompson; p. 56 – MCA TV; p. 71 – DHPC; p. 72 – Danny McBride; p. 76 – DHPC; p. 90 – DHPC; p. 102 – Danny McBride; p. 108 – DHPC; p. 129 – Danny McBride; p. 133 – DHPC; p. 134 – Fremantle; p. 144 – Fremantle; p. 159 – DHPC; p. 160 – Fremantle; p. 168 – DHPC; p. 178 – DHPC; p. 182 – Wade Hubbard; p. 184 – Fremantle; p. 201 – DHPC; p. 202 – John Giles (PA/Empics); p. 208 – Danny McBride; p. 223 – Peter Thompson; p. 224 – Danny McBride; p. 227 – *This Is Your Life*; p. 228 – DHPC; p. 241 – DHPC; p. 242 – Nickelodeon.

Receiving my at Guinness Book of World Records
certificate from editor-in-chief Craig Glenday

Baywatch starring David Hasselhoff became the most widely viewed TV
series in the world ever, with an estimated weekly audience of more
than 1.1 billion in 142 countries in 1996. Covering every continent
but Antarctica, all 232 episodes were seen by a combined audience of
5.7 billion – just short of the population of the planet.

Part I: DRIVEN

Part II: BEACHED

Part I: DRIVEN

The many faces of David Hasselhoff

Prologue: My True Story

'My image is someone else's perception
of what my life is like. It's not the truth.'

Broadway – Opening Night
Plymouth Theatre, 31 October 2000

The stage manager asked me, 'Are you all right?'
'Yes, I'm okay. Now remember – I'm going to come off stage in between scenes and you're going to tell me who I am.'
'Yes – I'll say, "Now you're Jekyll" or "Now you're Hyde".'
'You'll give me my first line and you'll point me in the right direction?'
'Yes. Are you sure you're okay?'
I was far from okay. After forty years in show business, my childhood dream was about to come true. It had been a long journey. *Knight Rider* had made me famous. *Baywatch* had made me rich. But Broadway had always been my dream.
When I had stepped on to the sidewalk that night I could see my name in lights over Times Square. At eight o'clock a hush would fall in the Plymouth Theatre, the overture would begin and I would step on to the stage as the lead in *Jekyll and Hyde: The Musical*. This would be the greatest night of my career, the pinnacle of my success.

And I was terrified.

I was terrified because I was not only an actor playing a role, I had something to prove. I had to prove I was more than a guy who talked to a car, that I was more than a guy in red Speedos running in slow motion across a beach. I had to prove my talent to the world. More importantly, I had to prove it to myself. Walking along Forty-Fifth Street, I remembered the saying, 'Luck is being prepared for opportunity when it presents itself.' The question was, 'Was I prepared?'

At the theatre, I looked in the dressing-room mirror and said to myself, 'What is wrong with you? Why do you put yourself through this? Are you crazy? You're in the hardest role on Broadway, singing fourteen songs, playing not one character but two. You're opening after only five weeks of rehearsals? You must be crazy.'

Yes, I *was* crazy – crazy with excitement, tension and fear. From the age of nine, I had dreamed of starring in a Broadway musical. And when it didn't happen for many years I had lived by these words, 'Never, never, never give up.'

Now I had made it – except I didn't know if I would be able to speak, let alone sing. I said a prayer, 'God, just get me through the first note.'

Then the orchestra started playing, the curtain went up and I caught a look at the audience and I realised this was not a dream – this was Broadway. My parents Joe and Dolores were there, my wife Pamela Bach was there with our younger daughter Hayley, my manager Jan McCormack, my lawyers Eric Weissler and Alan Wertheimer, my business managers Bob Philpott and Peter Stoll, my press agent Judy Katz, my friends, my peers in show business, including many other Broadway and Hollywood stars – all of them were there. My mother's words came back to me, 'You can do it, David, you were born for the stage.'

The first notes came out of my mouth, 'Lost in the darkness, silence surrounds you.' The fear dissolved. The adrenaline took over and I was off and running. I didn't miss a beat the whole evening, at least I don't think so – to be honest, I couldn't remember a thing about the show except a standing ovation and a tremendous sense of relief. We had a huge party at the Russian Tearoom to celebrate my opening night all those years after I had first dreamed of appearing in a Broadway musical.

This book is my opportunity to print something from my heart, to tell the truth about what happened to me on the long and winding road from Baltimore to *Baywatch* to Broadway – and beyond. And the truth is not to be found in tabloid stories but in my actions: I am a good father and have tried to be a good husband. I love people and the emotional rollercoaster that goes with human relationships. The truth is I love all of the bewildering, crazy and wonderful things that life has to offer.

Let's get this out of the way: my image is someone else's perception of what my life is like. My buddy Chuck Russell, director of *The Mask*, *Eraser* and *The Scorpion King*, says, 'They don't call them congratulators – they call them critics. They put themselves on a higher plane than everybody else. Their job is to criticise but inevitably the audience decides.'

The fact is that the critics have made a great number of assumptions about me, most of them untrue, while the tabloids have never missed a chance to stir up trouble whenever possible. Because I worked with the most beautiful women in the world on *Baywatch*, they assumed I must have had the greatest job in the world. This was true up to a point, although nobody knew that the sand was hotter than hell and the water was toxic; that every week we had to bow to the dictates of what was perceived as a horrible sexist show that was becoming more and more popular around the world. Every week we had a girl coming to work with a different breast size, or a different tattoo that had to be covered up, or a different personal crisis that had to be resolved.

I'd look out of my trailer when the assistant director shouted, 'Rolling!' and the girls would drop their towels and I'd go, 'Thank you, God.' It was assumed by the critics that I was bedding them all. But I didn't have a great desire to mess around because if I cheated on my wife I knew I would also be cheating on my children and myself. I loved my wife, I loved being married and I worshipped my children.

When I was touring with my band or filming on location, the guys would stay out all night and come back with stories about the girls they'd met in the bars and clubs, and I would grin and they'd say, 'What about you? What did you do last night?'

And I'd say, 'I had the minibar.'

Girls would be outside my trailer door clamouring to get in and I would drink the minibar. My assistants got all the girls and I got all the minibars. Many minibars later, it caught up with me. I needed to drink greater quantities to get a buzz. In the end, I got very close to checking out, permanently. Over the years I had this recurring dream that I wanted to get busted, I wanted to stop. I wanted this whole drama to end. I just didn't know how to stop it. I was running away from my problems and it was killing me. The truth is that I tried to save the world and forgot to save myself.

When people stop me in the street today, nine times out of ten it's because of *Knight Rider*. It was a show about heroes, about a man who could change things, about a man who helped others. *The Knight Rider* slogan was 'One man can make a difference'. I truly believe that I got the role of Michael Knight for a reason. I was given a power that could be used in a positive way, far greater than anyone could imagine, to help sick and terminally ill people, mainly children who watched the *Knight Rider* programme and believed in its hero.

The person who made me realise that helping others was my purpose in life was Randy Armstrong, a fifteen-year-old leukaemia patient who visited the *Knight Rider* set at Universal Studios in 1983. After his death, I received a letter from him begging me to help other sick children forget their pain. The letter came with a photograph of Randy in his casket dressed in the Knight Rider hat and jacket that I had given him as mementos of his visit. From that moment on, I felt it was a spiritual calling and maybe it explained why I had been chosen as the Knight Rider. It was a much bigger responsibility than playing the hero in a TV show; I actually had to be a hero. My quest, my calling, had begun. From then on, we opened the doors of the *Knight Rider* set to any suffering child.

On my travels I visited the children's wards of hospitals in forty countries: I rarely left a country without visiting sick children. It became a mission. The children had absolute faith in the Knight Rider; he was their hero and he could make them smile and forget their pain, if only for a few moments. I've held little children as they faced death with a courage that had to be seen to be believed.

There have been many disconcerting and humbling experiences. One Christmas Eve my mother called me. 'David, a boy was knocked down on a crosswalk,' she said. 'Somehow his parents got my phone number – will you go and see him?'

The hospital was right around the corner from my home in Los Angeles. The child was in a coma, oblivious to his surroundings. I asked the parents what they would like me to do. They said: 'Maybe you could hold his hand and the darkness won't seem so dark.' After being with the boy for half an hour, I turned to the parents and said: 'Can I ask you a question? How do you retain your faith in God when something like this happens to your son?'

They said: 'Because you came.'

'What?'

'David, we know there is no hope for our child but we prayed that his hero would come and, David, you came.'

I fought back the tears and stayed with that boy for another hour. He came out of his coma, looked up and said: 'Michael Knight' and gave me a hug. Twelve hours later he passed away.

It has always been the children who are the true heroes and to this day they are still my most loyal fans. SpongeBob rules!

Today I am listed in the *Guinness Book of World Records* as 'the Most Watched TV Star on the Planet', thanks to *Knight Rider* and *Baywatch*, pretty funny with a name like 'Hasselhoff'. I had never perceived Hasselhoff as a name with charisma and power like 'Steiger'; it was more like 'Humperdinck' – funny and a bit of a liability but now I love it. Alexandra Paul, my best friend on *Baywatch*, once said: 'You can't really be an American and not know the name David Hasselhoff.' On *The Simpsons* the first words out of Lisa Simpson's mouth were 'David Hasselhoff'. Why? Because Jeff Martin, head writer on David Letterman's *Late Show* and later, *The Simpsons*, met me at a wrap party where I posed for pictures with him and signed an autograph for his mother. Ten years later, he told me Lisa's line was a nod to me.

This book is also about my travels and some of the amazing people I have met along the way. I was at Madison Square Gardens for a big fight when somebody tickled my ear. 'You're pretty, Knight Rider,' a voice said, 'but you're not as pretty as me.'

I didn't have to turn around to know it was Muhammad Ali. Then another voice said: 'Yeahhhh, buddy, but we love you.'

When I turned around, I saw that Ali was sitting next to Lou Rawls.

Another time, I bumped into Sidney Poitier, star of one of my favourite movies, *Lilies of the Field*, in a New York elevator. 'My God, you look like a teenager,' he said. 'Don't you ever age – what's your secret?' I was amazed he even knew who I was.

But fame is a double-edged sword: you get the best table in a restaurant but everybody watches you eat. And there is a dark side. F. Scott Fitzgerald said, 'Show me a hero and I will write you a tragedy.' I really wasn't happy. I had nightmares about losing my marriage and ending up alone. I had nightmares about getting arrested and being in jail. Even though I had achieved worldwide success, there was an emptiness inside me, an aching loneliness. I secretly and desperately wanted to be found out. I wanted someone to make the decision for me; I wanted to get busted.

It took God's angels to bring me to the brink of disaster and death to get my attention so that I could finally stop drinking and walk away from a marriage that was slowly killing me. And when it happened I felt ten years younger, ten years cleaner. It had taken me so long because I was afraid I would let my public down. I was afraid I'd lose my power, my career and the respect of my friends, but they were all still there, especially the power – the power of love, the power of positive thinking, the power to go forward along God's chosen path. It was a power I had learned at home from the time of my earliest memories.

This book is about my successes and my failures, my strengths and my weaknesses. And, above all, it is about the hope contained in the *Knight Rider* slogan: 'One man *can* make a difference.'

I was destined for Broadway . . . but it took forty years

Outside my grandparents' house in Baltimore, the city of my birth

1 Southern Dreamer

*'I had blind faith that I was going to make it.
I never doubted I would be a star.'*

Growing up in Atlanta, I discovered the power of dreams from Martin Luther King. I met Dr King's children when they came to see a performance of *Peter Pan* in which I had played Nibs, one of the Lost Boys. Remember Peter Pan singing 'I won't grow up' to the Lost Boys?

> I won't grow up, I don't want to go to school.
> Just to learn to be a parrot, And recite a silly rule.

Those words struck a chord in me when I first heard them. Writing them down again brings back a flood of childhood memories. When I saw Johnny Depp in *Neverland* I cried like a baby because that was my childhood – dress up and pretend.

'Dress up and pretend' became my life, it became my armour, it became my security. It took away my fears because when I dressed up and pretended, everything was all right. And it was fun. I could pretend I was one of the Lost Boys in *Peter Pan*. I could pretend I was Brutus in *Julius Caesar*. Then I would go home from the theatre, change my clothes and, back in the real world, hide behind my sense of humour because I was really a shy, insecure, self-conscious little boy.

The theatre represented freedom, innocence and fun. In the theatre, we were surrounded by people of all colours, beliefs and sexuality, and we accepted them all. It was easy for me to fit in because there was no racial delineation in our house and no distinction between black and white in my mind. Dad was always talking about his best friend, Earl, but I didn't know he was an African-American until I met him for the first time.

My hero was Sammy Davis Jr, Mr Wonderful, the entertainer who endured racial jibes and threats from gangsters but who never gave up. 'Just remember,' he told me, 'that if you give 110 per cent, the audience cannot fault you. They may not like the repertoire, they may not like you, but if you give 110 per cent every time, you're a winner.' His autobiography *Yes I Can* became a second Bible to me. Here was a guy at the top of his career who lost his eye in a car crash, but who went back on stage with a glass eye and always gave 110 per cent.

Sammy taught me that human beings must have dreams or they will go nowhere; that if you believe in your God-given talent, great things will happen and you will be given the power to help other people make their dreams come true. I was fortunate. From the age of nine, I had blind faith that I was going to make it. I never doubted I would be a star. 'Yes I can' were the words I lived by then – and still live by today.

My parents were made for each other. Dolores Mullinex and Joseph Hasselhoff met on a blind date in 1947 and have been together ever since. They were married at St Edward's Church in Poplar Grove, Baltimore, on 4 June 1949 when she was twenty and he was twenty-five. Dolores was young and beautiful, with long dark hair and a flashing smile. She looked a lot like the actress Loretta Young.

Dad says the reason he and Mom are still married is that they never talked to one another. This is one of his jokes. If things had been different he might have been an entertainer – that was his secret ambition – but he never had the opportunity. He was a child of the Depression when the most important things in life were an education and a job. Dreams had to be sacrificed, although he never stopped working to create a better world in any space he occupied, no matter how big or small.

Me? I was born at Johns Hopkins Hospital, Baltimore, on 17 July 1952, which makes me a Southerner and a Cancerian. I was christened

David Michael and raised a Catholic. In our house, everyone talked. Dad was a salesman for Brinks Inc., the armoured car people, and he talked for a living. My sister Diane was two years older than me. At four, she could outtalk Dad. Mom said she should stop talking and give me a chance to say something.

'And what happened?' Diane says. 'David never stopped talking!'

My parents belonged to a generation that believed implicitly in their country and the economic opportunities of the postwar boom. World War II had ended and the troops had come home to start families and tackle the problems of racial inequality and social injustice that had bedevilled American society for generations. I was a baby boomer who grew up during the Civil Rights struggle.

Dad was born in Baltimore in 1925 and named after his father, Joseph Vincent Hasselhoff. His mother, Myrtle, was from a large Irish family, the Concannons, while Joe Senior was the seventh son of a seventh son and, although born in Baltimore, he was half-German. His mother had emigrated to the States from Munich and settled in East Baltimore. The Hasselhoff name is of German/Austrian/Dutch origin. *Hoff* means house or village; there's a town outside Frankfurt called Hasselhof. In Germany, people posed with my photograph and said they were related to me.

Young Joe grew up as an only child in a rowhouse at 3631 Kimball Road, Gwynn Oak Park. He went to grade school at St Patrick's and then to Mount St Joseph High School before being accepted into the University of Baltimore. Joe always regretted not having any siblings but he made friends easily and looked forward to the day when he could start a family of his own. By the age of eighteen, he had developed into a fast-talking, self-assured six-footer with a great sense of humour and a killer mischievous smile, but it was his athlete's physique that got him a job as a guard at Brinks Inc. for sixty-five cents an hour to help pay his way through college. After graduation, Brinks hired him as a sales representative in Baltimore and Washington.

In 1947, Joe was also working part time for the Baltimore Post Office. It was thanks to this job that he met Dolores on the blind date. One of his Post Office colleagues, Mike Johnson, invited him to his house on New Year's Eve to meet 'a girl you might like'. There were just the four of them: Mike and his girlfriend and Joe and Dolores. When the clock struck midnight Joe and Dolores just looked at each other and then shook hands. 'It was the first time we had met,' Joe says, 'and we were too embarrassed to kiss.'

Dolores Therese Mullinex was eighteen years old and lived with her parents, Gertrude Elizabeth (née Taylor) and Winfred Louis Mullinix, and two brothers, Kenneth and Paul, in West Baltimore. Joe and Dolores started dating and after a two-year courtship they were married in June 1949. The newly-weds moved into an apartment that had been built for them at the Hasselhoffs' house in Kimball Road. Tragedy almost overtook them when Dolores was admitted to Bon Secours Hospital in May 1950 to give birth to their first child. At midnight, Joe received a phone call saying he'd better get over there quickly because Dolores was bleeding badly and might lose the baby. Joe spent anxious hours pacing the waiting-room floor before a nurse informed him that he was the father of a baby girl and that his wife was going to be all right. He wept tears of joy.

Dad learned later that Dolores had almost died and it was only natural that he should be nervous when Mom became pregnant for a second time. Dad was at work when he received the call to go to Johns Hopkins, where he was presented with his son. I was a blond, blue-eyed baby and, according to Dad, I was tall for my age – so tall that, he jokes, I was born on the 7th, 8th and 9th of July. He nicknamed me 'Smokey' after my blond hair. Dad drove Mom and me home to Kimball Road and took a few days off work to look after us. He says: 'When people ask me about David, I say I created him – my wife produced him but I created him.'

I get my outgoing nature, my love of people and my good-natured outlook on life from my father. I also inherited a lot of his sensitivity. My daughters are always saying, 'Dad, are you gay?'

I say, 'No, why?'

They say, 'You cry at everything.'

It's true: I cry at game shows. A new car? – I break down.

My single-mindedness and my work ethic come from my mother. She's a strong woman, very determined, incredibly and brutally honest. She spotted my natural affinity for performance when I was nine years old and gave me all the encouragement I needed to get started in show business. 'I saw you had talent,' she says, 'and gave you a little shove.'

My first memory is a happy one. I was being bathed in the kitchen sink of Gramma Myrtle's house in Kimball Road near Memorial Stadium, home of the Baltimore Orioles baseball team. Gramma splashes water over me and I remember laughing at something through the open window – a horse! In those days, milk, vegetables and groceries were delivered to the back door by horse-and-cart. The tradesmen would ring a bell to attract the householder's attention and then run up the back stairs and dump their produce on the kitchen table. I remember hearing the bell and seeing this huge brown horse peering at me through the window. I was around two and a half years old at the time. I still smile when I think about it today.

Living in the family house at Kimball Road enabled Joe to save money and three years after his marriage he moved us to a typical rowhouse with white steps in West Baltimore. By now there were three children, Diane, me and baby Joyce. When I was four in 1956, Brinks offered Joe a promotion to general manager south, based in Jacksonville, Florida. He asked Dolores how she felt about moving away from her family and friends. It was a big move for Mom to make with three young children but she readily agreed that Joe should grab the opportunity. He moved us to a long, low house surrounded by trees at Holly Oaks, Jacksonville, and went on the road for Brinks, opening up new offices at Tallahassee, West Palm Beach and Miami.

For the next six or seven years, we returned to Baltimore to spend summer vacations with our grandparents. I used to stand by the bus stop waiting for Grandpop, as we called Grandpa Joe, to come home from his work at an attorney's office so we could play games. One afternoon while he was taking a nap I put my cap-gun to his ear and pulled the trigger. The gun went off with a loud bang and Grandpop woke up with a start. He yelled at me and I ran like hell, terrified that I'd done something awfully wrong. I hid in the closet for an hour until he had calmed down. It should have taught me a lesson about playing practical jokes on people, but I still had a lot to learn.

For kids in Baltimore, the best days of summer were spent at the amusement park at Gwynn Oak Park on the big dipper and the Ferris wheel. For me, nothing was more exciting than climbing one of the telephone poles outside Memorial Park to watch Brooks Robinson on third base for the Orioles. In winter, I travelled up to Westminster to see the Baltimore Colts football team at their training camp. Johnny Unitas, the legendary quarterback in the No. 19 jersey and black high-topped boots, was my main man. I pestered Mom for a 'Johnny U' crewcut.

I still rooted for the Orioles and the Colts after we moved to Jacksonville, a sprawling town on the St Johns River in north-eastern Florida. By this time, I had another sister when Jeannie was born in 1956. As the only boy among four children, I started playing up to attract attention. At Christ the King Elementary School, I couldn't resist making fun of the nuns. One of the Sisters of St Joseph would waggle her finger at me and say, 'If you don't stop talking, David Hasselhoff, you'll have to stay behind and clean the windows.'

I'd shake her hand and say: 'Gee, Sister, I love cleaning windows.'

There were moments of delicious humour, such as the day my friend Neil Bell was misbehaving in church. One of the nuns hissed, *'Neil!'* and every kid within earshot kneeled down. As an altar boy, I spent quite of bit of time with drinking, smoking priests but never suffered any form of abuse. At home, our house was filled with love and laughter. We never went to bed hungry and we never woke up in fear of our parents.

At age seven, I got my first taste of show business when an advertising agency that was looking for a family with a collie dog phoned Dad. We had a collie named Lassie and Dad agreed to hire her out for a $50 fee. The agency was making a commercial for Texaco, the gasoline people, and the idea was that Lassie would be filmed jumping through the window of our station wagon on to the back seat.

Lassie, however, refused to budge. The only person who could control her was me and the only way to get her to co-operate was for me to lie down on the back seat and call her. Lassie then jumped through the window and the cameraman got his shot. I was fascinated by the whole process of seeing this little movie being made – the camera, the lights, the slate – and then watching it on TV.

The feeling that I was destined to act grew stronger when I saw my first show at the Children's Theatre in Jacksonville. I looked at Mom and said: 'That's what I want to do.' I wanted to be a musical comedy star. I wanted to go to Broadway. I knew in that moment that this was my calling. Having been denied opportunities herself, my mother gave me every encouragement. We soon had a row of costumes and props in our basement at Holly Oaks. My sister Joyce recalls: 'There was always a lot of imagination going on in our house. Mom pushed us all and we all tried out for shows. The whole family was involved.'

I fell in love with performing. The first part I played was Major Domo in *Rumpelstiltskin* at the Children's Theatre. Mom made me a suit with an Elizabethan ruffed collar and pinned some medals she had bought in a thrift shop on my chest. I carried a broom handle with a painted rubber ball on top. My sister Diane also made her stage debut in that play as one of the Miller's children.

My one line in *Rumpelstiltskin* was: 'Enter the king.' These were the first words I ever spoke on stage. The date was 18 April 1962 and even at age nine I had no fear of being in front of an audience. This first experience of acting was more exciting than anything I had ever done, although I needed some reassuring words from Mom when kids at school teased me for having worn make-up on stage.

Off-stage, I craved the same buzz as I got performing. I became addicted to excitement. After reading a book about a great hunter in Africa, I went on safari around the garden, shooting squirrels and birds with a BB gun. Not having a brother, I converted Joyce into one; she became my buddy and, although she was too pretty to be a real tomboy, we did a lot of guy stuff together. She also became the butt of my silly pranks. I once had a pet alligator, which escaped in the house one day and created panic among my sisters. There were more hysterics when I threw the beast into Joyce's bath and she chased me out of the house screaming 'Are you crazy?'. 'I hated that alligator,' she says.

We'd go down to the river near our house and play with the giant toads while keeping a lookout for alligators. We'd see alligators – fully grown ones – walking down the street. Lassie was too smart to get caught, but another boy's pet dog went swimming in the river and was grabbed by a huge alligator. A bunch of the neighbourhood kids hopped into a boat with our BB guns and tried to rescue him. We shot the alligator many times but the pellets just bounced off his hide and it was too late to save the dog. Our parents went ballistic. 'What's wrong with you?' Mom said. 'If you fall in the water, you'll get eaten!'

My craving for excitement was getting out of hand. I set my parents' lawn on fire so I could see the firemen put it out. The fire didn't seem to take hold and I was walking down the street when one of my neighbours shouted, 'Hey, your house is on fire!' I ran back and helped to put the fire out with a hose but not before it had burned part of the garage. I didn't admit to that little prank for about forty-five years.

I was a pretty rough-and-tumble kid, although I wasn't into fighting. I spent all my spare time performing in plays while everybody else was into sports. As I hadn't grown up in Jacksonville, I didn't have a lot of close friends at school; most of my buddies were children I'd met in the theatre. The theatre was considered effeminate and one of the older kids in the neighbourhood used to come over and tease me. He would knock me down and sit on me and I'd cry and when he let me up I'd run upstairs to Mom.

One day I said: 'Mom, the kid across the street is really bullying me.'

She said: 'You can't come in the house until you go over and deal with it.'

I said, 'Mom, this kid is bigger than me and he is gonna kick my butt.'

But she would not let me in the house. I remember crying outside the locked door.

She said, 'You're going to have to stand up to this boy sooner or later.' I got so angry about being locked out that I ran across the street and absolutely jumped on this kid and knocked him down. Unfortunately, he got up and then he beat me up, but Mom said, 'Good – you stood up for yourself. You can come in now.' That kid never touched me again – I had learned a valuable lesson.

On vacation, we'd drive up to Baltimore for a few days and then the whole family would migrate to a sixty-acre farm at Eldersburg, near Sykesville, in the idyllic countryside north of Baltimore. The farm was owned by Mom's Uncle Herbie, who held open house over the summer. Gramma Myrtle knitted all five of us little berets to wear on the farm. They were supposed to be in the Orioles' colours of black and orange, but Gramma was colour-blind and they turned out purple and orange. We were the only kids in Maryland in purple and orange berets.

Uncle Herbie's farm was a mystical place way back in the woods beside a river. We'd go picking blackberries and strawberries in the fields. One of our expeditions ended abruptly when we disturbed a beehive and Jeannie was stung eighty times. Uncle Herbie also killed a black snake which was so long that fourteen people were able to hold it. We accumulated pets: apart from Lassie, we had Hoppity the rabbit and Sydney the squirrel. And then there was Ducky-poo, a duck that followed us all the way home from the river to the farmhouse and refused to leave. The big event of the week was when the ice-cream truck came bumping all the way out from town over that rutted dirt road just for us kids.

Every night I'd take a shower, yet wake up with muddy feet. I couldn't figure out why until Mom told me I was sleepwalking. They'd hear me get up and, as it was considered dangerous to wake a sleepwalker, follow me out of the house into the yard. Mom's brother, Uncle Kenny, followed me all the way across a field before he managed to turn me around and guide me back to the house. Other nights, they'd hear me get up and find me watching a blank TV screen. This was happening every night; nobody except me was getting any sleep. Finally, when they were all exhausted, they solved the problem by locking my bedroom door.

From the very beginning, Dad had been recording all of our activities with a movie camera. These home movies provide an unfailing picture of my childhood from the time we dressed as cowboys and cowgirls playing in the garden when I was a three-year-old. There's me in a white suit for my first communion; there we are playing croquet on the lawn; there's me making waves as a budding surfer (a forerunner to *Baywatch*); there's us trick-or-treating at Hallowe'en; there's a Fourth of July party; there's the whole family at Thanksgiving. There is a lot of hugging and everyone always seems to be laughing. Like my dad, I'd already adopted the persona of family clown, making faces at the camera and generally losing my self-control. Dad sometimes constructed little scenarios for us to act out: prisoners in a castle escaping from captivity, or a dozen kids walking in Indian file with our heads through the rungs of a ladder.

Joe travelled great distances for Brinks but he still loved taking the family on road trips. Most weekends we visited a sacred Indian site or a ruined monastery or some other landmark. We visited a six-column, pre-Civil War mansion at Stone Mountain Park, Georgia, which turned out to be eerily similar to the house I bought in California many years later with the money from *Baywatch*.

One film clip shows Mom getting into our red station wagon for one of these road trips. Her hair – now blonde – is neatly permed, her make-up perfect, the skirt of her print dress slightly flared. She is the epitome of the American mother of the 'Ike Era', that golden time when the American Dream became attainable for many ordinary people. It was also the era when African-Americans demanded equality. Gramma Myrtle came from a white society that had been raised on the Jim Crow system of segregation under which even the amusement park at Gwynn

Oak Park was off-limits to African-Americans. We'd pass a 'Coloured only' water fountain and I'd say, 'What does that mean, Gramma?'

And she would say, 'It's for black people. They're nice but . . .'

I truly didn't understand.

Joe and Dolores, however, belonged to a generation which was determined to change things; they voted Democrat and were big supporters of President John F. Kennedy when he was elected to the White House in 1960. They brought us up to respect people irrespective of the colour of their skin. Dad answered my questions whenever I read stories in the *Florida Times-Union* or saw TV news film of violence against the peace marchers or freedom riders. Jacksonville's most violent day was Axe Handle Saturday – 27 August 1960 – when children and young adults taking part in a peaceful protest against segregated lunch counters at two department stores were attacked with axe handles and baseball bats by members of the Ku Klux Klan.

At the end of 1962, we moved to Atlanta when Dad was promoted to regional manager for the whole of the South. The city was built on a granite ridgeline deep in the northwest Georgia woods. As the nerve centre of the Confederacy, it had been blasted to pieces by siege guns and then burned to the ground by General Sherman during his 'March to the Sea' in 1864. We lived on Harris Circle in the middle of a forest, with Civil War bunkers behind the house. We built forts of rocks, engaged in pine-cone fights with other kids and swung across deep ditches on vines. In late spring, the dogwood would burst into blossom and we could walk to our school, St Jude the Apostle in Sandy Springs.

Atlanta, home of *Gone with the Wind* and Coca-Cola (and later CNN), was no cotton-and-corn hick town; it was an ahead-of-its-time, thriving black-and-white metropolis with a rich culture. I threw myself into acting at the Academy Theatre, Buckhead, which had been founded in an old TV film studio as Georgia's first professional theatre. Under the guiding hand of actor/director Frank Wittow, it offered a wide range of traditional and experimental plays.

This was the age of Beatlemania, although my own tastes ran to Broadway musicals like *Oklahoma!* and *West Side Story*, in which the songs were acted out on the stage. My voice was trained to hit the back seats of the theatre without the aid of a microphone. With Diane and Jean, I auditioned for *110 in the Shade*, a musical based on the

Broadway play *The Rainmaker*, and all three of us were selected for the children's chorus.

The musical takes place during a drought in a dust-bowl western state and the music and lyrics were by Harvey Schmidt and Tom Jones, both Texans, who had perfectly captured the lilting rhythms of rural America. The Atlanta production featured Dale Robertson, star of the TV series *Tales of Wells Fargo*, as the fast-talking rainmaker Bill Starbuck, and the Broadway actress Eileen Brennan as Lizzie Curry.

The show was held at the open-air Theatre Under the Stars near Stone Mountain and, except for the final night, it rained throughout the two-week run. Dressed in raincoats and sheltering under umbrellas, the audience giggled while the actors complained about the heat and Dale Robertson sang about the possibility of making it rain. He thought it was the funniest thing that had ever happened to him.

One of the other child actors, Gary Enck, opened a theatre in the basement of his house – the Valley Circle Theatre, a full-blown, non-Equity, twenty-four-seat house, where we performed many shows including *Annie Get Your Gun, Blithe Spirit, Oliver!* and *Once Upon a Mattress*. We even had our own little orchestra. Gary became my hero because I was eleven and he was all of thirteen. I remember thinking, 'Wow, this kid is cool.'

My greatest acting experience was in *The Fantasticks*, which to this day is my ultimate fun experience on the stage. Written by Tom Jones and Harvey Schmidt, *The Fantasticks* had opened at the Sullivan Street Playhouse in New York in 1960 and when it closed its forty-two-year run in 2002, it had become the longest-running production in the history of the American stage. After watching my performance in *The Fantasticks*, Mom had kissed me and said, 'You've got it, David – you're going to be a star.'

Our musical director knew Tom Jones and Harvey Schmidt and we travelled to New York to see the performance and meet the composers at Joe Allen's restaurant on West Forty-Sixth Street. On that trip, I stepped on to Broadway for the first time. From the moment I saw it, my dream was to appear in a musical comedy on a Broadway stage.

Back in Atlanta, I met Martin Luther King's children, Yolanda, Martin Luther III, Dexter and Bernice. Dr King, an Atlantan by birth, had led the public sit-ins and bus boycotts that had forced civic leaders to desegregate the city. On 30 August 1961 nine black children had been enrolled in all-white high schools. That afternoon, President Kennedy praised the city and urged other communities 'to look closely at what Atlanta has done to meet their responsibilities'.

I was in my schoolroom two years later in November 1963 when news of JFK's assassination in Dallas, Texas, was broadcast over the public address system. Children burst into tears. Our teacher told us to get down on our knees and pray for the President and his family. JFK was a Catholic and the news hit me hard: our hero was dead.

In ninth grade, I graduated from St Jude's and went to the Marist School at Chamberlee-Dunwoody on Atlanta's urban fringe. The school, owned and operated by the Society of Mary, or the Marists, was both Catholic *and* military. The worst students were enrolled there because no other school would take them, but it also had the brightest students because it offered the best education available in that area.

The mission of Marist School was 'to form the whole person in the image of Christ through instruction grounded in religious values, the teachings of the Catholic Church and the spirit of the Society of Mary'. The school motto, I used to joke, was 'Genuflect and salute.' I had the dubious distinction of getting terrible grades but was also considered one of the top students because I was the lead in all of the school plays. I was an outstanding student with a C average – and a D in self-control.

The night before my thirteenth birthday I slipped into our garage in the middle of the night and pulled aside a blanket. There it was: the hottest little go-kart you could ever see. I went back to bed but couldn't sleep, knowing I would have to fake surprise in the morning. Everything in this life is connected in some way and that go-kart was an omen that driving was going to figure large in my future. I was the only kid on Harris Circle with his own set of hot little wheels. I built ramps and made jumps and roared down the street with Joyce or Jeannie between my legs. The ramps got higher and higher and I'd turn the kart over or crash it. It got to the point where you could only turn left because the right steering bar had been so badly bent. I was a crazy driver but I had a knack for it. I was King of the Road – the Atlanta Flash. Obviously it was prophetic – I was the Kid Knight Rider.

The saddest memory of all these years was walking into my parents' room in our Jacksonville house to find my father sitting on his bed. He was crying. Dad told me that Grandpop had died. The sight of Dad's pain somehow took away my own tears. I hugged him and prayed that

I would never have to go through the same experience. Grandpop was only sixty-two when he passed away in 1961. Both of Mom's parents were already dead. When Dad had heart trouble in his seventies, he had a quintuple heart bypass that saved his life. He's still my best friend, my mentor and my guide; to this day, we see each other or talk on the phone every day. His positive attitude and sense of humour have always seen me through rough times. He is The Man.

Sandy Burke, my first love and high school sweetheart

2 This Thing Called Love

*'All I wanted was to act. That didn't
frighten me. Girls did . . .'*

Sex was a mystery to me. Girls would tell me I was good-looking and
it was like they were speaking a different language. It never
occurred to me to take advantage of them. I was a funny, outgoing kid
but I was also sensitive and painfully embarrassed about my skinny
legs. I didn't wear shorts for six years because somebody made a remark
about them.

My first girlfriend was Lucy Nouse when I was twelve years old. I was
so shy that I'd write down things to say to her on the phone but when
the big moment came, I'd panic and fluff my lines. It was agony. One
night she had a party and the lights were turned down low so we could
dance and I could kiss her. The Beatles were singing 'And I love her' but
I was too scared to make a move. Self-consciousness was a curse and I
was sure it had something to do with sex.

An older boy said sex was all about hormones. 'What are they?' I
asked.

'I don't know,' he said, 'but something is giving me pimples. It's got to
be hormones.'

Then Mary Ellen, the girl next door, kissed me in our laundry-room
and I started to think there might be something in this sex business

after all. When a crop of pimples broke out on my face and I grew some fuzz on my chest, I figured that my hormones were finally working.

There was no time to explore the possibilities of Mary Ellen before we were on the move again. Brinks promoted Dad to executive vice president in Chicago, and in early 1968 we moved into a large house at 222 South Spring Street, La Grange, Illinois. Diane stayed in Atlanta with Gramma Myrtle to finish her senior year of high school, then they both joined us in Chicago. Mom was expecting another baby and my fourth sister, Lisa, was born in July 1968.

The move meant that I went from a Catholic military school in Atlanta to a Chicago public school, a fairly traumatic experience. We lived close to my new school, Lyons Township High School, whose motto, *Vita plena*, meant 'the quest for a fulfilling life'. There were problems with my schoolmates from the very first day when I turned up wearing a red sweater and matching red socks. I thought I looked cool, although I soon changed my mind when guys nudged each other and said, 'Hey, who's the dork in the red sweater and red socks?'

Hasselhoff? What sort of a name was that? I took a lot of stick for my name but I told Dad I would never change it. In 2000, I showed him a copy of the *Guinness Book of World Records* and said, 'You've got one of the most famous names in the world.' Payback is a wonderful thing.

Meanwhile, Chicago was full of surprises. My sisters and I burst out laughing when we heard Midwesterners saying 'ruff' instead of 'roof'. But it was no laughing matter when I boarded a bus and heard people use the word 'Nigger'. It absolutely floored me. Living in the South, especially in Atlanta, had given me a completely different attitude towards black people. We would *never* use that word under any circumstances. I soon learned that Chicago was the most heavily segregated city in the North.

In all my previous schools, I had been brought up to believe that you had to be a Catholic to get into heaven; if you didn't believe in Jesus Christ you were going to hell. After my first week at Lyons Township, I said to Mom: 'Gee, there's a lot of people in my class who are going to go to hell. They aren't Catholics and some of them are real nice. I think I'm gonna go to hell with them.'

Our house was two storeys with porches front and back and a large basement. It was about a hundred years old and looked like the spooky house in *Psycho*. Jean was convinced the basement was haunted and we older children fed her fears with lurid ghost stories. 'You guys sure liked to scare me a lot,' she says. Uncle Herbie now lived with us. He wore a brown sweater and a mischievous grin and claimed to see Spaniards in his bedroom.

The sex thing was still bothering me. In church, I became aroused every time I kneeled down prior to taking communion. It was incredibly embarrassing. I wore long blue pants, shirt and tie and I'd try to arrange my clothing so no one noticed. Luckily, this only lasted for a short time, but I missed a lot of communions.

I still couldn't have a conversation with a girl without blushing. I did plays with girls but I didn't know how to date them. It was strange; I could perform a solo song-and-dance routine on stage or recite Shakespeare in front of hundreds of people but I could not go in front of my class and give a vocal report without playing the clown. I guess it was because I wasn't very confident in my schoolwork.

At sixteen years old, I was six foot three inches tall. I threw myself into the theatre morning, noon and night. My ambition was to get to Broadway as quickly as possible and I learned the scores of the latest musicals playing on the Great White Way. My grades started to slip but it all seemed worthwhile when, in my junior year at Lyons Township, I was awarded an apprenticeship with the Troupe of American College Players. That summer, I worked in three main stage productions with the troupe at Grand Lake, Colorado.

All through my junior year my parents drove me to acting classes, singing classes, dancing classes and music classes (I played the guitar and drums). They also drove me for an hour and thirty-five minutes after school to the Shady Lane Dinner Theatre at Marengo, Illinois, where I took part in dinner theatre. The manager would bus in senior citizens and we'd do shows like *When to Water the Milk*. I always played a kid's part; it was paying work and I was good at it. I found a real sense of peace, freedom and security on stage. Homework? I'd do that in the car on the way to the theatre.

The following year Jerry Wilcox, the high-school basketball coach, grabbed me on my way to class. 'You're a sophomore and you're six foot three inches tall – my God, it's incredible. You should try out for the team.'

I was up for the lead in *I Remember Mamma* and was spending all my spare time learning my lines. 'I'm an actor,' I said. 'I'm not really a basketball player.'

'No, no, no – you don't understand. We have a fantastic team but we really want you to try out for it.'

'Look, guys, I am an actor, I am not a basketball player. I know I'm tall but I've got white man's disease – I can't jump, I can't shoot.'

But they insisted so I tried out for the team. After about half an hour the coach came over to me and said: 'You know what? You're an actor!'

I still can't dunk.

Our acting coach (and director of most of our shows) was David L. Thompson, who lived two doors from us in La Grange. Mr Thompson believed in me. As my first mentor, he taught me commitment, dedication and hard work. He was a rough, tough guy but we became friends and he cast me in a new show every month, an invaluable experience for a budding actor. I was Brutus in Shakespeare's *Julius Caesar* and beat the two top contenders to take over the leading role in *I Remember Mamma*. Performances were held at the student-owned recreation centre of the Lyons Township Youth Organization, known as the Corral, in Willow Springs Road, adjacent to the school's South Campus. At the Corral, I reprised my favourite show *The Fantasticks* with a cast including Bill Stetz, now a talented Los Angeles photographer and still a dear friend.

It was in 1968 that I fell in love for the first time. Sandy Burke was the blonde, blue-eyed daughter of conservative parents. Her father was a former marine, a real ball-breaker of a guy with a handshake that could crack walnuts. Sandy and I started dating after she had given me a little help with my schoolwork. I could read *Julius Caesar*, work out the plot and memorise the lines but I could not figure out what algebra was all about; algebraic symbols looked like hieroglyphics to me. Sandy helped me. I sat behind her in class and started sweet-talking her so I could look at her maths tests. She let me cheat off her and I invited her out on a date.

Sandy was petite and very cute, and didn't know anything about sex either. On prom night we'd both had too much to drink and decided to experiment. We went back to the basement of her house but she passed out at the vital moment. I started to panic; visions of her ex-marine father bursting into the room and finding me with his naked daughter ran through my mind. There was only one thing to do. I knew that Sandy's bedroom was on the second floor so I loaded her on to my back and carried her upstairs. We had to pass her parents' bedroom on the way but fortunately the door was shut. I carried Sandy into her room and dropped her on to her bed. She didn't wake up, so I pulled the covers over her and sneaked out of the house.

Next day, I called her to see if she was all right.

'Did anything happen?' she asked.

'No, it didn't – but some of your clothes are under the couch in the basement.'

'Thank you for looking after me.'

Unfortunately, Mrs Burke was listening in on the other line and we were busted. The ex-marine ball-breaker started looking at me in a curious way, but didn't try to break us up. Sandy was quiet and reserved, while I was quite shy around people and that provided us with a strong bond of togetherness. We became inseparable, although after that one false start, we never got around to consummating our love affair. We remained virgins.

After graduation, Sandy's parents were relieved when she went off to college in Denver and I headed for Michigan. Next time I came back to Chicago I had grown a moustache and had an Afro haircut. Sandy, who had gone to a very conservative university, thought I was either gay or out of my mind on drugs. I was neither – I had just turned into a long-haired thespian who loved blacks, greasers and hippies. I didn't smoke dope or drink heavily – only beer at parties – but I knew our relationship was doomed. Next time there was a dance, I was performing in a show and couldn't accompany her. She went with another guy and ended up marrying him.

In 2000 I was doing *Jekyll and Hyde* on Broadway when a guy and a girl walked up to me after the show. It was like a flashback.

The girl said: 'Hi, I'm Sandy Burke's daughter.'

And the guy said: 'And I'm Sandy Burke's husband. I married your girlfriend.'

I said: 'Congratulations.'

The daughter looked like a clone of Sandy. Let's do the time warp again!

Back in Chicago in May 1969, I donned a green cap and lederhosen with long socks and trod the boards at the Corral as the star of a musical called *Wooden You*, based on the Pinocchio fairytale. According to the show's posters, *Wooden You* was about 'Pinocchio and Esmeralda searching for the path to Truth, Justice and the American Way'. For me, however, it was excruciatingly embarrassing, standing there in my shorts with my finger in my ear.

I graduated from Lyons Township High School in 1970 at a time of great social upheaval. Martin Luther King and Bobby Kennedy had been assassinated; America had put a man on the Moon and the country was divided over the Vietnam War. The cult movie was the druggie road odyssey *Easy Rider*, starring Dennis Hopper, Peter Fonda and Jack Nicholson.

David Thompson talked me out of going straight to New York to pound the boards of Broadway. 'You've got a terrific amount of talent but it's raw,' he said. 'It needs to be developed and the way to do that is to get a well-rounded college education.' Mr Thompson had already shown me that an actor needs discipline to be really successful. The reason that many successful actors behave like children is that we are misguidedly allowed to do anything we want. We have people to cover up for us because we are making money for the producers and investors: we're the engine that's pulling a massive train worth millions of dollars and they need to keep that train running, sometimes to a fault. I tell my children, 'It's show business, with the accent on business.'

My high-school grades were too low to get me into an accredited university – something I regret to this day – but I dreamed of being accepted by the Julliard School, the prestigious music, dance and drama academy in New York's Lincoln Centre. I travelled to Manhattan and stayed with an actor friend who was pursuing his dreams on Broadway. On my first night, he informed me that he was gay and took me to a gay bar, the Pickle Barrel, to meet his buddies.

The experience of being in New York and knowing that my future was hanging in the balance overwhelmed me – and so did the gay bar. I'd never been in a gay bar before and it was quite an eye-opener seeing guys with their shirts off kissing one another. For my audition the following day, I had chosen the monologue from Tennessee Williams's *The Glass Menagerie*. I'd performed it many times without a glitch but that day I suffered an attack of nerves and confusion, and was unable to do myself justice. I think I was still freaked out about my visit to the Pickle Barrel. Julliard accepted seventeen of the prospective students, including Christopher Reeve and Robin Williams (who became roommates and good friends). I was named as first replacement and, as nobody cancelled, I missed out on a place.

It was with a heavy heart that I enrolled at the Academy of Dramatic Arts at Pontiac, near Detroit, Michigan – a racially tense area. My abiding memory is how angry the blacks were with their lot in a white-dominated society. I had never experienced reverse racism and would have found it hard going had it not been for the friendship of two black students, Demene Hall and Bob Wright. We just clicked and called ourselves 'the Three Musketeers'. Demene and Bob showed me respect and unwavering friendship.

To help pay for my tuition, I got a job at a Clark's gas station. The workforce at General Motors was on strike and a spate of robberies had broken out in the Pontiac area. I was on my own at 11 p.m. one night when two guys pulled up in a car. When I went to serve them, one of them put a gun in my face. I had often wondered how I would react in such a situation; I was too petrified to do anything.

The robbers marched me into the office to get the money, most of which was kept in a secret safe, with only a handful of dollar bills in the till. They took the money from the till and I automatically walked over towards the safe. What was I doing? Fortunately, I stopped in time. The gunman ordered me to get down on the floor.

'Don't get up for ten minutes,' he said.

'Buddy, I ain't getting up at all.'

I heard them drive off and I was still down on the floor when another motorist burst in. 'I saw what happened,' he said. 'I'm going after them.'

He dashed out to his car and I got up and went to the payphone. We kept a dime on top of it to call the cops in an emergency but I was shaking so much that I dropped the coin and couldn't pick it up. Next day, the story of the robbery was in the local newspaper. I posted a copy of the paper to Dad.

He phoned me up and said: 'Okay, come home.'

'Dad,' I said, 'I'm already packed.'

I had been away from my family for six months and was greatly relieved to be back in Chicago. While I was applying to other colleges, I performed in dinner theatre at the Pheasant Run Playhouse at St Charles with Robert Urich (*Spenser: For Hire*) and Rose Marie from *The Dick Van Dyke Show* (my all-time favourite TV show). Rose Marie (her real name was Sally Rogers) had worked with all the greats from Jackie Gleason to Milton Berle to Red Skelton. I learned a lot from her professionalism. She always wanted the audience to feel that they had got their money's worth. If she felt the performance hadn't been up to par, she would stay behind and do half an hour's stand-up comedy. I'll never forget her – what a dame.

I was getting $35 a week but knew I had to complete my education if I wanted to make it in the theatre. Then Demene Hall and Bob Wright turned up at my house and suggested that 'the Three Musketeers' audition for the California Institute of the Arts at Valencia. Auditions were being held in Chicago and my parents put Demene and Bob up in our house while we performed in front of the adjudicators. Demene and Bob didn't get a place but I was accepted and made the trip to the West Coast. My fellow students at Cal-Arts included Ed Harris (*The Right Stuff*), Paul Rubins (*Pee-wee Herman*), Michael Richards (*Seinfeld*), Katey Segal (*Married with Children*), Lorraine Newman (*Saturday Night Live*), and Frank Darabont (*The Shawshank Redemption*).

Cal-Arts, founded by Walt Disney, wasn't the university I expected it to be; it had no recognisable theatre tradition and there was no great camaraderie among the students. This college was so bizarre that the faculty once showed up naked at a meeting with the owners. They were saying: 'We want the freedom to be who we are and to teach what we want.' Their idea of drama was esoteric plays like Buchner's *Woychek* and Alfred Jarry's *Ubu Roi* (*King Turd*), whereas I wanted to do one of Shakespeare's comedies or *Oklahoma!* or *Annie Get Your Gun*.

One of the heavyweights among the staff was Professor Herbert Blau, a respected experimental theatre director, very innovative, very academic, very avant-garde. Blau had staged some of the country's first productions of Samuel Beckett, Jean Genet and Harold Pinter. He was co-founder of the Actor's Workshop of San Francisco and co-director of the Repertory Theatre of Lincoln Centre.

But I wasn't ready for this school, where some of the students were tripping on LSD and eating magic mushrooms. Every week an ambulance would roar on to the campus to pick up somebody who had smoked too much dope or was having a bad LSD trip. My roommate dropped acid one night and announced he could fly. The only problem was that he *did* fly; he jumped out of a second-storey window and disappeared. We thought he had flown away. I told people, 'Wow, Bob just flew away like Peter Pan!' Three hours later he was found in a flower-bed, laughing his head off.

We said to him, 'We thought you flew.'

He said, 'I'm still flying.'

He was lucky he didn't break his neck.

It wasn't as though everybody was there to do drugs; drugs were just rampant at that time. Someone would say: 'Let's drop acid and go play football.' I'd say: 'Let's not drop acid, let's just go play football.' Coming from a conservative Midwestern background, drugs were a big downer for me. It was mind-boggling that people wanted to take stuff that would keep them awake for twenty-four hours and see monsters. I couldn't see the point.

The first year I stayed in the university dormitory and hated it. I'd seen so many people get wasted that I hooked up with one of my friends, David Stafford, and in the second year we roomed together in a ranch-style house. We bought a motorcycle and we'd take it up giant hills and do stunts just for the fun of it. We were glad to be away from the campus, where there was a lot of sitting around getting stoned to George Harrison records. I had dabbled in getting high occasionally but came to the conclusion that it was a waste of time.

Cal-Arts was a fully accredited four-year college course but after two years I felt as though I'd wasted my parents' money. 'We studied real hard,' David Stafford says, 'at having a good time.' I didn't feel I was learning anything worthwhile and I had an itch to see whether I could earn a living as an actor. Dad had bought me a red Pontiac Firebird for my first car and I drove to Santa Monica, where Demene Hall and Bob Wright were living in a commune on the beachfront after missing out on Cal-Arts. They were doing plays by Pinter, Joseph Heller and J. P. Donleavy with South Coast Repertory, a nearby actors' group.

Demene and Bob invited me to move in with them. In the beginning, there were seven people in that little wooden house at the edge of a broad beach overlooking the Pacific, but others soon drifted in until we had a big happy family of thirteen, ranging in age from seven to thirty-seven and including musicians, actors, dancers and people who were into psychic awareness. It was Alice B. Toklas to the sitar. The house had only three bedrooms so we knocked out the ceilings and created lofts, then converted the porch into another bedroom. No one had much money, so we did a deal with Safeway to pick up milk, fruit and groceries that had reached their expiry date and were headed for the garbage can.

One day I'd wake up and have nothing to do, so I'd work on the house. Next day, I might ride waves or lie on the beach all day. I had two pairs of blue jeans and a couple of shirts, and that was all I needed. We held group therapy sessions in which we lowered our defences to find out what each of us wanted out of life and how we could best relate to one another. Although I came from a loving family, we never said, 'I love you' to each other. It seems amazing because today those words are part of my everyday vocabulary with Mom, Dad, my children and my friends.

I sometimes visited the King's Head, an English pub just off the seafront on Santa Monica Boulevard, where I learned to drink warm beer and play darts – 'arrows' – with expatriate Englishmen. This was the time when Nixon resigned over Watergate and there were anti-Vietnam War demonstrations across the nation. The Summer of Love was long gone, the Flower Children had disappeared and we were wearing sunglasses in our hair.

One day there was a knock on the door and I found myself looking at a long-haired guy with a moustache who introduced himself as Chuck Russell. Chuck was from Park Ridge, Chicago, and our mutual friend Bill Stetz, who had starred with me in *The Fantasticks* at high school, had suggested he look me up. We became good buddies. The future director of big Hollywood films had arrived in Los Angeles in a Ford Pinto with $250 in his pocket. 'We were broke,' Chuck recalls. 'I was sweeping stages, yet we were plotting to take over Hollywood.'

However, I started feeling increasingly anxious that my career wasn't going anywhere. In search of work, I drove along the Pacific Coast Highway to Topanga Canyon, then – as now – Hippie Central, to visit Will Geer's repertory theatre. Will, America's favourite grandpa as Zebulon Walton in *The Waltons*, had opened the Theatricum Botanicum among groves of eucalyptus and oak after being blacklisted during the days of McCarthyism. Defying brushfires and torrents of floodwater that flowed right under the stage, his company had developed a fine reputation for its Shakespearean productions. In that leafy amphitheatre, I watched *A Midsummer Night's Dream*.

It inspired me to audition for a part in *As You Like It* in the Free

Shakespeare Festival at the John Ford Theatre. I got the role mainly because I could sing and there was a small part for a singing page. There was no money in it but it gave me a chance to work alongside John Ritter, twenty-four-year-old son of Western star Tex Ritter and the man who would later rule TV comedy with *Three's Company*.

Chuck Russell and I hung out together. I was clued-up and had a certain amount of Southern charm that could get us into clubs and parties. It sometimes backfired. One night at the Whisky-a-Go-Go, I quickly scanned the guest list at the door and spotted the name Pierre Cossette.

'I'm Pierre Cossette,' I told the doorman.

He looked me up and down and laughed. 'Pierre Cossette,' he said, 'produces the Grammy Awards on TV and he's short and fat.' But my chutzpah must have amused him because he added, 'Anyone who has enough guts to pretend to be Pierre Cossette deserves to go to the party. You can go in.' (Later in life, I met Pierre and told him the story. We became good buddies.)

All the while, Chuck and I were scheming our way into show business. We had no family connections and no funding, and encountered the usual prejudices. When you come from the outside, people want you to think Hollywood is something else, but I had a single-minded vision of what I wanted to do and it didn't overwhelm me. When people tried to make me feel insecure, it just made me stronger. I never lost the belief that I would make it.

After three months, I moved from the commune into a house with David Stafford and his girlfriend Judy on 7th Avenue at Montana. I looked around for an agent and found one who believed in me. Jack was a gentleman of the old school who drove me around in his Eldorado to meet all the casting directors. To broaden my cultural education, he took me to plays, the ballet and art galleries. Then he went to Spain on vacation and I didn't hear from him again.

After six months, I called his office. 'Has Jack died or something?'

'Yes, he had a stroke and died.'

I was so unimportant no one had bothered to tell me.

While I looked for a new agent, I became what everybody in Los Angeles becomes at one point in their life: a waiter. I was working at the Riviera Country Club when, lo and behold, Sammy Davis Jr walked in. I was so much in awe of him that I kept out of his way. He was with

Dean Martin and other members of the Rat Pack, all very funny gentlemen. They were also pretty good golfers and, I heard, huge gamblers who would place a bet on every ball, on every hole. Dean drank tall whiskies and soda. Later that night I found him wandering around in the bushes outside the clubhouse.

'Are you okay, Mr Martin?'

He assured me he was okay, so I led him to his car, a Stutz Bearcat. He climbed behind the wheel and drove off without a hitch. I didn't last long at the Country Club, however. On Christmas Eve, I mixed up a drinks order and the customer got shitty with me, so I jumped up on a table, stripped down to my shorts and then made a dramatic exit, saying, 'Merry Christmas to you all and good night.' I got a round of applause from the other members.

I took my waiting talents to the Marina City Club in Marina del Rey. The club consisted of three big circular towers, which were opening up to new residents. I worked in the main restaurant – the Gourmet Room – with a lot of other out-of-work actors. The clientele consisted primarily of divorced women who took a friendly interest in the waiters, all of whom were young, virile and single. After work, we were invited on to their yachts to party.

We had little scams. There were so many lobsters in the club's kitchens that rather than see them go to waste we'd put them in the dessert cart, push it into the elevator and press 'Park'. Someone down below would remove the lobsters and send the cart back up.

One of my fellow waiters was Bob Woods, who had returned to his native California in 1971 after fighting with the Green Berets in Vietnam. A few years on he became the Emmy Award-winning actor Robert S. Woods in the role of Bo Buchanan, the dashing police commissioner in the soap opera *One Life to Live*.

By day, I went body-surfing at Venice Beach on Santa Monica Bay, the huge stretch of open water that would later figure so prominently in my life. After work, I entertained one or other of the divorcées. Some of them were hooked up with slick, cool guys who had made a lot of money doing deals in South America. One girl invited me to her apartment while her boyfriend was away 'on business'; they were having problems, she said, and maybe I could cheer her up. I opened the refrigerator to get some ice for a drink and there were some big bricks of white stuff, property of the boyfriend, sitting on the shelves. I got the hell out of there without waiting for an explanation.

Chuck Russell was working his way up from sweeping sound stages to line producer and assistant director on low-budget films for schlockmeister Roger Corman. He got me a job on the set of *Death Race 2000*. 'I was the guy getting the coffee,' Chuck says, 'and I ended up directing the second unit. If you ran over a scene, they cut the scene. I saw they were falling behind and said, "Give me a camera and I'll do it." That was how I got started behind the camera.'

One of the girls in the commune who had been cast in a B-movie mentioned that the producers were looking for a male lead. I met with them and they said, 'We'll put you in the Screen Actors Guild and pay you scale if you take the part.' It was a big thing for a young actor to be accepted into the Guild, so I made my film debut in *Revenge of the Cheerleaders*. One reviewer described the movie as 'this 88-minute, mind-rot spectacular', while another commented that 'David Hasselhoff probably wishes he could excise this one from his résumé'. Sure, I would have preferred to play Hamlet at the Old Vic but *Cheerleaders* was a lot of fun. We were young guys and we had beautiful girls kissing us. It wasn't porn, it was all very innocent and, most importantly, it got me my Screen Actors Guild card.

My height had now reached six foot four inches and I was constantly being told that I was too tall for most roles. Most of the stars of the existing TV series were quite short – such as Robert Blake in *Baretta* – and none of them wanted to be upstaged. I got so desperate that I sent out photographs of myself in a moustache and told everyone I was Errol Flynn's nephew. It worked. Julian Davies of 20th Century Artists asked me to come in for an interview. His wife Dianne Davis made an appointment for me to see Joyce Selznick, niece of the legendary *Gone with the Wind* producer and founder of 20th Century Fox, David O. Selznick. Joyce and her partner Jan McCormack were casting the role of Elvis in a biopic about the King of Rock-'n'-Roll. By coincidence, she came into the Gourmet Room at the Marina City Club the day prior to my appointment but it was a hectic time for us waiters and I was too busy to speak to her.

I was due to meet Joyce at her office in Paramount Studios but after waiting for four hours there was no sign of her and I thought she must have forgotten about me. On the second day, she finally showed up, looking very tough, after I'd waited for another three hours. The first thing that happened was that her dog, Shamus, bit me on the leg, an inauspicious start. While I held a handkerchief to my leg to stop the bleeding, Joyce flicked through my book.

'Can you act?' she snapped.

'Yes, ma'am.'

'Bullshit! If you're this good-looking and you could act, you'd be working.'

'Look, your dog just bit me in the leg. I didn't wait four hours yesterday and three hours today to be insulted.'

'Sit down and shut up. You've got it, kid, so I'll take you on as a client. I'm going to make you a star. I'm a casting director but I'm also a manager and I only manage stars.'

Joyce had either discovered or helped to develop the careers of Faye Dunaway, Robert De Niro, Tony Curtis and many other big Hollywood names. At that moment, she glanced out the window and saw Al Ruddy, producer of *The Godfather*, heading for his car. She ran out of her office, jumped into her car and literally drove him off the road in her haste to introduce me.

'Here's the star of your new series, *How the West was Won*,' she excitedly told the bemused producer.

That was my introduction to the real Hollywood, the one that took me behind the security gates of Paramount Studios. I didn't get the job but Al and I later became good friends. I also auditioned for the Elvis part at the old David O. Selznick Studios – but missed out to Kurt Russell. Joyce, however, became my manager and introduced me to Joel Thurm, a casting director, who gave me a minor role on *Police Story*, the LAPD series created by author (and former policeman) Joseph Wambaugh. I played a valet at the Smoke House restaurant in Burbank, just opposite Warner Brothers studios where the show was filmed.

The Hasselhoff family had moved from La Grange to Somonauk on Lake Holiday, and Mom had alerted the whole town of 1,100 people to the fact that I was going to be on television that night. Just as I was about to appear, an announcer cut in to report that Mayor Richard J. Daley had won the 1975 Chicago mayoral election. His announcement blanked out my twenty seconds. My youngest sister Lisa, aged six, had been given permission to stay up late to watch the show. She cried herself to sleep that night.

I made amends with a walk-on role in a TV movie titled *Griffin and*

Phoenix: A Love Story, starring Peter Falk (taking time off from *Colombo*) and Jill Clayburgh. The plot involved two terminally ill people falling in love and acting out their wildest fantasies, knowing that they won't be around to answer for their actions. Joyce Selznick was casting director for this film and she cast me as a hang-gliding instructor who appears on screen for about five seconds and utters a single line: 'Be your turn in a minute, mister.'

My big break came in December 1975 when Joel Thurm suggested I audition for a role in the daytime soap *The Young and the Restless*. One of the stars, William Gray Espy – who had played one of the main characters, Dr Snapper Foster, since the show started in 1973 – was quitting.

'Go for it, kid,' Joyce Selznick said. 'This is your big chance.' Then she said, 'You've got to decide now whether to change your name or stick with Hasselhoff.'

I said, 'How about "David Michaels", after my middle name?'

'No,' she said, 'there is already a David Michaels.'

A few hours later while I was still deciding whether I needed a new name, Joyce burst into the room and, with a gorgeous, disarming smile on her face, announced, 'I've got it! It's perfect. "Eric!"'

'Eric? What – "David Eric"?'

'No – "Eric Hasselhoff". It sounds like you just got off the boat from Norway.'

'Thanks, Joyce,' I said, 'but I think I'll stick with what I've got. I took a lot of crap for that name when I was growing up and I'm proud of it. I'm going to make it famous.'

My first break on television was in a soap opera –
The Young and the Restless

3 Young and Restless

'Someone said youth is wasted on the young
and, boy, were they right.'

Just before Christmas 1975 I gunned the Firebird down Beverly Boulevard to CBS Television City, Hollywood, to audition for *The Young and the Restless*. Joyce Selznick had pumped up my confidence and spoken to Jon Conboy, *Y&R's* executive producer, but I was still feeling tense when I walked in. This was a golden opportunity and I couldn't afford to blow it. I had to psyche myself into becoming Snapper Foster, a dashing young medico from the wrong side of the tracks.

Television City had an awesome reputation in the history of American television. One of the gods who had performed there was Elvis Presley when he appeared on the *Ed Sullivan Show* for the first time in 1956 and rocked everybody with 'Heartbreak Hotel'. This was the home of such TV classics as *I Love Lucy*, *Dragnet*, *The Jack Benny Show* and *Gunsmoke* in the 1950s; *The Andy Griffith Show* and *Candid Camera* in the 1960s; and groundbreaking sitcoms such as *All in the Family*, *M*A*S*H* and *The Mary Tyler Moore Show* in the 1970s.

The Young and the Restless, created by the husband and wife team of William J. Bell and Lee Phillip Bell (and still going strong in 2006), revolves around the rivalries and romances of the residents of the fictional Midwestern metropolis of Genoa City. Since its launch on 26 March 1973, Y&R had revolutionised daytime television drama with its strong characterisation, socially conscious storylines and beautiful cast members.

Bill Bell heard my reading with mixed feelings. He said later that he thought I looked like 'an Adonis' but when he heard that I was 'an Adonis working as a waiter in Marina del Rey' and didn't have much TV experience, he wasn't so sure I could do the job. There was, however, something about me that made him take a chance and I was given an audition.

After rehearsing in an upstairs room, we moved to the set, where a disembodied voice commanded, 'Okay, David – hit your mark.' I looked around and couldn't see anybody, so I asked the stage manager, 'Excuse me, where is the director?' I discovered that the director was sitting in a booth like a command module and issued instructions to the cast over a loudspeaker system. This was not going to be easy, but I survived the audition and a few days later Joyce called me to say, 'Congratulations – you've got the part.'

One of the most difficult things for an actor is to replace the star of a successful show. After I had appeared in a few episodes, a sack of mail was delivered to my dressing-room. The first letter read, 'Dear David Hasselhoff, Every time you open your mouth I want to be sick . . .' It transpired that every letter had been written by a fan of my predecessor, William Gray Espy, who had been extremely popular with the housewives who watched The Young and the Restless. In fact, he was the show's Number One star. I said, 'How do I replace the Number One star – and why didn't anybody tell me?' Without exception, the letter-writers detested me; they wanted me to go blind, to have a car crash, to die of a horrible illness. The thought crossed my mind that these fans took their soaps so seriously that one of them might be deranged enough to take a pot shot at me.

The studio people tried to put me at my ease but these anonymous attacks had destroyed my self-confidence. The nerves came back when the cameras started rolling for my very next scene. The set was dressed with various props including a bowl of salted peanuts. Without hesitation, I reached into the bowl and put a handful of peanuts into my mouth to calm myself down. I spent the entire scene trying to say my lines through a mouthful of half-chewed peanuts, much to the dismay of my fellow actors. The scene ended in complete disarray with the disembodied director screaming 'Cut! Cut! Cut!' from his command module.

'What's with the peanuts?' he demanded.

'I have no idea,' I said. 'I just grabbed them.'

'Well,' he said, 'we have two minutes of footage of you picking them out of your teeth. Now, shall we go back and do it again as it was rehearsed?'

It was a bad start and things got worse. When they said, 'Five, four, three, two . . .' to cue me in, I would go, 'Five, four, oh my God, what's my line? Three – I can't do this!' And I'd freak out. I was psyching myself out of a tremendous chance to become a star on daytime TV. I thought, 'You're not making it here. You've got to do something about it.'

Working on a soap opera is tough enough without stage fright; it's a long day and there is a lot of dialogue to learn. Soap actors are gifted actors; it takes nerves of steel to do it day after day. I was in danger of losing the battle when Bill Bell asked one of the best actors in the business, Jeanne Cooper (Katherine Chancellor, the grande dame of Y&R): 'Will you work with him?'

Jeanne, mother of LA Law star Corbin Bernsen, was a marvellous coach of young talent and she agreed to take my career in hand.

'Your job is on the line,' she told me. 'You've got to deliver.'

Jeanne took me to her house and gave me acting lessons. After a few sessions, there was a marked improvement and I've always been grateful to Jeanne for her friendship and dedication. The nervousness persisted, however, and I thought I would have it forever until I ran into an acquaintance – another angel – who provided the remedy. This girl had been very fat but had lost a huge amount of weight and become a successful model. I asked her how she had done it.

'I read this book,' she said. 'You programme yourself.'

The book was titled The Power of Your Subconscious Mind, by Dr Joseph Murphy, and it changed my life. Murphy's programme was all about psyching yourself into the role. When I said, 'I'm going to be sick', I was giving my subconscious mind a statement and it believed it. So I tricked myself into believing I was calm and that I was here for a reason. It really worked for me. I learned how to programme my brain with a simple mantra: Five – you're here for a reason; four – take it easy; three

– believe in yourself; two – you can do this; one – let go, have fun. With this technique and Jeanne Cooper's incredible help, I turned it around and became the Number One daytime television star. I moved into my own apartment, a studio on Ocean Avenue for $325 a month. I thought I was rich.

Snapper Foster got his nickname because he snapped at people; his real name was William. When I took over the role, I turned Snapper into a more sensitive and charming person. I guess I gave him a heart and played him as a more sympathetic character, but it wasn't my acting that did it – I was just trying to remember my lines and put one foot in front of the other. Pretty soon, however, my dressing-room was full of sacks of mail from fans who actually enjoyed what I was doing.

My success had a big impact on my family. My sister Jean says, 'The rest of us wanted to kill Mom and Dad because all they did was talk about you for two long years. They got better after we threatened them.' Joyce, who was at Iowa State University, says: 'My sorority sisters and I sat around the TV set watching *The Young and the Restless*. The whole room was filled with girls watching David. It was embarrassing.'

Suddenly, the whole world seemed to love me because I was this tall young kid on daytime TV. Snapper was a very romantic doctor who never cheated on his wife Chris, played at that time by Trish Stuart. He had an Afro haircut, a disarming bedside manner and was very popular with the ladies because he was always taking his wife to bed.

I soon discovered that when you become a star, you don't change – everybody around you changes. When you go home, all your parents' friends say: 'Hey, how are you? Great to see you. What's it like out there?' When I went to visit them for the first time since I started work on *The Young and the Restless*, there was a big sign outside Somonauk saying: 'Welcome home Snapper'. I drove past thinking: 'How weird is this?'

One day on the set, a dream came true.

'I love you, Chris, but I must work in the ghetto.'

'But, Snapper, we have no furniture.'

The director called, 'Okay, guys, cut – next scene.'

I heard applause. Looking over, I saw a little guy wearing a cowboy hat, dark glasses, a lot of jewellery, tight pants and cowboy boots. And he called out: 'Hey, Snapper!'

The visitor was my hero, Sammy Davis Jr. He now knew who I was.

The Young and the Restless was his favourite TV soap and Snapper was his favourite character. I just melted. I said, 'You have no idea.' I started singing 'What kind of fool am I?'

Sammy started laughing. 'Don't be tall, don't be good-looking and don't sing,' he said.

We hit it off and became good friends. We came from completely different backgrounds but we were both driven by the same need for applause and success. 'You wear the hat of success well,' he said. 'Don't mess with the hat of success or it'll be taken away.'

Coming out of the Artists Entrance at Television City one day, I heard someone shout, 'Snapper' and saw seven squealing girls descending on me, pens in hand, asking for autographs. It took me a long time to adjust to being recognised whenever I stepped outside the front gate. Adulation messes with your head and the exaggerations in the studio's press releases made things immeasurably worse. I hated giving interviews to reporters who had read one of these hyped-up releases. I was beginning to feel as though I was a pin-up doll and not a real actor because of all the stereotyping that goes with the soaps. 'I'll never be happy until I respect myself as an actor,' I told one reporter. 'I don't want to be just another TV personality. I want to say, "I'm an actor: a learning actor." Just recently, I've been feeling I'm off the track again, and I get very self-pitying when I feel I'm not doing well.'

My girlfriend at the time was Linda, a twenty-five-year-old manicurist. We had a great relationship, or so I thought, because we didn't live together: I didn't have to call home and say, 'Look, I'm going to be late . . .' Very much in the spirit of the 1970s, she did her thing and I did mine. I wasn't ready to be tied down; neither could I stand feeling guilty or being dishonest, so instead of making up some lie because I wanted to spend an evening with another girl, I would just say upfront: 'I'm going out with someone else.' Usually, the other date turned out to be a bummer and I would end up thinking about how much better it would be if I was with Linda. But I knew that if I had stayed at home with her, I would have wondered what the other girl was like and it would have ruined our whole evening.

Confused? You bet – still am. I had a lot of painful lessons to learn about relationships . . . still do.

Most of my spare time was dedicated to becoming a recording star, with my own nightclub act like Sammy Davis Jr's. My first appearance as a singer came on *The Merv Griffin Show* in 1977. Backstage, I was with the other guests, Bob Hope and Shelley Winters. Shelley had a couple of drinks and started flirting outrageously with me. This – and the fact that I was on the same show as these huge stars – made me very nervous.

'And now,' Merv Griffin announced, 'here's David Hasselhoff making his auspicious debut singing the theme song from *The Young and the Restless*.'

I went on stage with all the bravado in the world and all I could think of was, 'What the hell does auspicious mean?'

I got through the song without mishap and I'm grateful to Merv for the opportunity. To this day, he says, 'I remember you on that show – you looked like a tall glass of milk with big hair.'

My voice teacher told me: 'Don't open your mouth unless you have something to say.' I had nothing to say so I stopped singing and devoted my pent-up energy to playing hard. I'd go out dancing and drinking and partying with girls – the whole trip. But it bothered me. I really wanted to use this energy singing on stage, so it seemed like a waste. I set myself a target five years hence to get my singing career off the ground.

We had a saying on *Y&R* that 'when the ratings are low, all the clothes go'. One of the show's most popular themes was Snapper's troubled marriage. He and Chris were always breaking up and this gave the writers an opportunity to conceive passionate love scenes between them whenever they were reunited. We had lines such as:

Snapper: 'I wasn't sure you were ever coming home.'

Chris: 'I am home now.'

Snapper: 'What am I supposed to do about it – welcome you with open arms?'

Dissolve to bedroom . . .

When I was doing *Baywatch* later on, I was half-naked most of the time but in *Y&R* I was very shy and found it difficult to take my shirt off and jump into bed. Then the writers came up with the scenario of a love triangle between Snapper, his wife and another Genoa City medico, Dr Casey Reed, played by Roberta Leighton. Casey tries to seduce Snapper away from Chris and the audience loves him because he resists the temptation. He's more interested in helping his patients than jumping into bed with this foxy blonde. The reason his wife has left him is that he has sold their furniture to help people in the ghetto.

'I want to fall in love, of course,' I told another interviewer. 'I'd like to have a one-to-one relationship with someone. Success, if you have no one to share it with, means nothing. So I'm looking to find someone to share it with. My basic goal, I think, is to be happy and respect myself. If I look in the mirror and like what I see, then I'm happy.'

I started dating Roberta Leighton and was surprised to discover that my private life was of even greater interest to the viewers than what was happening to Snapper on the screen. Some of the viewers separated the character from the actor and while they didn't like to see Snapper getting married on TV, they got a real kick out of reading in the magazines that I had fallen in love.

Roberta and I got engaged and moved in together. It was a dramatic relationship, very wild and passionate. We were young and free and full of young hormones. I could stay up all night long and go to work after an hour's sleep, yet still memorise my lines. I was my biggest enabler – not a good thing – but I'd worked very hard for my success and took full advantage of everything on offer. But after a while it became apparent that I'd been given too much too quickly; I became complacent and started to take my work for granted. Roberta, meanwhile, was having trouble keeping up with me. Our relationship began to crumble when I realised that I wasn't ready to get married and settle down. I wasn't in love; we split up.

This created difficulties because we still had to work together. The day after the break-up I had to film a love scene with her in which Casey tries to seduce Snapper, even though she knows he's married and faithful to his wife. It was very disconcerting. I was waiting for the ultimate slap – I knew it was coming and I knew I deserved it. When I rejected her advances in the scene, she let rip with an almighty whack that rattled my brains. Then she stormed off the set.

The director came up, concerned. 'That wasn't in the script.'

'It's okay – don't ask.'

I was lucky to get out of it with a slap.

By the time I was twenty-six I was burning the candle at both ends – partying all night and working all day. When you're on a show like Y&R you're on top of the world but there are problems. I saw many people on the show spin out of control and become substance abusers because they had no time to unwind. As Robin Williams wisely observed about that period, 'Cocaine is God's way of telling you you're making too much money.'

The scripts were invariably concerned with conflict and drama – there was rarely anything happy – and we would be crying and fighting all through the working day. Then we'd have to go home and learn the next forty pages of dialogue for the following day's shoot and, in the morning, bring our emotions up to the required pitch. As I say, I saw people spin out on the set and eventually it happened to me.

I had reached the point where I found it impossible to go home and learn my lines every night. Instead, I drank and partied and chased girls and came home at 3 a.m. and thought, 'I'll learn my lines in the morning.' I got so good at it that I could stay out until 3 a.m., go to bed and get up at six. With three hours' sleep, I'd drive to the studio, learn my lines, get through the first rehearsal coffee'd up, and then sleep between seven and nine to take the edge off it. When I woke up, I'd be ready to work and I'd be perfect – or so I thought.

When we wrapped for the day around four o'clock, the thought of going home and being alone was just too much. Even though I'd said to myself that very morning, 'I'll never do this again', I'd start to change my mind. The little guy on my shoulder would say, 'Hey, that wasn't so bad – let's party. You can do it – you deserve it.' So I'd hit the bars again, with similar consequences. There's a saying that repeating the same failed experiment expecting a different result is a definition of insanity. I was living that saying.

It was a lonely experience but the loneliness was internal; even when I was surrounded by other people, I felt as though I was alone. Beer and tequila and scotch were my thing in the clubs. I'd wake up across town with someone and think, 'Oh-oh, I've got to go to work.' When I finally addressed the issue, I realised that the alcohol problem wasn't a sudden phenomenon but that it had caught up with me over many years. I realised that even back then, in the 1970s, I had been drinking to kill anxiety and loneliness.

At the time, I solved the problem of learning my lines by taking cue cards on to the set. After a hard night's drinking and chasing girls, I'd go straight to work. The director didn't like my attitude and took the cards away but when I signed for another year I made it a condition that I could use them. I cleared it with the other actors and made sure I was never late and never missed a scene. We called it 'beat the light' –

when the light was on Trish or Roberta, I knew I was off-camera and I would quickly read my next line before it turned on to me. It wasn't much fun for my fellow actors and I regret that, but I was frustrated with my job. I craved more challenging work – I wanted Broadway.

Meanwhile, my private life had taken a dangerous turn. I'd invited a young woman to move into my house in the San Fernando Valley. One morning she held up a knife.

'I could have killed you in your sleep.'

'It's a beautiful morning,' I said. 'Why don't I make breakfast?'

I got up and fled to the kitchen. I realised my new lover was psychotic and that I had to get out of this relationship and slow down a bit. That afternoon I closed a deal on a house in the Hollywood Hills. I went home and told her that I was moving out and she wasn't coming with me. My sister Joyce had moved to Los Angeles and moved in with me. She ran the house on Coldwater Canyon and acted as my secretary, taking care of my fan club and my diary. Joyce has been an angel in my life and has helped me through some troubling times.

After four years on *The Young and the Restless*, I'd gone as far as I could go with Snapper Foster. I was desperate to escape from *Y&R* but I was locked into a cast-iron contract. However, nobody could stop me from taking the occasional movie part. Joyce Selznick got me a tiny role in *California Suite*, the Neil Simon comedy with a huge star-studded cast including Maggie Smith, Michael Caine, Jane Fonda, Alan Alda, Richard Pryor, Bill Cosby and Walter Matthau. I played Maggie Smith's lover in her attempt to win back the affections of her homosexual husband (Michael Caine). It was only a walk-on role and I had forgotten all about it until, years later, I saw the film on TV and recognised myself.

I was offered a bigger role – and a $10,000 fee – in *Star Crash*, a cheap Italian rip-off of *Star Wars* directed by Luigi Cozzi in which I play Prince Simon, son and heir to the Emperor of the Galaxy (Christopher Plummer, light years away from his triumph as Captain von Trapp in *The Sound of Music*). The heroine, Stella Star (former Bond girl Caroline Munro in a spectacular leather bikini) has to rescue Simon from the clutches of Count Zarth Arn (Joe Spinell), evil leader of the League of the Dark Worlds who has a doom machine which projects red monsters into space that drive astronauts mad . . .

We filmed these scenes at the Cinecita studios, Rome, in spray-painted star buggies on a plastic set surrounded by flashing neon lights and exploding papier-mâché planets. My parents flew over and I joined them for a sightseeing trip of Florence. I have always included my family in all of my travels around the globe. We also did location work at Bari in southern Italy, where I was struck down with food poisoning but it didn't stop me working. The director just wanted me to say the alphabet to get my mouth moving so he could dub something else in there. The film was released in 1979 to universal derision (it was so bad it has since become a classic example of the spaghetti space opera).

My chance to break away from Y&R came in September of that year when the producers decided to extend the show from half an hour to an hour, an eventuality that wasn't covered in my contract. It meant I could not automatically be committed to the new format, so an escape hatch had opened up. I was offered a role in the pilot episode of *Pleasure Cove*, a series that hoped to cash in on the popularity of *Love Boat* and *Fantasy Island*. Tom Jones, the immensely popular Welsh singer, was one of the stars. In one scene, we spent half an hour or so floundering around in the water. 'I'm an entertainer,' he complained, 'not an effing frogman.' Tom's worries were needless, *Pleasure Cove* disappeared into the place they call 'busted-pilot purgatory', never to be seen again.

I tried again in spring 1980 when producer David Merrick sold the idea to ABC of converting his successful big league professional football movie *Semi-Tough* into a prime-time TV series. The film centres on the comic misadventures of two womanising members of the luckless New York Bulls football team. The two teammates and roommates, Billy Clyde Puckett (Burt Reynolds) and 'Shake' Tiller (Kris Kristofferson) find their lives upended when they both fall for the same woman, Barbara Jane 'B. J.' Bookman (Jill Clayburgh).

The pilot episode had been aired on ABC on 6 January 1980 featuring Mary Louise Weller as Barbara Jane, Douglas Barr as Billy Clyde, and Josh Taylor as Shake Tiller. When the first episode was shown in May, however, there were three new leads: Markie Post as Barbara Jane, Bruce McGill as Billy Clyde and me as Shake Tiller. It was a big leap from daytime to prime time, but I was confident that with a lot of hard work I could make the transition. I'd made a deal with CBS that if *Semi-Tough* was a success, I'd quit *Y&R* but in the meantime I'd do both shows at the same time. It was an insane arrangement. I filmed *Semi-

Tough during the week at ABC and, because Snapper was so popular, CBS filmed me in *Y&R* at weekends.

Semi-Tough, however, didn't work out; it was only semi-funny. It fizzed briefly and then fizzled out completely after only four episodes. I returned to *The Young and the Restless* feeling like a failure after thinking I'd broken free. You get typecast as a soap star and very few people succeed in making the break – Tom Selleck had been in *Y&R* for two seasons before he had broken out in *Magnum, PI*, while Gwyneth Paltrow and Meg Ryan both made it big in the movies through sheer talent. Going from soap opera to prime time and then to feature films is intimidating: it's made out to be such a different world and there is a great deal of prejudice and animosity towards soap actors.

'Oh, you're a soap star – that's not good enough for prime time.' Or: 'Oh, you're a television star – you're not good enough for the movies.'

Subconsciously, no matter how hard I tried to ignore it, this negativity took up residence in my head and, as I didn't seem to be getting anywhere, it stayed there. In 1981, I tested for three prime-time shows, *T. J. Hooker*, *Today's FBI* and *Strike Force*. I didn't get any of them. Since only one of the series survived, that was probably a blessing.

These setbacks were nothing compared with the shock I got when Joyce Selznick was diagnosed with cancer. She was dying when I visited her in hospital. I promised her: 'I will be the star you always said I would be.' Joyce Selznick died on 17 September 1981; her young partner Jan McCormack took over as my manager.

My sister Diane rang me from her home in Houston. 'I've got a small lump on my breast,' she said. 'The doctor says if it's not cancerous they'll remove the lump. Otherwise, they'll take the breast.'

Next day, she called me up from hospital. 'I woke up and there was no breast.'

I was heartbroken. I flew to Houston and dressed up in my doctor's uniform to visit her in hospital. When I walked into her room, I held a clipboard in front of my face.

Diane said, 'Are you a new doctor?'

'Yeah.'

I dropped the clipboard.

'I'm Dr Snapper.'

I hugged her and we shared a few tears. Then I went back to Los

Angeles. She rang me. 'Don't ever come and see me again,' she said. 'I haven't slept since you've been here. Every nurse wants to know, "Are you David Hasselhoff's sister?" '

My life was at a crossroads. I wasn't happy on *The Young and the Restless* and I had no personal life, although I had met a gorgeous girl at the Daytime Emmy Awards in New York where I'd presented David Letterman with an award. At the Emmy party, about twenty guys were hitting on a beautiful blonde in a cowboy hat. She was a picture of lust – mine. In the face of such competition, however, I acted aloof in the hope that she would notice I wasn't interested in her. After about an hour, she came over to me.

'You remind me of Bo Derek in *10*,' I said.

'You remind me of a Ken doll,' she replied.

Her name was Catherine Hickland and after we had consumed a couple of drinks she invited me to go on a sightseeing tour of New York the following day.

Catherine was a Southerner from Fort Lauderdale, Florida, who had thrown herself into acting at an early age. While at high school she had attended so many theatre classes that she described herself as a 'drama nerd'. Her first professional job had been as a stewardess in the 'Fly Me' advertising campaign for Pan-American Airways. She was now playing Dr Courtney Marshall in NBC's soap *Texas*, a pre-Civil War costume drama that was struggling to find an audience on daytime television.

Back in Los Angeles, I pestered Catherine with long-distance phone calls for several months until she flew out to see me. We had a brief fling, although she wasn't at all sure about getting involved with me. I found out why when she suddenly announced that she was getting married. This set me back a bit, but we said our goodbyes and she flew back east. I looked at her picture on the wall of my home and said to myself, 'It's okay – I'm not in love with you.'

Catherine's marriage lasted only a very short time. Six months later, she moved to Los Angeles and turned up on the set of *The Young and the Restless*. I had broken up with Roberta Leighton, although we were still attracted to one another. Every time I'd see her I'd lure her back in and we would have wild, passionate sex. She would think we were back together again, but I would say, 'No, that's not where I'm at.' It was an up-and-down, rollercoaster ride for her and it made her quite bitter. I knew it wasn't fair but every time I saw her my libido would go into overdrive.

Then Catherine walked on to the set and, after we had wrapped for the day, she invited me back to her apartment, where she was incredibly passionate and loving. I thought, 'Boy, you really are single!' We established a relationship and I asked her to move in with me. Catherine had no agent and no career, so I hooked her up with Dianne Davis of 20th Century Artists. My home life settled down into a pleasant routine of work and fun times with Catherine. The problem was that I had now been doing *The Young and the Restless* for six years and, professionally speaking, I was going through the worst period of my life. I was tired of playing the self-righteous Snapper Foster; tired of reading forty pages of script every day; tired of being turned down for parts in prime-time series.

When I begged the producers to give Snapper a new challenge, the writers brought back Sally Roulland (Lee Crawford), a young woman from his past. Sally has a terminally ill son, Chucky (Marcus Bentley), who is actually Snapper's illegitimate son. They become close and our scenes together were among the best I had done on *Y&R*, but it was a case of too little, too late. I was finished with the world of soap operas. In March 1982, I turned my back on $2,000 a day and quit the show. In my final appearance, I donate one of my kidneys to Chucky and make a tearful exit.

The theme of my farewell party to the cast was 'Still young . . . and still restless'. I was going to New York to pound the pavements looking for work. Steve Stout, the guy I had replaced in *I Remember Mamma* back at high school, was in New York and doing quite well, so I intended to hook up with him.

Dad said: 'Are you crazy?'

'No, Dad. I've got $40,000 in my pocket – I'm going to Broadway to follow my dream. I can't do this anymore. I've been here six years, I've done 890 shows – I feel as though I'm going to die here.'

First, I had agreed to go to Las Vegas for the industry's biggest event, the NATPE convention – the National Association of Television Programming Executives – to sell a *Soap World* show about soap stars on vacation. Dozens of excited ladies swarmed around the *Soap World* booth yelling, 'Hello, Snapper!' A lot of them didn't even know my name until I autographed photos for them. They said, 'David who?'

I enjoyed myself gambling and swimming, although we had no success in selling the show. I was looking forward to my move to New York when Jan McCormack called my hotel and said, 'Get on the next plane – you've got a 10 a.m. meeting at NBC with Joel Thurm.' Joel Thurm was the casting director who had given me my first TV job, through Joyce Selznick, on *Police Story*. He was now casting a top-secret new series for the network that invariably occupied last place in the ratings.

I hopped on an LA-bound plane and almost immediately noticed that a young, dark-haired man a few rows in front kept looking back at me. I said to my seatmate, an entertainment lawyer: 'Who's that guy who keeps staring at me?'

'Don't you know? That's Brandon Tartikoff, president of NBC Entertainment.'

Tartikoff, a New Yorker and self-confessed 'child of television', was a programming genius, the brilliant, charismatic Irving Thalberg of the small screen. He had been the youngest entertainment president of a major network when he took over the reins at NBC at the age of thirty-one and had transformed it from a laughing-stock into a formidable contender for the network crown. During his time at NBC, Tartikoff developed (alongside a couple of dismal flops) *Hill Street Blues* (1981), *Cheers* (1982), *The Cosby Show* (1982), *Family Ties* (1982), *The A-Team* (1983), *Miami Vice* (1984) and *LA Law* (1986). Tragically, he was already fighting the lymphatic cancer that would kill him at the age of forty-eight.

On the plane, I straightened my tie, fixed my hair and got up to make a pitch to Brandon Tartikoff. I had no way of knowing that Tartikoff was sitting next to Earl Greenberg, an NBC executive who knew me from *The Young and the Restless*. He had asked Greenberg: 'Who is that kid back there? I saw women at the convention leave their slot machines to mob him.'

'That's David Hasselhoff,' Greenberg replied, 'the biggest star on daytime television.'

'He's the guy I want to test for the Knight Rider.'

Synchronicity again – right time, right place.

With my best friend and mentor, my Dad, Joe

Michael Knight was a dream role and I grabbed it with both hands

4 Ride of a Lifetime

'One role can make all the difference . . .
but you've got to get it first.'

At that precise moment, lightning raked the sky and the cabin was buffeted by high winds as the airplane flew into an electrical storm over the Nevada Desert. Just as I was heading towards Brandon Tartikoff, the seat-belt sign flashed on. A stewardess intercepted me in the aisle.

'Please sit down, sir, we've encountered some turbulence.'

'No, no, you don't understand – I just quit *The Young and the Restless* and I'm going to New York, but I need to talk to that man upfront.'

'Sit down, sir.'

'But . . .'

'*Sit down, sir.*'

So I sat down.

The same thing happened three more times when I tried to get up. I never left my seat during the entire flight. When the plane landed at Burbank, I ran after Brandon Tartikoff, but he climbed into a waiting limousine and took off.

I said to myself, 'I've blown it again.'

I got to baggage claim and Catherine picked me up.

'Do you know some guy named Brandon Tarty-something?'

'Brandon Tartikoff?'

'Yeah. Who is that guy?'

'He's the head of NBC.'

'I think he noticed me on the airplane.'

'Well, did you go and speak to him?'

'No, I didn't. I couldn't get up because of the turbulence.'

'You, the greatest self-promoting man on the planet, did not meet Brandon Tartikoff?'

'No, I couldn't get up – but I think he noticed me.'

Next day, I showed up at NBC for my appointment with Joel Thurm. I didn't know that Brandon Tartikoff had walked into Joel's office that morning and said: 'I saw all these women mobbing this guy in Vegas – he's got a funny name.'

Joel turned the photo on his desk around.

'David Hasselhoff?'

'That's him.'

'He'll be here in thirty minutes.'

Everybody at NBC was whispering about *Knight Rider*, the hot new show that was going to take on *Dallas*, the biggest and most successful series of the 1980s. *Knight Rider* was being developed by Glen A. Larson, a member of the 1950s Four Preps singing group and a former writer/producer at Universal Studios. Joel explained to me that the hero of *Knight Rider* was named Michael Knight and that he would be driving a talking car. He sent me to see Glen Larson, who was now operating out of 20th Century Fox.

Glen had tested a large number of hopefuls, including Don Johnson, in his projection room at Century City. He gave me a reading and then filmed my test. After the tapes of all the auditions had been sent to NBC, Dick Lindheim of Universal Television phoned Larson.

'They didn't like anybody. We'll have to go back and start over.'

'Wait a minute, what do you mean – they didn't like anybody?'

'They didn't like anybody.'

'Well, what was wrong with Hasselhoff?'

Larson had looked at the scene in which I was introduced to the talking car. I had burst out laughing. I was sceptical about the whole idea, so I had given the car a pat on the bonnet as though it was a horse and called it 'Buddy'. Glen loved that little touch.

'The look on his face and his tone of voice are perfect,' he told

Lindheim. 'He's saying, "You gotta be kidding me!" It's just what I want.'

Larson sent the tape back to NBC. Three hours later the phone rang. 'You've got Hasselhoff.'

But they wanted to test me again. I'd gone to Boston for the wedding of Jan's brother Buddy McCormack when I got word that I was going to be retested for the *Knight Rider* role. I hopped on the next plane for Los Angeles. I wasn't cutting it this time either, so I said to Glen Larson: 'Excuse me, can I have five minutes – I need to do something?' I went outside and screamed: 'I am the Knight Rider, I am the Knight Rider. Get it together, man – you're here for a reason. C'mon!' Using the 'Power of Your Subconscious Mind' technique, I came running back in and said, 'Now roll the tape!' And I got it on the second screen test.

I called Dad. 'I've left *The Young and the Restless* and I'm making the pilot for a new TV series,' I said. 'It's about a talking car.'

'A talking car? You've been making good money, David, and you're going to do a series about a talking car?'

'Yep, it's going to be great.'

Dad thought I was crazy.

The script for the two-hour pilot episode of *Knight Rider* was sent over to my house. It glowed in my hand. This was James Bond with a sense of humour and a talking car; it was *Police Story meets R2-D2*; it was *The Lone Ranger* with the car as Silver and its on-board computer as Tonto. I absolutely knew this was my ticket to prime time.

I made everybody call me 'Michael Knight' for two weeks. I put it on my answering machine. I said: 'I'm Michael, I'm no longer David.' When the cameras started rolling, I was the Knight Rider. And because the show's concept was so outrageous, I got a mischievous gleam in my eye as if to say: 'You're not going to believe this, but lean back and enjoy it anyway.'

The origins of *Knight Rider*, one of the campest, most unforgettable shows of the 1980s, have become part of TV folklore. NBC was looking for a new contender to put up against *Dallas*, J. R. Ewing and his fellow Texans having destroyed all previous rivals in the 9 p.m. Friday slot. Sceptical about the young male talent around, Brandon Tartikoff felt it would be difficult to find a handsome male star who could act well enough to carry a new series. Why not have a series, he mused, called *The Man of Six Words*, which would begin with the guy getting out of a woman's bed and saying, 'Thank you.' Then he would chase after some villains in a supercar with artificial intelligence and say, 'Freeze!' Finally, the grateful victims would thank him and he would murmur, 'You're welcome.' End of show. In between each of these scenes, the super-intelligent car would take care of all necessary dialogue.

Nevertheless, Tartikoff was willing to apply his Midas touch (and NBC's money) to developing a new series, and word went out to Universal Television that NBC was looking for a new action/adventure show. It was Universal's Dick Lindheim who contacted Glen Larson after eight other producers had turned him down. Larson was the veteran creator/writer/producer of a mixed bag of TV series including *Quincy* (1976), the ill-fated *Battlestar Galactica* (1978), *Buck Rogers in the 25th Century* (1979), *BJ and the Bear* (1979), *Magnum, PI* (1980) and *The Fall Guy* (1981). Lindheim recalled that Larson had used a computerised supercar in an episode of *BJ and the Bear* entitled 'Cain's Cruiser'. He suggested that Larson base the concept of the new series around a similar car.

Larson had a firm understanding of the likes and dislikes of Middle America. His style was family entertainment: humorous, tongue-in-cheek scripts with simple storylines, little violence, no bad language and a likable, charismatic lead character. He responded to the challenge by taking the supercar idea and turning it into the most sophisticated vehicle ever built, a computerised 1982 Pontiac Trans Am with a personality similar to Clifton Webb in *Life With Father*. 'It had to be tongue-in-cheek,' Larson says, 'like Sean Connery did in the James Bond pictures and Christopher Reeve in *Superman*. If we had played it straight, it would have been ridiculous.'

The Trans Am was called Knight Industries Two Thousand, while KITT – an acronym for Knight Industries Two Thousand – was the on-board computer. Larson never considered KITT to be the car's name, but to me the car and the computer were indivisible: they were one and the same.

In early 1981 while I was exiting *The Young and the Restless*, Larson took himself off to Honolulu, where he holed up in a hotel room for ten days and wrote the pilot episode of the as-yet-untitled new series. Most of the elements came together in this first script: the hero was named Michael Knight and he dashed after a bunch of criminals in a computerised supercar. The title *Knight Rider* was dreamed up shortly afterwards by both Larson's wife Janet and Universal Television's vice president Kerry McCluggage after they had read the script.

Larson's inspiration for KITT's computer was HAL, the evil talking computer in Stanley Kubrick's phenomenal sci-fi movie *2001: A Space Odyssey*. Unlike the malevolent HAL, KITT has been programmed to protect human life; virtually indestructible inside his molecular bonded shell, he is forbidden to kill even the bad guys.

The oscillating red-light scanner on the front of the car that acts as KITT's eyes was based on similar scanners on the evil Cylons in Larson's *Battlestar Galactica*. The car itself was a variation on the production line model Pontiac Trans Am of 1982, modified by General Motors at a cost of $18,000. George Barris's company, who had styled the TV Batmobile, were commissioned to streamline the bodywork, while the dashboard was customised in Styrofoam by a toymaker named Michael Scheffe.

'It's like Darth Vader's bathroom,' Michael Knight says when he gets his first look at KITT's controls.

'It's a one-of-a-kind car,' he is told, 'operated entirely by microprocessors, which make it virtually impossible for it to be involved in any kind of mishap or collision – unless, of course, specifically so ordered by its pilot.'

'Pilot?'

Not only could KITT talk but he could also think, work out problems, intercept police calls, drive himself, propel me through the roof on to the top of high buildings, smash through walls and, when necessary, use his turbo-booster to fly fifty feet through the air. The 'jumping car' was a hollow fibreglass Trans Am, which crumpled on landing. The 'auto-cruise' car was a right-hand drive Trans Am driven by a stuntman, usually Jack Gill, who was hidden from the cameras. Whenever Michael Knight would say into his wrist transmitter, 'KITT, come get me', Gill would be driving the right-side blind-drive car and I'd jump in the left side and take over a second steering wheel on my side. With an electronic brain and a top speed of 300 m.p.h. (actually 120 m.p.h.), KITT could do ten times as much as the General Lee, the Dodge Charger in *The Dukes of Hazzard*.

Larson's pilot episode was entitled 'Knight of the Phoenix' and was directed by Dan Haller, former art director for Roger Corman. The pilot tells the story of Michael Long, an LAPD cop who is working under cover in Las Vegas to smash an industrial espionage ring. When his partner is gunned down by the villains, Long chases them into the Nevada Desert. With him is Tanya Walker (Phyllis Davis), a beautiful blonde woman whom he believes to be an ally. However, when Long apprehends the killers, Tanya produces a gun and shoots him at point-blank range – she is secretly a member of the gang. Long is left for dead and the gang takes off.

However, Wilton Knight (Richard Basehart), altruistic head of Knight Industries Inc., has flown to Las Vegas in his helicopter to see Long, whom he wants to recruit for a special assignment that Knight Industries has been developing with Professor Devon Miles (Edward Mulhare). Wilton finds Long's body on the desert road. 'My God, we're too late,' he cries. But Long is not dead. Wilton flies the stricken cop to his headquarters, where his own surgeon performs a life-saving operation. Long, a Vietnam veteran, has been saved by a metal plate in his forehead. The bullet from Tanya Walker's gun has hit the metal plate and ricocheted through his face.

During extensive reconstructive surgery, Long's shattered appearance is remodelled in the image of Wilton Knight's estranged son Garthe. When he recovers consciousness, Wilton, who is dying, tells Long of his mission to launch the Foundation for Law and Government (FLAG), which will hunt down criminals who are above the law. 'One man can make the difference,' he says. Long is given a new identity as Michael Knight and is introduced to the supercar, the Knight Industries Two Thousand. Wilton Knight then dies and Devon Miles takes over the running of FLAG, later referred to as 'the Foundation'.

A dead body from a mortuary has been substituted for Michael Long in the desert and everybody, including his fiancée Stephanie 'Stevie' Mason, believes that he has perished. Instead, Michael Knight and KITT are on the trail of Tanya Walker's gang to bring them to justice . . .

With funky synthesised theme music composed by Stu Phillips and Glen Larson, the pilot was aired on 26 September 1982 opposite *Matt Houston*. I count my lucky stars that Richard Basehart and Edward Mulhare, both exceptional actors with impressive stage credentials, had been cast as my two male co-stars. They gave the show a touch of class that made it believable. In less skilled hands, the plot of *Knight Rider* would have sounded preposterous. We would have been laughed off the screen. Glen later surrounded me with veteran actors he had used in other shows, including Richard Anderson from *Six Million Dollar Man*.

Richard Basehart had started life as a reporter on his father's newspaper at Zanesville, Texas, but acting was in his blood. During a forty-year career, he played heroes, villains, the mentally disturbed and many other types, often in a rugged and forceful manner, including a long stint on *Voyage to the Bottom of the Sea*.

Edward Mulhare was an Irishman who spoke with the most perfect English accent. He had played opposite Orson Welles's Othello in a London stage production directed by Laurence Olivier and had replaced Rex Harrison as Professor Higgins in *My Fair Lady* on Broadway. He had starred in many other stage shows before turning up in the popular TV series *The Ghost and Mrs Muir*. In *Knight Rider*, Edward was adamant that he would not be upstaged by a computerised car. Even before the pilot had been shown, he had gone to great pains to tell reporters that he was not co-starring with an automobile. 'I do not compete with machinery,' he said. 'David Hasselhoff and I are the stars of the show.' Edward and I grew so close that he became an honorary member of my family.

One of the high points of 'Knight of the Phoenix', however, was the way in which the relationship developed between Michael Knight and KITT. Unaware at first that KITT can talk, Michael muses aloud about listening to some taped music.

'What would you like to hear?' KITT inquires.

These are his first words in the series. Michael is nonplussed and looks round for the source of the voice. He soon gets the hang of it and lets KITT do the driving while he takes a nap. This is the beginning of the love/hate interplay between them. In no time, KITT chides Michael for his behaviour (hanging out in bars and places of 'low morals') and Michael responds that KITT is 'a smart-alec car' and 'about as much fun as a divorce . . . which is not a bad idea'.

From the very beginning of the show, KITT brought in an audience of young children, while the adventure stories brought in their fathers, who mostly didn't want to watch *Dallas*. Meanwhile, women were tuning in to watch me because Snapper Foster had a lot of fans among *Dallas*'s female audience. After all, *Dallas* was just another soap.

We were equally fortunate in the actor chosen as KITT's voice. William Daniels, a Brooklyn-born actor with a superior New England accent, had played Dustin Hoffman's father in *The Graduate* and was a regular on *St Elsewhere* as Dr Mark Craig. William was nowhere near the set when we were filming, so we had a script girl or PA throwing me his lines. William would then go into a booth with a recording engineer and a microphone and record KITT's part of the dialogue. He had only the script pages for his scenes in front of him and had no idea what was happening in the rest of the show. 'It was phenomenal,' William says. 'I was doing two ongoing series, each totally different from the other, and they were both successful. I played KITT for laughs and Dr Mark Craig as a serious surgeon. I sometimes did a funny scene as KITT and then would go and do a heart transplant on the set of *St Elsewhere*. It was quite a challenge.'

Universal Studios, who produced *Knight Rider* for NBC, had completed principal photography on the pilot episode when it was decided that a new opening sequence was required to make sense of the bizarre plot. New scenes were quickly written and Larry Anderson, who had the same physical features as me, was phoned late in the afternoon to come to a casting session at Universal to meet the producers. He got the call the same evening to report to the set the next day.

The new scenes showed Michael Long, played by Larry Anderson, tracking the gang of industrial spies in Las Vegas. The location was a mocked-up casino in the lobby of a hotel near Los Angeles airport. The make-up and hair department curled Larry's hair to match mine and everything happened so fast that he went on to the set with his script pages in his hand. 'All I knew was that I was to run out of the casino, jump in a car and start driving,' he says. My voice was dubbed over Larry's and his name did not appear in the screen credits.

After substituting the opening sequence, it was discovered that the pilot had fallen seven minutes short. Glen Larson wrote three short scenes in which two car thieves make several failed attempts to steal KITT. One of the thieves is an uncredited William Daniels.

'Knight of the Phoenix' ends with Richard Basehart's closing narration: 'One man can make a difference, Michael. Michael Knight. A lone crusader in a dangerous world. The world of the *Knight Rider*.' The pilot rated an excellent fifth in the Nielsen Media Research ratings for the week with 30.3 per cent of households. Most industry insiders, however, predicted that when *Knight Rider* moved to the 9 p.m. slot on

Friday night against *Dallas*, it would vanish without trace. As 75 per cent of all new shows fail, the odds were heavily against us.

Our first episode in that slot, 'Deadly Manoeuvres', in which Patricia McPherson is introduced as KITT's mechanic Dr Bonnie Barstow, scored 19 per cent but was still higher in the ratings than any NBC series had scored against *Dallas* in four years. No other NBC show had ever survived in that slot and the TV critics, who had unanimously panned the pilot – Tom Shakes in the *Washington Post* described me as 'a hood ornament' – never forgave us for becoming successful.

'Hey, we got bad reviews,' I told anyone who mentioned them. 'That means we're going to be a hit.'

When *Knight Rider* had settled into its home in one of the big sound stages on Alfred Hitchcock Drive, I roamed around the studio in my black Trans Am. One day I drove on to the lawn at the base of the Black Tower for a photo shoot. The Black Tower was the executive skyscraper just inside the front gates. Peering down from the fortieth floor, Lew Wasserman, the head of Universal Studios, spotted this act of sacrilege. Lew never wrote memos, but he sent a message to the set, 'If I ever see that guy or his car on my grass again, I'll have his show cancelled.'

To boost our visibility among viewers, I went on a forty-city promotional tour around the States. Soon, my face was on lunch boxes and posters. Kids ran up to me and wrapped their arms around my legs and refused to let go. 'KITT is like ET to children,' I told one reporter. 'He's a source of non-stop love and affection – and a protector.'

I was paid $500 to appear with KITT at an automobile show in a small town up near the Canadian border. Hundreds of young kids turned up to see the Knight Rider and his talking car. Other invitations followed. I'd go out every weekend and my fee went up from $500 to $50,000 – how sweet it is! Even after I'd paid my taxes, I was earning a nice piece of change for these appearances. I'd take my father and Buddy McCormack in black leather Knight Rider jackets, jeans and black sequin ties.

At each auto show it was advertised that Michael Knight and KITT would be appearing in two shows that afternoon. We'd look out and see thousands of people in the arena who had each paid a $5 admittance charge, and hundreds of them were in line to meet me. All the kids really thought I was Michael Knight. It was endearing and great fun: we knew it was making their day and also helping us find an audience.

I wore a special pair of parachute pants with zippered pockets to store the money we'd made from merchandise. 'If this plane goes down,' I told the girl sitting next to me on the flight back to Los Angeles, 'and I don't make it, grab my pants – it's not what's in the pants but what's in the pockets that matters.'

No one gave *Knight Rider* a chance except me, Dad and Buddy. We did forty auto shows that year and without them I am convinced that we would not have succeeded in making *Knight Rider* a hit. You create your own destiny. You *can* make a difference. And we did. My sister Joyce answered the Knight Rider's fan mail until it got too big for her to handle. When I was on *The Young and the Restless*, most of my letters had been written by lonely divorcées, women who were looking for a special man in their lives. I was now getting 16,000 letters every week mainly from kids who dug the Knight Rider.

There was, however, a downside to my popularity. All of my absences dashing across the States to promote *Knight Rider* had damaged my relationship with Catherine. Her own career had stalled following the cancellation of *Texas* and she was having trouble adjusting to my sudden new fame. When I got home from each trip, I'd put the money from the latest auto show on the bed, but Catherine wasn't impressed; she wasn't part of these excursions and hence there was no camaraderie between us, only work. One night she sat me down and calmly told me: 'I'm ready to take this to the next level, David. I want to get married or else I want to move on.'

I heard myself say: 'Well, why don't you move on because I'm not ready to get married.'

Apparently I did say that because she moved on. I was so caught up in a round of filming, promoting and enjoying the ride that it took me weeks to realise that Catherine was gone, let alone not coming back. It upset me greatly, but there were plenty of women at Universal City and inevitably I started to play around. I had my own executive trailer and my own dressing-room.

'What style of décor do you want?' they asked me.

'Moroccan?'

'You got it.'

Every Friday night we'd have a party on the set and then go back to the divans and exotic drapes in my Moroccan dressing-room. Scotty, the legendary guard on the studio's front gate, would escort 'secretaries' to my trap. 'Gee, Mr Hasselhoff,' he said after the umpteenth girl had turned up at the gate, 'it's really difficult for you to keep staff.'

We were kings of the lot. I'd take one of the black Trans Ams – we had four picture cars – and grab the guest star of the week and we'd party in the *Psycho* house, or on the *Spartacus* set, or on Elm Street. I took one actress to the *Leave it to Beaver* House, parked the Trans Am outside. We were enjoying ourselves when the studio's guided tour came by in one of the special trams.

'And now we have the house used in *Leave it to Beaver*,' the tour guide said. 'Oh – and we've got the Knight Rider's car in the driveway. Wonder what's going on here?'

Inside the house, I whispered, 'Don't move!' We kept out of sight while a bunch of tourists fired a battery of Nikons at us. After the tour tram had moved on, we rolled around on the fake floor, laughing.

Whenever we had a break or I was bored during filming, I'd say to my best buddy on the set, my diabolical double and king of the make-up and hair department, Allen Payne, 'Let's go raid the tram.' This involved following the tour tram from the Parting of the Red Sea to the Ice Tunnel and then down to the seaside village in *Jaws*. We'd drive up behind a tram and then watch the reaction as one row of tourists after another would see us and freak out with excitement at seeing KITT and the Knight Rider in person.

There were a couple of close shaves that showed me this wasn't always a good idea. Once, we were driving two children from the Make-a-Wish Foundation through the Ice Tunnel when the car started to revolve – or at least it appeared to. Actually, it was the tunnel that was revolving around the car but the illusion was so realistic that I really thought we were going to turn over. The kids started screaming and I drove madly to get us out of the tunnel before we were all killed. I resolved never to try that particular trick again.

Then one Sunday I was driving Catherine and a next-door neighbour through the Red Sea when the car stalled. At that moment, the Red Sea ceased to be parted and water started gushing around the car.

'It's okay,' I said, 'we can escape through the roof and swim for it.'

Security guards alerted the fire department that we were stuck and in danger of being swept away. The firemen turned up on the scene with sirens blaring. A crowd gathered to see what was happening. Just as the firemen were preparing to rescue us, the car started and I drove clear.

'I'm going to kill you!' Catherine hissed in my ear. I loved it.

But my antics had impressed Lew Wasserman. 'I've seen Hasselhoff jump on to the tram and talk to people,' he barked. 'He's the only star who understands that people take the tour to see stars. He can have whatever he wants on this lot, except my grass.'

Meanwhile, *Knight Rider* had developed into a very particular series. Apart from the pilot, 'Deadly Manoeuvres' was the only episode without Richard Basehart's famous opening narration: 'Knight Rider – a shadowy flight into the dangerous world of a man who does not exist. Michael Knight, a young loner on a crusade to champion the cause of the innocent, the helpless, the powerless, in a world of criminals who operate above the law.'

This was introduced at the opening of episode two, 'Good Day at White Rock', a cross between the Spencer Tracy movie *Bad Day at Black Rock* and Marlon Brando's *The Wild Ones*. In our version, Michael Knight's tranquil rock-climbing vacation is interrupted by a motorcycle gang, the Scorpions, who take over a town with a weak sheriff. One of the cast was Alex Daniels, a six-foot-three-inches-tall actor from Blythewood, South Carolina, who appears as Big Lonny Spencer. I didn't get to know Alex then but we met in Hawaii the following year. For many years since then, he has been my friend and stunt double on both *Knight Rider* and *Baywatch*, and has also rescued me in my private life several times.

It was just after the sixth episode had aired in early November 1982 that Ron Alridge wrote in the *Chicago Tribune's TV Week* magazine: 'Although it's much too early to draw conclusions, early ratings suggest that *Knight Rider* is finding a place in the hearts, if not the minds, of the viewers.' We were the second most popular newcomer on NBC after *Family Ties* with a 26 per cent audience share. We knew we couldn't beat *Dallas*, so the objective was to finish second in our time slot. Despite its early promise, however, *Knight Rider's* ratings started to slip and *Dallas's* picked up again.

We were in danger of cancellation when Jan McCormack contacted her connections at Universal and pleaded, 'Give us another four weeks.' She got us a reprieve and in those four weeks we pulled things around, thanks largely to an episode called 'Trust Doesn't Rust' in which writer Steven de Souza introduced KITT's evil twin KARR, an acronym for Knight Automated Roving Robot. This was Wilton Knight's prototype for KITT which had been deactivated and kept under lock and key in a storeroom prior to being displayed as an exhibit at the Knight Museum of Technology.

The 'Trust Doesn't Rust' title had absolutely nothing to do with the plot, in which two thieves, Tony (Michael MacRae) and Rev (William Sanderson), break into the storeroom and accidentally activate KARR's computer. KARR is identical to KITT in every respect except that he has been programmed for self-preservation. The two cars bicker like two brothers. KITT sniffs, 'That other car is going to give Trans Am a terrible reputation', while KARR describes KITT as 'the inferior production line model'.

'Trust Doesn't Rust' was probably the best episode of the first season and one of the best in the series' entire run. It certainly was the Jekyll and Hyde of talking cars. In December, *Knight Rider* got better numbers for NBC on Friday nights at 9 p.m. than its twenty-six previous shows in that slot. The TVQ ratings which measure how much audiences like all of the series on the air also ranked it as the second most popular show of the season after *M*A*S*H*.

I met William Daniels for the first time at the *Knight Rider* Christmas party.

'Hello, I'm Bill Daniels – I play KITT.'

'Hello, I'm David Hasselhoff – I play Michael.'

'We have a hit.'

'Yes, sir, we do.'

I poured him a glass of champagne.

'Nice to meet you, KITT.'

'Nice to meet you, Michael.'

To this day, we have never done a scene together but we have a great relationship.

Knight Rider's average share for the entire 1982–3 season was a respectable 25 per cent. The *New York Times* reported: 'With tongue firmly in cheek and a remarkable lack of violence or mayhem (despite all the fast action, few characters were killed, not even the bad guys), *Knight Rider* raked in ratings and goodwill for NBC.'

In January 1983, I won the People's Choice Award for Favourite Male Performer in a New Television Program. The awards, based on annual results from Gallup Polls, are one of the few awards shows to be based on popularity. As I was walking to the stage to collect my trophy, I suddenly remembered a dream I'd just had in which I was looking around the audience for Joyce Selznick and couldn't find her anywhere. This was quite a premonition. On stage, I said, 'I was managed by a lady by the name of Joyce Selznick. She's no longer with us . . . This one's for you, Joyce.' As I walked off stage, my eyes filled with tears.

Burt Reynolds, one of my role models with his great heart and offbeat humour, said to me: 'That was nice what you did for Joycie.'

Then the star of *Smokey and the Bandit* said, 'Hey, take good care of my Trans Am.'

Wherever I went . . . Everybody seemed to love the Knight Rider

I'd gone to pick up a contestant for a TV show – and now I was in jail!

5 Travels with the Hoff (I)

*'Knight Rider swept around the planet and
I went along for the ride.'*

Knight Rider was my passport to the world. From the very first
season, the show was riding high in foreign markets. It went on to
be syndicated in eighty-two countries, some of which are still showing
it to this day. In South America, *Knight Rider* was renamed *El Auto*. In
Turkey, it was *Kara Simsek* or 'Black Lightning'. In Israel, the title
translated into Hebrew as *Abir al Galgalim* or 'Knight on Wheels'. In
Italy, we were *Supercar*; in Poland, *Nieustraszony* ('Fearless'); in
Portugal, *O Justiceiro* (roughly meaning 'the bringer of justice'). The
French settled for *K 2000*.

Buddy McCormack and members of my family were my travelling
companions to most of the forty countries I visited. Wherever we went,
Knight Rider opened doors and helped me to make friends. But in the
mid-1980s there was one occasion when *Knight Rider's* popularity
almost led to disaster. I had flown to Puerto Rica with Dolores, Buddy
and my press agent at the time, Jonni Hartman, to appear with KITT on
a telethon to raise money for a children's charity. On our first night in
town we went to a club and there was a near riot when people jumped
over tables to meet me. My mother was sitting next to me and I had to
protect her from these crazy people, most of whom were women.

Back at the hotel, a group of air stewardesses had arrived in the lobby and this led to an all-night party in my room with what seemed like the entire staff of the airline. I don't remember if anything was consummated – there was a lot of drinking and hugging and laughing and no one got any sleep. I went straight from the party to the studio for the telethon, sang a couple of songs and conducted a conversation with KITT.

Part of the show entailed me picking the name of a contestant out of a barrel. Not only would the winner, a teenaged girl, appear on the show, but I would go and collect her from her home and escort her to the studio. With TV cameras broadcasting live pictures of our progress, we headed into the winner's neighbourhood. People who had been watching the show streamed out of houses, bars and places of work to see the Knight Rider drive past.

So many people gathered in the street that the producers decided it would be safer if we picked up the contestant at the local police station. We only just made it inside the gate of the police compound when a huge crowd descended. The gate looked solid – it was seven feet high and made of iron bars – so I went over to it thinking I'd calm things down a bit. I had learned in the past that the most important thing about surviving as a celebrity is to keep moving; if you stop, you're dead. So rather than stopping to sign autographs for a line of fans, I always carried a handful of signed photos of myself to hand out as I walked past. Thus I kept moving and the fans got their autographed pictures. (I still carry photos, although today they are *Baywatch* and *SpongeBob*.)

I started chatting to these people at the gate and was handing photos through its iron bars when a full-scale riot broke out as fans started to clamber up on to the gate trying to get at me. Outside in the streets, people were hanging off balconies in a block of flats to get a better view and the noise was so loud that I couldn't hear myself speak. The police pulled me back, saying '*Alto, alto!*' – 'Stop, stop!' I looked up and saw that the gate was starting to collapse under the weight of bodies clinging to it.

As it crashed down, crushing people under it, the police hustled me inside the police station and locked the door. Hundreds of people streamed into the compound and angry faces were pressed against the window, while the door itself was being broken down. The police chief took me and Buddy out back, put us in a cell and locked the door. I sat there thinking, 'I came down here to pick up a contestant and I'm in jail.'

Half an hour later, a policeman came in to say, 'We think we have it under control. We'd like to take you back to the studio in a police car.' TV cameras had filmed the whole drama of the riot from outside in the street; they were still running as a four-car convoy, sirens blaring, moved out of the police compound and tried to thread its way through the milling crowd. When people started surging around our car, looking for me, the police freaked out. Our driver pulled out his gun and was about to shoot someone when I reached over and grabbed his hand. 'What are you going to do?' I screamed. 'Shoot 10,000 people? You fire that gun and we're dead.'

He put the gun back in his holster and we reached the television studio without further mishap. The show went on . . . but it was a miracle that somebody hadn't been killed. It was also a lesson to me about the potency of fame and its potential for disaster. And it was my first time in jail.

After a couple of false starts, Catherine Hickland and
I made it to the altar

6 My First Marriage

*'The single life was killing me so I hatched
a plot to win Catherine back.'*

Without Catherine at my side, I was desperately lonely in my big
house at 4310 Sutton Place, Sherman Oaks – the house that KITT
built. I was working horrendous hours on *Knight Rider*, leaving home at
4.30 a.m., starting work at 6 a.m., working until sundown and getting
home exhausted. From Sunday evening till Friday evening, I didn't
drink. I made a point of never being late and was always prepared.

The worst time was walking into an empty house. My sister Joyce had
got married and was running a restaurant in Atlanta with her French
husband, Philippe Corjon. I missed Catherine enormously, but she was
showing no signs of wanting to return. In bed, I tossed and turned until
it was time to go back to work again. For the first time, I started using
alcohol to numb the pain – drinking was no longer any fun, it had
become medicinal.

At work, I complained to producer Robert Cinader that it was
ridiculous for KITT to get more lines than a fine actor like Edward
Mulhare. He took the point and told the writers to slant a lot of the
stories away from the car. It seemed I was always fighting for someone
else. I also argued with the producers to stop *Knight Rider* becoming a
fender-bender like *The Dukes of Hazzard*. *Knight Rider* was about saving

lives, not killing people. It was based on the theme of 'One man can make a difference', so it had to be a show about heroes.

We were given a chance to practise what we preached in 1983 when Jan McCormack's sister Lori received a request from Dream Makers Inc., a Nashville charity that granted last wishes to terminally ill children. Dream Makers said that the last wish of a dying teenager was to meet the Knight Rider. I told Lori, 'Send him over.' The boy's name was Randy Armstrong and he was from Booneville, Mississippi. He was a good-looking fifteen-year-old with short hair because he lost most of it receiving chemotherapy for leukaemia. We took him for a ride in KITT and spun it around on jumps; we put him behind the camera. For three days, the crew and the stuntmen made sure he had a great time.

Just before Christmas, one of the assistant directors knocked on my trailer door. He said, 'A letter has come in for you from Randy Armstrong.' I hesitated to open it. I knew Randy had passed away on 4 December but I had declined an invitation to attend his funeral, not wanting to see it turned into a media event. His father, J. C. Armstrong, later told me that Randy had written to me. I opened the envelope and out fell a photograph of Randy in his Knight Rider hat and jacket in his casket. The letter read: 'Dear David, Please tell the cast and crew of *Knight Rider* that you taught me there was more to life than pain. Please go out and see other kids. You guys are truly real heroes.' The whole cast and crew just broke down and we couldn't finish the day's filming – we wrapped early.

I called Randy's father, 'I promise you I will carry out his request for the rest of my life. Is it okay if I use his name as my inspiration?'

He said: 'Absolutely.'

Maybe this was the real reason I got the Knight Rider role. Maybe I could be a real hero. From that day on, I opened the door to any sick child from anywhere any time. Requests for visits to the *Knight Rider* set came in like meteorites. We took Polaroid pictures of every visiting child and gave one print to the child, while I stuck another on my make-up mirror to remind me of my promise to Randy. By the end of the season, my mirror was covered in dozens of photographs.

Working with sick children and talking to their parents only emphasised my loneliness and the lack of a family of my own. I missed Catherine so much that I hatched a plot to win her back. I figured that if we worked together the chemistry between us might start to work again. Everybody on *Knight Rider* liked her and respected her as an actress, so I saw to it that she was brought in to play the female lead in 'White Bird', an episode about people and human emotions, rather than the show's staple fare of action/adventure.

Catherine plays Stevie Mason, Michael Knight's fiancée when he was LAPD undercover cop Michael Long. Stevie is a lawyer's assistant whom Michael bails out after she is framed in a gangland conspiracy. He takes her to the Foundation's retreat but there is a big complication: Michael is still in love with her. From the moment he lays eyes on her, the viewers can see how deeply he cares for her.

Stevie soon catches on that Michael Knight is her supposedly dead fiancé but Devon Miles urges him not to reveal himself to her and thus damage his future effectiveness as an agent. When an attempt is made on Stevie's life, Michael rescues her and catches the gangsters. His secret is saved when Stevie is sent into a witness relocation programme. This is the first case to touch Michael on a personal level and it was made easy for me because but I didn't have to act; I used my real feelings to let Catherine know how much I loved her.

'White Bird' was the last episode produced for the first season and the end-of-season wrap party fell on Catherine's birthday, 11 February 1983. I went down-town and bought a fantastic ring. Then I got a toy replica of KITT and put it on top of a birthday cake with the words 'Look under the hood' written in icing. I presented the cake to her in front of the entire cast. When she looked under KITT's hood, there was the ring.

Then I said, 'Catherine, will you marry me?'

Catherine burst into tears.

She thought it was a very cool, romantic proposal and accepted. That night we were driving down the road quite fast when the hood of the car flew up and we couldn't see anything. I managed to steer the car to a stop but it was a near miss and we could have been killed. We both took a deep breath. We realised that life was a gift and took this as a sign that getting married was the right decision.

We flew down to the Caribbean for a romantic ten-day vacation on Peter Island. I'd turned over a new leaf and had become more considerate of Catherine's feelings. We were getting along very well when a hurricane hit the island. We tried to escape by driving to the port in a bus but I took one look at the harbour and said to Catherine,

'Looks like we're spending the night here.' The seaplane had been hit by gale-force winds and had been turned upside down in the water. We checked into a bed-and-breakfast place run by a born-again Christian and her heavy drinking husband. That night while the hurricane howled around us, Catherine prayed with the wife and I drank with the husband.

When we returned to Los Angeles, she moved back into Sutton Place. In June 1983, *TV Guide* reporter Bill Davidson found that I was enjoying life as the Knight Rider. 'Hasselhoff earns an estimated $15,000 per episode,' he wrote, 'and lives in a unique Hollywood Hills house filled with hundreds of wind-up toys, which he assiduously collects and which distract his fiancée, the beauteous Catherine Hickland of the expired soap opera *Texas*.'

Life was wonderful when I kissed Catherine goodbye and visited South Africa for the first time to do promotional work for a chain of South African retail stores. I had decided to go ahead with the trip even though my fellow actors warned me to stay away from that controversial country. In July 1983, South Africa was still in the grip of apartheid, the system of government under which a minority of 4.5 million whites ruled a majority of 21 million blacks, many of them confined to squalid 'townships' outside the big cities. Nelson Mandela was still in jail and the country was in a state of chaos. *Knight Rider*, however, was the Number One television show and a lot of people, black and white, wanted to meet me.

In my lifetime, I had witnessed the Civil Rights movement destroy segregation in the Southern States and it made me angry that people were criticised for going to South Africa. Among the American musicians who had played in South Africa since the 1968 United Nations' ban were the Beach Boys, Glen Campbell, Cher, the Osmonds, Sha Na Na, Tina Turner and Frank Sinatra. The most recent trans-gressor was Linda Ronstadt, who was attacked for giving six concerts in Sun City for a fee of $500,000 after standing in as a last-minute replacement for Sinatra. I thought I could go to South Africa because I wasn't a political figure. It took me quite a while to realise that this attitude was naïve; that in South Africa, *everything* was political, whether you were a businessman, footballer or entertainer.

Controversy was the last thing on my mind when I arrived at Jan Smuts Airport in Johannesburg on 12 July 1983 with Mom, my fourteen-year-old sister Lisa and Buddy McCormack. I was astonished that 10,000 people had shown up to greet me. When the crowd showed signs of restlessness, the police sent a van on to the tarmac to collect us and drive us to our hotel. Everywhere I went there was pandemonium. I made a personal appearance at a disco and when I tried to leave there was a riot. I posed for a photograph with three black girls for a black newspaper. Next day, the headline was, 'KNIGHT RIDER CAUGHT IN RACE ROW'. I laughed – it was so wrong.

I told reporters that I was in South Africa on behalf of a human being whose mission was to save lives; there was nothing racial or political about it. The people of South Africa, black and white, were the same as human beings in the United States or anywhere else, so why make it political? Reporters looked at me as though I had just arrived from Mars.

I had been in South Africa for only twenty-four hours when I noticed that black South Africans would always shake my hand in such a way as to show they had no weapons up their sleeve. I walked on to a segregated bus, even though people warned me not to. I said to myself, 'Hasselhoff can't go on that bus but Michael Knight can!' To the consternation of the security guards, I boarded the bus. Every passenger was black and they began hugging and kissing me; everyone wanted to shake my hand.

I put the power of Michael Knight to work at the SANTA Tuberculosis Hospital in Johannesburg. The child patients sang, 'Thank God you're here.' They were wearing little hats made out like KITT cars and had hung my picture on the walls beside their beds. One little boy was so shy when I came up to him that he covered his face. So I said, 'Come on, give Michael Knight a smile' and like magic the hands came down and I got a big grin.

Everywhere I went in South Africa – and I visited all the major cities: Johannesburg, Cape Town, Durban, Pretoria, Bloemfontein – my audiences were filled with blacks, whites, Indians, Afrikaners – everyone. On 17 July, 35,000 people sang happy birthday to me. Another 10,000 gathered in Pretoria city centre and traffic snarled down Vermeulen Street when I showed up to open a new shopping centre.

Dad joined us during the tour. We were walking down the street when a man smiled at me and said, 'Hello, Hasselhoff.'

I turned to Dad. 'Did you ever think you'd be walking down a street in South Africa and somebody says "Hello, Hasselhoff"?'

'Unbelievable,' he said.

Flying into Bloemfontein, we looked down from the helicopter and saw in huge letters 'Welcome Michael Knight' written out in sand on the ground. When we landed, the words were blown away, but 10,000 people had turned up to see me, many of them clutching little stuffed giraffes. A twelve-year-old girl handed me one. I found out many years later when we both appeared on the *Tonight Show* that her name was Charleze Theron.

Another riot was waiting to happen around every corner. In Cape Town, we weren't able to clear a path through the crowd, so I stayed on stage for another half an hour because I was afraid some of the kids would get hurt in a stampede if I tried to leave. In Durban, the promoter introduced me and then ran off the stage. The audience were going wild. I went on and said, 'This is the Knight Rider – calm down.' It worked – they really thought I was Michael Knight.

Johannesburg, the heartland of apartheid, looked a lot like Toronto. In the 1950s, the government had evicted 60,000 black residents and resettled them in the grey, four-roomed dwellings known as 'matchbox houses' at Soweto (an acronym for South-Western Townships). Soweto had grown into a ghetto of more than half a million people, many of whom had to travel the ten to fifteen miles to J'burg (and back) every day to work in the white suburbs.

It was in Soweto that much of the struggle against apartheid was being fought. Student anger had exploded there in June 1976 when more than 10,000 students, who were protesting against Afrikaans as a compulsory school subject, had been fired on by police, triggering an uprising that had spread to other parts of the country. I was determined to see Soweto for myself, although I had been told, 'You can't go there – no way.'

I said, 'Get me five black armed guards – I'm definitely going.' Next day, five black policemen armed with machineguns arrived at my hotel in a van at 7 a.m., followed by a busload of reporters and photographers. With the cops riding shotgun, Dad and I drove into Soweto and headed straight for the Chris Hani Baragwanath Hospital, the largest hospital in the southern hemisphere. Conditions in the wards were unbearably hot, but we got a rapturous welcome. In the tuberculosis section, the kids and the nurses smiled at me and sang, 'Thank you, Jesus.' They said, 'We love you, Michael Knight!' It was very emotional. Dad and I both burst into tears, fighting over a pair of sunglasses to hide our feelings.

From the hospital's footbridge, there was a view of the rows of tin shanties, piles of garbage and rutted, unmade roads that formed the bulk of the township. Yet despite living in these disease-ridden slums, the people were beautifully dressed and were singing harmoniously as they set off for work. It was an inspiring sight. I realised this was where Motown began. Dad and I stayed back to talk to two white doctors in the TB section, while the bus carrying the journalists set off for Johannesburg. On the way back, it was stopped by an armed gang and all of the photographic equipment was stolen.

I turned down $200,000 to perform in Sun City, the Las Vegas-style conglomeration of luxury hotels and casinos created by Sol Kerzner in the barren African homeland of Bophuthatswana. I received a letter saying I would be put on a blacklist if I went to Sun City, but I went anyway when I was invited to compere an Ironman competition. 'Put me at the top of the list,' I said. 'I don't believe in sanctions against my freedom to go places.' I was donating my salary to charity, but they didn't seem to care about that. I was surprised to discover that the visitors to Sun City were both black and white. In the hotel disco, black and white people danced together and no one tried to stop them. Integration of a sort was already starting to happen.

My trip ended with a visit to the wonderful wildlife at Kruger National Park, where someone suggested a game of golf. We watched elephants lumbering up and down the fairway knocking down trees, and we drove golf balls over a lake full of people-eating hippos. South Africa was a magical place with so many problems that only the animals seemed to be at peace. As we flew home, I was glad I had made the visit and looked forward to going back again. I had visited nineteen cities and loved every minute of it. More than anything, however, it opened my eyes to the evils of apartheid and human cruelty.

Back home in Los Angeles, Patricia Nolan in TV Magazine decided I was 'definitely not a Hollywood playboy'. 'I love the life I share with Catherine,' I told her in an article published in December 1983. 'Sure, it's tough sometimes, having two busy careers in one household, and last year we even broke up for a while because the stress and strain became too much. But now Catherine and I are back together again, very much in love, and we plan to get married next year.'

But other reporters just couldn't accept that *Knight Rider* had succeeded where others had failed. Gail Williams wrote in the *Hollywood Reporter*: 'Kids like fast cars and computers. How are they supposed to relate to a talking car with a male voice that has a crush on its driver? It has the kind of flaws that make you wish you were a network executive or a producer.'

It was comments like this that provoked the producers into swinging the axe in the fall of 1983 when the *Knight Rider* cast were gearing up for our second season. The axe, however, didn't fall on KITT or me – instead, the producers sacked Patricia McPherson as Bonnie Barstow, quoting a 'lack of sizzle' in her character. When I questioned the decision, executive producer Robert Foster told me: 'We want to try something different, something glitzy.' I didn't agree – I was devastated, but unfortunately the 'powers that be' won out. I vowed that one day, if I ever had that power, I would pray to God I wouldn't abuse it.

They hired Rebecca Holden, a stunning redhead who had done a lot of guest-starring roles for NBC and Universal Studios, to play April Curtis as the mechanic responsible for maintaining and programming KITT's systems and driving his mobile workshop. The producers figured Rebecca would bring more sex appeal to the Foundation's rather staid image and thus attract older male viewers.

Everyone was downcast about Patricia's departure, but the second season started strongly with an episode entitled 'Goliath', the two-hour season première that scored a Nielsen rating of 30.9 per cent, slightly higher than the original pilot episode of the previous year. Goliath is a fourteen-ton, eighteen-wheeled semi-trailer that has been reinforced with a molecular-bonded shell identical to KITT's to crash through the defences of an American defence base and steal nuclear missiles for a renegade African dictator. The evil mastermind behind the plot is Michael's evil 'twin brother', Garthe Knight, Wilton Knight's psychopathic son whose photograph was the template for Michael's surgical reconstruction. I played the roles of both Michael and Garthe Knight.

Garthe wore a small tuft of hair on his lower lip and carried a stick. I played him with a sardonic curl of the lip and a harsher tone of voice. Dad watched this episode and told me with his funny smile: 'Michael

Knight's evil twin is a better actor than Michael Knight.' In fact, I enjoyed switching from one role to another. In 'Goliath', Garthe has escaped from an African prison where he was serving three life sentences and is determined to destroy the man who has been given his face. 'Michael Knight is a living, breathing insult to my existence,' he says. Wilton Knight's ex-wife Elizabeth (Barbara Rush, star of *It Came from Outer Space*) has thrown in her lot with her son and lures Devon Miles to her home, where he is drugged and kidnapped.

'Goliath' maintained *Knight Rider*'s improved figures and the producers' judgement in replacing Patricia McPherson seemed to be vindicated. In fact, the battle between Michael Knight and his evil twin proved so popular with viewers that both Garthe and Goliath were brought back in a two-hour episode, 'Goliath Returns', near the end of the second season during the February sweeps period, when ratings are assessed for advertising. Once again, Garthe escapes from prison and this time he joins up with the wicked Adrianne Margeaux (Ann Turkel), the villain from an earlier episode, 'Soul Survivor'.

The most expensive items in filming *Knight Rider* were the fighting scenes between Goliath and KITT. To keep costs down, some of the key scenes were filmed using miniature models. I felt that this cheapened *Knight Rider* and protested to the producers about the loss of quality. When my protests fell on deaf ears, I talked to Tom Greene, writer and producer of many of the second-season episodes, about leaving the show. One day I went into Greene's office for a chat and saw a script titled 'The Death of Michael Knight' on his desk.

'What's that?'

'I'm just following your request to be written out of the show.'

Then he laughed and lifted up the script to show me that it was just a cover page and not an actual script. I never talked about leaving again. I'd learned a valuable lesson: never walk away from a winner.

My five-year search for a music career had failed – I had been turned down by every major label in the USA. In early 1984, I took a cassette of my work to music producer Joel Diamond, who saw the possibilities of promoting me as a singer on the back of *Knight Rider*. He put up $40,000 of his own money to record my first album, *Night Rocker*. The album inspired Catherine and me to do another episode of *Knight Rider* together in which we would sing some of the *Night Rocker* songs. This episode, entitled 'Let it Be Me' after one of the tracks, was aired in May 1984 and served as a springboard for the release of the *Night Rocker* album.

Catherine's television career then took off when Jon Conboy cast her in the political series *Capitol*, the first soap opera to commence production in Los Angeles since *The Young and the Restless* in 1973. We also started to plan our wedding. Catherine's parents had been divorced when she was six years old and, with one failed marriage behind her, she was determined that we should start our married life with a memorable ceremony. She had become a born-again Christian, so we asked her pastor, the Reverend Henry Cutrona, to conduct the service, even though I was a Catholic.

I gathered together all the people I loved in my life – my mother and father, my sisters, aunts, uncles, Jan, Lori and Buddy McCormack, Jonni Hartman, the talented Allen Payne and Carlos Yeaggy from the hair and make-up department, and Carlos's actress wife Melanie Thomas. We drove up the coast in a bus, stopping at the Hearst Castle at San Simeon and then at Monterey, where we lunched, bonded and played with sea lions. It was great fun and I was very excited about getting married.Catherine had a tight schedule on *Capitol* and had to fly up to Carmel after work on the eve of the wedding, which was due to take place at the Highlands Inn on 24 March 1984. Word had leaked out to the press that we were getting married and a dozen reporters and photographers descended on the hotel, hiding behind bushes and trying to photograph us. The Carmel Police Department saw to it that their cars were towed away or mysteriously rolled downhill.

Catherine was estranged from her father, so Edward Mulhare stepped in to give the bride away. Chuck Russell was my best man . . . still is. During the ceremony, helicopters hovered overhead and reporters crept up the hillsides. 'It was like an invasion of that little piece of turf,' Chuck Russell says. 'Catherine and David had to shout their vows to be heard above the commotion.' We hired our own photographer and sold the pictures to Rupert Murdoch's *Star* magazine to pay for everything. Our wedding night was spent at the Tickle Pink Inn, a beautiful little place on top of a rugged cliff overlooking the Pacific. From our room, we could see the waves crashing over the rocks down below. We both had to get back to work, so we delayed our honeymoon until the end of the second season of *Knight Rider*.

My first surfing lesson, 1954

With sisters Diane and Joyce

An early eye for fashion

A STAR IS BORN: with Joyce and Diane as Major Domo in my
first acting role, 18 April 1962

Our house in Chicago

My parents Dolores and Joe Hasselhoff

Joe and Dolores with the family
Chevrolet, 1948

Our house in Jacksonville, Florida

With Joyce, Diane and Lassie

All dressed up with Diane

The Lone Ranger…

… and the Slow Ranger

The stylish schoolboy

The high school actor

Michael Knight meets KITT, 1982

Knight Rider creator Glen Larson

Camera-clad KITT poses for his close-ups

KITT, the car that made me famous

Patricia McPherson and Edward Mulhare

Edward Mulhare and Rebecca Holden

Reunited with Edward, Patricia and Peter Parros on *This Is Your Life* with Michael Aspel in Los Angeles in 1993

Michael Knight's evil 'twin', Garthe

Down memory lane in London 1995

My first wife Catherine Hickland at our
1984 wedding

Taylor-Ann, our first-born daughter toured
Germany with Pamela and me in 1990

Pamela and I renewed our vows on our fifth wedding anniversary in Hawaii with the girls

On the beach with my niece Alexis,
Hayley and Taylor-Ann in 1995

With Hayley, Taylor-Ann and Pamela
at Christmas 1994

The Berlin Wall and Brandenburg Gate, December 1989, and with Pamela at the Wall

Allen Payne III was my hair and make-up man on *Knight Rider*… we're still great buddies and travel everywhere together. Here we are in Cologne

My Tara-style house in Encino, California

Joe Ballesteros, my right-hand man

TOGETHER: Joe and Delores and my four sisters (from left to right)
Joyce, Diane, Lisa and Jean on my fortieth birthday

IN THE SPOTLIGHT: family and friends caught me unaware, on *This Is Your Life*, 1993

After Randy Armstrong had sent me his 'Please help more kids' plea, I devoted much of my free time to visiting children in hospitals all across the country. I also invited terminally ill children to spend the day with me on the *Knight Rider* set to bring some happiness into their lives. Universal had given me a mini replica of KITT as a wedding present and the kids loved to drive it.

There were hundreds of dying children out there whose last wish was to meet me. It was a big responsibility and I took it seriously. I'd had a terrific childhood and I'd been successful in my career. All my life, I'd been healthy and I had so much going for me that I wanted to give something back in return. I visited kids who had rare and terrible diseases, kids who were dying of cancer, kids who were mentally and physically challenged. In return, they gave me unconditional love. They really believed that I was Michael Knight and somehow he had just jumped out of the television set.

With Ralph Hansen, I launched my own charity for terminally ill children called Race for Life, which was centred on the Indianapolis 500. We built our own racecar in the *Knight Rider* colours of black and gold. Our driver was Arie Luyendyke, the Flying Dutchman, one of a handful of drivers to win the title twice. Art Grunevelt was the team owner and Lori McCormack ran the charity for me. We brought in children from all over the States and made them grand marshals on race day. They met all of the stars, including Paul Newman, Carl Haas, Nigel Mansell and Mario and Michael Andretti.

Later, we moved the charity to Newman/Haas Racing, where Paul Newman was always a gracious partner. Paul was notorious for not signing autographs but he made an exception for our little visitors and just melted in their hands. To this day, he has his own project for chronically ill children, the Hole in the Wall Camp, financed by the sale of food products bearing his name. Paul is a fantastic actor and a tremendous human being.

Catherine and I were in great demand from the media. As one of Hollywood's beautiful couples, we posed for the cover of *Us* magazine in July 1984 with Catherine draped around my shoulders for an article on our 'sexy honeymoon shape-up'. 'I was a wild, crazy man before I met Catherine,' I said. 'I was partying too much and staying out all night because I couldn't face a lonely home life. But our love has turned my whole life around.'

Having taken the big step from daytime to prime time, I was determined to make it as a movie actor. Between *Knight Rider* seasons I was cast opposite Joan Collins – the English actress who had achieved worldwide fame as the power-dressing bitch Alexis in ABC's *Dynasty* – in a made-for-TV film, *The Cartier Affair*, produced by Joel Dean, my present agent, and Len Hill. Joan had made her first appearance in *Dynasty* when a mysterious stranger removed her sunglasses to reveal Alexis Carrington, the scheming, vengeful ex-wife of Denver oil millionaire Blake Carrington (John Forsythe).

Alexis terrified me and I feared that Joan Collins would have the same effect. In *The Cartier Affair*, she plays Cartier Rand, a TV soap opera queen known as 'the Love Weapon' in a fictitious series called *Storm Watch*. Cartier is so hot that her jealous fiancé insists on hiring a gay man as her secretary. My character, Curt Taylor, is a conman who poses as a homosexual in order to get the job. Curt has to pay off prison blackmailer Phil Drexler (Telly Savalas) by getting his hands on Cartier's collection of jewellery. Curt and Cartier, however, fall in love when he confesses all to her. They run away to Mexico with Drexler's men in pursuit . . .

It was a funny concept and I was looking forward to playing the part, but I had heard terrible tales that Joan was an egomaniac who needed constant flattery or else she would throw tantrums. If the tabloid headlines (and her autobiography, *Past Imperfect*) were to be believed, she had dallied with virtually every male actor in Hollywood, including heavy hitters like Warren Beatty and Ryan O'Neal.

The only way I could overcome my nervousness was to go on the offensive. I knocked on her dressing-room door and walked in, carrying a bottle of champagne and a couple of glasses. I slammed the champagne down and said: 'I hear you're a bitch but I love your work and I respect you and I'm terrified.'

She just roared. 'Oh, I *like* you!' she said. 'Sit down and pop that cork.'

Joan was living with her Swedish lover Peter Holm and had given him a Rolls-Royce as a love gift. She was in tremendous shape and our love scenes left nothing to the imagination. Peter Holm got so jealous that he drove the Roller through one of the sets while we were shooting.

'What do you think of Peter?' Joan asked me.

'Joan, I don't know him very well, but he seems kind of sleazy.'

She sighed. 'It's the best sex I've ever had, darling.'

'In that case, sleep with him but don't marry him.'

But Joan was hooked. During the filming of my close-up scenes, she'd say, 'Do you mind, darling?' and disappear for a romp with her Swedish lover. Every love scene I did was with the director, Rod Holcomb. I'd say, 'I love you.' And he would say: 'Even though I'm engaged, I love you, too.' It felt weird doing a love scene with a man.

Joan soon married Peter Holm and he later sued her for a big chunk of her fortune.

I admired Telly Savalas for his hard-boiled, kind-hearted, lollipop-sucking detective in the *Kojak* series. In *The Cartier Affair*, he taught me an important lesson about acting when my character goes to see him in jail.

He said: 'Are you listening?'

'Yeah!'

And *bam!* He slapped me. 'Now are you listening?'

'Yeah, I am – but don't ever do that again.'

'You know what? It was your close-up and they got a great shot.'

He was right. The biggest problem I had was that while I was ready to say my lines in close-ups, I wasn't really listening to the other actor. Listening is the key to being a good actor; it took me a long time to learn that.

The Cartier Affair was aired by NBC in November 1984, running head to head with *The Best Little Whorehouse in Texas* on CBS starring Burt Reynolds and Dolly Parton. The reviewer in *TV Chronilog* commented, 'David Hasselhoff shows signs of a flair for comedy.' Great reviews – lousy ratings.

Our break-up was painful and it took me a long time to get over it

7 Love and Loss

'I thought marriage was for life and
the break-up nearly destroyed me.'

Catherine and I were beautiful California people living in a mansion in the Hollywood Hills with a pool, Jacuzzi, screening-room and four dogs and three parrots. I was driving a car with the number plate NITE RDR and earning more money than ever. I was devastated, however, when I realised that our marriage wasn't working. It had been built on the dubious foundations of not being able to live without each other. We had never given it a chance to develop into a strong commitment and now it was falling apart.

The main problem was that an unhealthy degree of competition had crept into our relationship. When we had started dating, Catherine was a big star in *Texas* and I was on *The Young and the Restless*. After I became the Knight Rider, it was an eye-opener for both of us because everywhere we went fans were asking me for an autograph and asking Catherine for a pen.

Now that Catherine was working again, in *Capitol*, she was determined to make the most of it. Her work had become more important to her than spending time with me. I felt neglected. When she was at home, she would invite friends from her church around to the house and I would be excluded, or I'd come home from work on

Knight Rider and find her studying her lines or doing publicity. I'd ask her when we were going to spend time together and it became more and more apparent that it wasn't going to happen.

At my insistence, Patricia McPherson was brought back to *Knight Rider* when we started filming the third season in September 1984. Edward Mulhare and I had lobbied Robert Foster, the producer who had dismissed her, and he had finally relented. 'We all began to realise that we hadn't done any favours for *Knight Rider* by firing Patricia,' he admitted. The fans had felt that Patricia was a sympathetic and accessible woman. They had flooded NBC with letters demanding that Patricia be brought back. I had nothing against Rebecca – in fact, she did a great job as well as being gorgeous – but I felt an allegiance towards Patricia as one of the original ensemble.

The show itself had to change to keep *Knight Rider* one step ahead of innovations within the automotive industry. The two-hour première, 'Knight of the Drones', reflected a hard new scientific approach. Michael and KITT are alerted when a murderer escapes from jail in an armoured car that appears to drive itself. After Michael fights off some radio-controlled robots, two drone cars armed with rockets bear down on KITT. Realising that he is going to be destroyed, KITT ejects Michael moments before one of the rockets hits its target. KITT's interior is destroyed.

The purpose of the high-tech plot was to give the engineers a chance to re-equip KITT with new sci-fi equipment, including 3D video screens, an audio synthesiser, laser seatbelt and new laser shield system, all of which were intended to appeal to young viewers.

'Knight of the Drones' was filmed on location in San Francisco. Over breakfast, I got into an argument with Robert Foster and another producer, Gerald Sanford, when I said that Jan McCormack and my lawyer Alan Wertheimer were negotiating with Universal to improve my original contract.

Fortunately, Jan and Alan had a very good working relationship with Pete Terranova, head of business affairs at Universal TV, and they worked out a lucrative new contract for me. I'd been overdoing things a bit, but a new regime of exercise and diet soon dealt with that problem.

Meanwhile, my *Night Rocker* album had failed to set the world on fire. The only place where we scored a Number One hit was in Providence,

Rhode Island, with 'Crazy on a Saturday Night'. I promoted the album around the country and was beaten up pretty badly by the disc jockeys. *Knight Rider* was a joke because it was about a guy who talks to a car and they thought I was trying to capitalise on its success. It wasn't a pleasant experience.

I was away from home again when I accepted the role of a police chief in *Terror at London Bridge*, an unlikely NBC thriller about Jack the Ripper turning up in Arizona. These absences meant that Catherine and I had become one of those married couples who behaved as though they were still single. Questioned on the TV show *Cover Story* in July 1985, she tried to cover up the cracks. 'I think that any two people who are career-orientated, whether it's show business or any other type of business, have a tougher time than the norm,' she said. 'The fact we have a lot longer hours doesn't help, but you have to really work at a marriage no matter what position you're in. It's been harder for us because he's been out of town a lot and I've been working a lot, but we manage it make it work pretty good.'

Creatively, *Knight Rider* was going through a tough time. With the storylines becoming repetitive and the ratings showing signs of fatigue, the producers decide to give KITT a complete makeover. The fourth season began in September 1985 with a two-hour episode, 'Knight of the Juggernaut', in which KITT is completely destroyed after his molecular-bonded shell is neutralised. NBC added Peter Parros to the cast as Reginald Cornelius III (RCIII), a young streetwise mechanic who is given the job of fitting a brand new KITT with a Super Pursuit Mode which enables him to go faster than 300 m.p.h.

The scriptwriters, Robert Foster and Burton Armus, described the new KITT in this way: 'The rear fin converts to a new aerodynamic shape as the rear end lifts up to expose two jet exhausts. Side vents slide outward. An air intake vent pops up from the hood. The Super Pursuit Mode transformation complete, we see a whole new KITT – sleeker, meaner, a car out of the future dropped into today.'

Peter Parros was a lovely guy whose offbeat character sparkled in every episode, but neither KITT's makeover nor RCIII's intelligence could slow down the decline in ratings. The axe fell in November 1985 when Brandon Tantikoff thanked me for a great four years and then informed me that *Knight Rider* would not be returning for the 1986–7 television season. I went home and cried. Michael Knight was the greatest role ever and I was stunned and bitterly disappointed for the cast, the crew and myself. The show was still the best action/adventure series on TV, but it shared the same fate as other action series, such as *Hardcastle & McCormack*.

For *Knight Rider*'s final episode, I asked the producers to bring back Catherine as Stevie Mason. I knew from *The Young and the Restless* that a TV wedding was a sure-fire ratings booster and I wanted the show to go out on a high. The producers liked the idea and commissioned 'The Scent of Roses' in which Michael and Stevie would get married.

In this episode, Michael is shot by a would-be assassin and seriously injured. He falls into a deep depression and wants to quit the Foundation. Devon, fearing that Michael has lost the will to live, contacts Stevie Mason. Michael embraces her and, after spending time together, asks her to marry him. Michael and Stevie are married in a small outdoor ceremony. As in our wedding, Devon gives the bride away and the ceremony is conducted by Catherine's pastor, the Reverend Henry Cutrona.

The bride and groom have exchanged vows when the gunman returns to finish the job. Stevie, seeing that Michael is directly in the line of fire, shields him with her body. She is hit in the back and dies in Michael's arms. The episode takes its name from Stevie's last words: 'You may shatter the vase . . . but the scent of the roses will hang round it still. The scent of the roses will linger forever. Forever . . .'

Instead of holding 'The Scent of Roses' for the final week, NBC aired it mid-season in early January 1986, even though it contained many end-of-series elements. I had expressly wanted it to be the last one aired but the network held all the aces. The Knight Rider made his final bow in an episode entitled 'Voodoo Knight' which still pulled a respectable share of the audience with a Nielsen rating of 13.8 and a 22 per cent share. But it was small consolation for the fact that, at thirty-four, I was out of work.

The higher you climb, the harder you fall. I'd been on top of the pile and suddenly I was at the bottom again with no idea of how to start over. I was in Portugal with the KITT car earning a few dollars on personal appearances when Jan McCormack called to say I'd got a guest spot on a *Perry Mason Movie of the Week* entitled 'The Case of the Lady in the Lake'.

'They wanted Dirk Benedict from *The A-Team*,' she said, 'but he was unavailable, so you got the part by default.'

I found out on that movie that other actors also used cue cards. Raymond Burr said to me: 'It's not that I can't learn my lines, David, it's just that I don't want to. So when you're off camera, David, you don't need to be there – I'm going to replace you with my lines.' David Ogden Stiers, one of the doctors in *M*A*S*H*, was playing the district attorney opposite Raymond Burr and they both used teleprompters. It was the funniest thing I'd ever seen: two well-known actors shouting at each other while looking over each other's shoulders at a teleprompter.

My marriage didn't look like it would survive the wreckage. Working together on *Knight Rider* had been one of the things that had driven us further apart.

One time, Catherine said to me, 'How was that take?'

'I think you should do another one.'

'What do you mean, "Do another one?" You've never won an Oscar.'

Sometimes honesty isn't the best policy.

After two years of marriage, Catherine sat me down and said calmly: 'This is not working and we need to separate.' We broke up because we were more concerned about our careers than each other. I was devastated when she moved all her belongings into her own house, but left me with all of the pets she had collected during our time together: four dogs and three parrots. I had made a big emotional commitment to our marriage and had really wanted it to succeed. I felt, 'Okay, the love will come', because it was almost there anyway. We were soulmates and we had a good time together, but it had turned into a contest rather than a marriage.

As fate would have it, we had both been cast in a horror flick called *Witchery* which was to be filmed in Massachusetts. I still had hopes of a reconciliation when we flew to Boston to join the cast. *Witchery*, however, was a disaster in every sense – an Italian movie with an Italian director and an Italian crew, none of whom seemed too bothered about the script or even whether our lines or the plot made any sense.

The female lead was Linda Blair, who was quite at home with the forces of darkness following her experiences in two *Exorcist* films. In *Witchery*, a group of people are stranded in an old hotel off the coast of Massachusetts, where they incur the wrath of an evil witch (Hildegarde Knef). As the hotel guests begin to die off in gruesome ways, Gary, a young photographer (me) and his girlfriend Leslie (Leslie Cumming) struggle to find a way to defeat the witch. There are corny lines such as:

Leslie: God, you scared me.

Gary: Who were you expecting? The Phantom of the Opera?

I left Boston as soon as I'd shot my scenes, while Catherine stayed on. Suddenly, I heard that she was making another movie and had gone to the Philippines to shoot it. Jan McCormack and Jonni Hartman had received a call from *People* magazine asking for a quote about how I felt about my wife shacking up with an Italian. Catherine called up in tears saying the story wasn't true, so Jan and Jonni convinced the reporters that they had been misled and they didn't run the story. What a nice guy I was – a stupid, idiotic, naïve nice guy.

Catherine came back to Los Angeles and bought a house at Encino in the San Fernando Valley. I had not allowed myself to get emotionally involved with anybody because I still thought it was quite possible that we would get back together. There was a great attraction there and I felt she was just doing to me what I had done to Roberta Leighton. I'd drop by her house like a little doggie and say, 'It'll work out', but she would keep me at arm's length.

Then stories started coming back to me that Catherine was having an affair. I intended to ask her whether this was true when she asked me to meet her for lunch at a restaurant in Encino. Her first words, however, were, 'I don't think this separation is working and I want a divorce.'

Next thing, an obnoxious kid was poking a pen and paper at me. 'Hey, Knight Rider, sign this.'

'Just a minute.'

Kid: 'Mom, he said, "Just a minute." '

Mom: 'Give my son your autograph.'

Me: 'I can't even get a divorce in private.'

In that moment, the failure hit me. I felt, 'Oh God, I'm not going to be married. We're not going to have any kids. Am I going to be one of these guys who gets married twice?'

I said to Catherine, 'Let's work this out.'

She didn't want to work it out.

I went home. It was a difficult time. I never expected to ever be divorced – I was a Catholic and I was supposed to be married for life. I was going to go to hell. I couldn't throw myself into my work because

I was unemployed and I couldn't find a job. I'd see casting breakdowns that said 'David Hasselhoff-type' and I'd ring up and say, 'I look just like him' and they'd say, 'Yeah, I know – but not you.'

Chuck Russell called round.

'I can't get any work,' I said.

'Hollywood eats its young,' he said. 'They use you up and toss you aside. But you'll be back.'

My neighbours Randy and Heather Hill, who worked as directors on *The Young and the Restless,* saw me sitting under my avocado tree with a bottle of scotch. They saw me killing myself and knocked on the door.

Randy: 'Okay, the shit stops here.'

Heather: 'We're your friends and we won't lie to you.'

Randy: 'We saw Catherine with a guy from the soaps.'

I invited this guy to have breakfast with me in a restaurant. I walked in wearing a long, light-weight overcoat like someone out of *The Godfather.* He was a big guy and I wanted to frighten him. I said, 'You know, it takes a real man to show up here. I want to talk to you man to man. Are you having or have you ever had an affair with Catherine?'

He looked stunned and said nothing so I continued.

'If you have, it's okay – I just want to know. I promise you that I won't go crazy, but I've got to have some closure on this – nobody is admitting anything and I'm hearing stuff from other people and it's making me doubt some of my friends. If you don't tell me the truth, I'm very well connected to a group of people who will make your life incredibly unpleasant.'

The guy got very worried. He said: 'It sounds like you're trying to build a case for divorce.'

'I'm not trying to build a case – I'm trying to tell you that I'll walk out of here if you tell me the truth. But if you don't tell me the truth and I find out later that you're lying you're not going to want to live in this city.'

'Well, we were really close.'

'Really close – how close?'

'Very close.'

'What's my wife's Trans Am doing at your house?'

But he wouldn't admit to an actual affair.

I got up and said: 'If you haven't had an affair with my wife but you're very close then I find that inappropriate. If you really want my wife, why don't we just get it over with right now?'

'What?'

'Right now – let's go.'

I picked a fight with him because I wanted to release the anger that was burning inside me, but he wouldn't fight me and the funny thing is that he probably would have kicked my butt. To this day, they maintain nothing happened.

Catherine would visit my house to ask for something she needed and I would always give it to her. She came over to the house when the divorce was about to take effect to sign some papers. I said: 'I won't sign these papers until you tell me the truth.' Even then, she still denied that anything had happened. She walked out and I signed the papers. Game over.

Three years later when the pilot episode of *Baywatch* had aired, a huge bouquet of flowers was delivered to my house. I had a new series and I was starting to get my life back together. I opened the card and it said, 'David, Congratulations on *Baywatch*. It was great and you were great in it.' The flowers were from Catherine. Could she possibly want a part on *Baywatch*? Go figure – but by then I wasn't playing that game any more.

All through the New Year of 1986 I spent a lot of time feeling sorry for myself and looking out of my window at my avocado tree. Suddenly, I decided to go to a pet store and buy a wiener dog – I'd always wanted a wiener and I bought one. I brought him home and said, 'Well, Wiener, it's you and me against the world.'

When the divorce papers arrived at my home, I invited Mom and Dad and eight friends to a divorce party at La Cage aux Folles, the nightclub on La Cienega Boulevard where people went to get super-loaded while watching drag acts. The female impersonators had great fun getting the Knight Rider up on stage and singing Judy Garland songs to him. When I stepped off stage, the maître d said, 'Mr Hasselhoff, Mr Liberace would like to buy you a drink.'

I looked over and saw Liberace lit up like a Christmas tree in the middle of a group of young blond men. He waved at me.

'Ask him if he would like to join our divorce party.'

Liberace and his pompadoured toupee came over to our table, where he introduced himself as 'Lee'.

'I'm such a big fan, David,' he said. 'Who's getting divorced?'

'I am.'

'Well, I'm available – let's party.'

Liberace was drinking gin and tonic and smoking Carlton cigarettes. He was sixty-seven years old and had had a lot of plastic surgery; he was very gracious and very sociable.

'I can see you are upset about the divorce,' he said.

'I'm a little sad.'

'Oh God, darling, put it behind you – life goes on.'

Over the next few months, I got to know Liberace fairly well. Both his parents were dead and he formed a close bond with Joe and Dolores. He was a generous host who loved to surround himself with family, friends and other entertainers. My career was going nowhere but Liberace said, 'You'll be back. I've done it and so will you.' He knew how I felt about the cancellation of *Knight Rider* because he had suffered a big setback when his half-hour daytime show had been scrapped by ABC after only six months.

His personal credo was contained in the pages of *The Magic of Believing*, a self-help book by Claude M. Bristol which extolled the virtues of converting negatives into positives through the power of thought. 'As you stand before the mirror,' the author advised, 'keep telling yourself that you are going to be an outstanding success, and nothing in the world is going to stop you.' (I tried this technique but burst out laughing.)

Everyone in Los Angeles knew that Liberace had lived in a Sherman Oaks mansion with a piano-shaped swimming pool, but he had sold that house and bought another one in Harold Way in the Hollywood Hills, then a penthouse on Beverly Boulevard. He also owned houses in Malibu, Palm Springs, Lake Tahoe, Lake Arrowhead, New York and several in Las Vegas. His main residence at the time I knew him was 'The Cloisters', a converted hotel in the heart of Palm Springs.

My father Joe asked him: 'How many houses do you have?'

Liberace replied: 'Oh Joe, who's counting?'

Lee delighted in showing people around 'The Cloisters', mainly to see their reactions to his lavish style of decorating. On arrival, you were driven into an ornate glass-fronted ballroom with glittering chandeliers, which turned out to be the garage. The entry hall contained Liberace's collection of Greek and Russian icons and the gilt mirror of a Spanish king. In the two-storeyed dining-room, the table was set with silver and crystal. The silverware was engraved with the letter K – it had once belonged to President John F. Kennedy – while the gold-rimmed Moser crystal was identical to Queen Elizabeth's with the exception that it bore the letter 'L' and a crown instead of 'E' for Elizabeth.

Lee's bedroom had so many French objets d'art that he called it 'the Napoleon suite'. It housed probably his most treasured possession, the Louis XV desk on which Nicholas II, the last tsar of all the Russias, had signed the Franco-Russian Alliance of 1893. His bathtub was a sunken marble Jacuzzi and the toilet was modelled in the shape of a throne. There were mirrors everywhere to enable Liberace to carry out his guru's injunction about telling himself that he was going to be an out-standing success. And dogs! – he had nine miniature poodles scampering around the house, plus a vast collection of porcelain canines in nearly every room.

Liberace had so much jewellery that I asked him where he bought it.

'Oh, come to my show in Vegas,' he said, 'and watch the encore.'

Liberace was appearing at Caesars Palace. With the help of a young blond man, Liberace struggled in and out of an assortment of jackets, capes and crowns and paraded in front of his adoring audience. 'I never wear clothes like this off-stage,' he assured them. 'Oh no, I'd be picked up for sure.' Referring to a Norwegian, blue-shadow fox cape with a train twelve feet wide and sixteen feet long, he said: 'There are only two of these in the world and I've got both.'

In between flashy renditions of standards such as 'The Impossible Dream', 'Send in the Clowns' and 'Raindrops Keep Falling on My Head', played on a glass-topped grand piano crowned with his trademark candelabra, he would leave the stage 'to slip into something a little more spectacular' and return swathed in furs and feathers to roars of approval. 'I'm glad you like it,' he chuckled, 'you paid for it.' After two-and-a-half hours of non-stop kitsch, he announced, 'I've had such a marvellous time I'm ashamed to take the money – but I will.' He exited to his signature tune, 'I'll be Seeing You', and a final quip, 'I'm no good – I've just got guts.'

For his encore, Liberace appeared in a pink suit of spun glass embroidered with silver beads which lit up with winking lights. He walked around the stage, shaking hands and kissing middle-aged and elderly women who took off their necklaces, rings and bracelets and handed them to him. He would say, 'Thank you for coming, dear – oh, thank you so much!' and hand all this loot to a little guy from La Cage aux Folles who was dressed up as a monkey with a bellman's hat on. Over in the corner was an armed Brinks guard who took the jewels to Liberace's dressing-room.

Between shows, Liberace showed me all the jewellery he had been given from the first house. 'This happens every night,' he said with a wry demeanour. 'I've made millions. I never asked for it – they just give it to me. I can't turn them down. It gives them such pleasure and it would be insulting.' All of the items were then locked in the safe which had been installed for that very purpose.

After two weeks in Las Vegas, Liberace went off to play the Radio City Music Hall in New York. I never saw him again. Within a year he was dead from the AIDS virus that was secretly destroying him. I was one of many actors and entertainers to whom he had shown kindness and who refused to condemn him when the truth about his death on 4 February 1987 was finally revealed. He was a one-off, a very special guy.

Buddy McCormack saves me from
a fate worse than death in New Zealand

8 Travels with the Hoff (II)

*'I looked at this cute girl's toes and said,
"Buddy, get me outta here!"'*

I accepted an offer from K-tel to make a new album entitled *Lovin'
Feelings*, a compilation of love songs that was a complete change of
pace from *Night Rocker*. Having succeeded in selling items like non-
stick pans on television, K-tel was now marketing albums of past and
present hits to consumers through flashy, high-powered TV advertising
campaigns. *Lovin' Feelings* was to follow this formula. I would cover
songs such as 'Always on My Mind', 'Stand by Me' and 'How Deep is
Your Love', plus a couple of numbers in Spanish to attract the big
Hispanic market.

To keep costs to a minimum, the album was to be recorded by
Festival Records at a recording studio in Auckland, New Zealand. The
prospect of spending four or five weeks away from Los Angeles at the
other end of the earth appealed greatly and I asked Buddy McCormack
to accompany me. We flew into Auckland on a Saturday and the entire
city seemed to be asleep. All I could think of was Michael Rennie in *The
Day the Earth Stood Still*. I looked around and thought, 'There's no
people here.' This was deceptive; I soon learned that Auckland was
quite a lively town beneath its reserved exterior.

Nobody knew I was in town so I enjoyed the freedom of not having to worry about the paparazzi. Every day I'd drive across town from my rented apartment to visit my voice teacher and then go to the studio to record. One afternoon I had stopped at some lights when I saw a boy and a girl walking home from school wearing *Knight Rider* backpacks. I rolled down the window.

'Excuse me, have you seen KITT?'

'Errrrrrr, no.'

'My name is Michael Knight and I seem to have lost my car.'

They seemed rooted to the spot.

'Well, guys, if you do see my car please say I'm looking for him. Here are some pictures to remember me by.'

As I drove away, I looked in the mirror and the kids were screaming and jumping in the air. Then they ran off to tell their parents that Michael Knight was in the neighbourhood. To this day, I wonder whether their parents believed them.

One weekend we took a break from recording and flew back to the States to take the Race for Life children to an Indy race in Milwaukee. The flight was so turbulent that sleep was impossible and the road to the race meeting was shrouded in fog, so we were running late. We needn't have hurried, however – we arrived to find that the event had been rained out. Wearily, we returned to the airport and caught the next plane back to New Zealand to resume our work on *Lovin' Feelings*. It was thirty-six hours flying time there and thirty-six hours back.

I was still devastated about my failed marriage and was amenable to female company. I chatted to an attractive young waitress in a restaurant and invited her back to the hotel. We spent a very pleasant night together and I was keen to repeat the experience, but the following night I sensed that something was wrong and asked her what the problem was.

'I'm really attracted to Buddy,' she confessed. 'Maybe we could have a threesome?'

I got up and looked out the window. 'I think that's your taxi outside,' I said.

Buddy and I went off to a nightclub and were having a few drinks when a good-looking girl started flirting with me. Buddy pulled me to one side. 'David, it's a guy.'

'She's really cute, Buddy.'

'David, it's a guy.'

'No, it's not a guy.'

'Yes it is, David, look at her shoes.'

I looked down and said to Buddy, 'Get me out of here!'

'She' was wearing open-toed shoes which revealed big thick masculine toes. The guy grabbed Buddy, who decked him with one punch. This provoked all of the other guys at the bar to start hitting us because they thought we had just hit a woman. We had to fight our way out of the door. The nightclub was five storeys up and we made it to our car just ahead of an angry lynch mob. Since the car was a right-hand drive, in his haste Buddy mistakenly slammed the car into first gear instead of reverse and crashed into the car in front. While many transvestite fists beat a furious tattoo on the roof, I managed to find reverse and we shot backwards before finally driving off. It was pouring with rain and we lost our pursuers somewhere on the bridge that separates one side of the city from the other. By this time, we were both roaring with laughter.

'Nobody is going to believe this,' Buddy said.

'Who cares?' I said. 'It's just another day in the life of the Knight Rider.'

The high point of my stay was a charity rugby match in aid of the Make-A-Wish Foundation. After the game, John Kirwin, the All Blacks star winger, presented me with his shirt 'as a memento of your work with children'. I was honoured to have the shirt and wore it around Auckland until a beefy guy stopped me in the street.

'John Kirwin is a god here, mate,' he said. 'It's irreverent to wear that shirt.'

I got the point and packed the shirt in my luggage – I've still got it.

While I was in Auckland, I got a call from Darren, a twelve-year-old Canadian boy who was in hospital with a cancerous tumour the size of a grapefruit. I had become friends with Darren after making him honorary grand marshal of the Toronto Grand Prix earlier that year.

'Are you okay?' I asked him.

'Don't worry, I'm not dying,' he said. 'The nurses don't believe that I know you. Will you speak to them? Maybe I can get lucky.'

I spoke to the nurses.

'This is the Knight Rider,' I said. 'Look after him – he's a spiritual angel.'

But Darren did die a year later. His mother called me and said they found him in his bed listening to one of the tapes I had sent him. 'Thank you for always being there for my son,' she said. It was a humbling moment and I regard it as an honour to have known this brave little boy.

After *Knight Rider* had finished its run, I had gone back to South Africa with Buddy and my parents. There's a saying that 'once you go to Africa you must return'. Since my first visit in 1983, I have returned many times and always marvelled at the mystical beauty of the country. The first time I saw the Victoria Falls, I thought to myself, 'How close to God can you get?' Standing on the edge, I had an insane desire to jump into the foaming water but something stopped me. It was as though God was saying, 'Enjoy my beauty – you are one of my children.'

The purpose of this trip was to shoot a commercial in Afrikaans for Royal Dutch Shell. At a party following a press conference about the TV commercial, I found myself in the middle of a group of Afrikaners discussing the rebellion in the African townships. The African National Council had called on the people to make Soweto and the other townships ungovernable. As resistance became more militant, the South African rulers had declared a national emergency and sent out death squads to eliminate rebellious blacks. One of the Afrikaners said to me, 'The biggest mistake we made with "the bleks" was taking them out of the jungle and educating them instead of shooting them.'

I walked away and proceeded to drink a lot of Grand Marnier. I started talking to a female reporter.

'You seem bored,' she said.

'Yeah, I am.'

'What would you like to do?'

'I'd like to take you out of here and have some fun.'

'Let's go.'

We drove to the nearest forest glade, where we steamed up the car. When we got back to the party, looking guilty, everybody was furious that I'd disappeared – except my parents; they understood. They didn't like these people either.

After Mom and Dad had flown back to the States, Buddy and I went on safari in the bush with an Australian friend, John Bonnin. We were driving down a narrow track with thornbushes on either side of our Range Rover. I was in the front, next to the guide, while Buddy was in the back with John. The Curse of Buddy was about to strike . . .

The guide said, 'Whatever you do, don't stick your head out of the window – there's thornbushes everywhere.'

With the wind whistling past the open window, Buddy couldn't hear what he had just said.

'What was that?' he said, sticking his head out of the window. He reeled back in, holding his face, with blood dripping through his fingers. The thornbushes had got him really good. Poor Buddy – I'm afraid we laughed. It was the Curse of Buddy.

The tables were nearly turned when, on the way back to camp, we stopped at a lake where some elephants were taking a bath in the muddy water. John Bonnin was photographing a baby elephant from the edge of the lake when I looked behind him and saw a huge elephant angrily flapping its ears. We had inadvertently got between a baby and its mother.

'John, John,' I hissed.

'Shush – you'll spoil the shot,' he said.

'John, look behind you.'

John took one look and froze.

The guide was nearby. 'Pretend you're bushes,' he whispered.

We dropped to the ground and remained motionless while the elephant walked past us. She was so close we could feel her body heat. To her, we were just a couple of bushes.

Back at camp, we retold this story several times. Then, in the middle of the night, Buddy had to go to the bathroom. On his way back to his tent, he bumped into a rogue elephant which had wandered into the campsite in search of food. Buddy remembered the words, 'Just be a bush.' He dropped to the ground and froze. The elephant walked right past him and Buddy, not daring to breathe, crawled to his tent.

We left South Africa with mixed emotions, not knowing that the days of apartheid and white supremacist rule in South Africa were drawing to a close. By the time I returned, things had irrevocably changed.

Suddenly, I was a rock star performing in huge concerts all over Europe

9 Looking for Freedom

'I was Number One in Austria . . . it was a chance and I grabbed it with both hands.'

I celebrated New Year 1987 in Los Angeles with my pets, now numbering six dogs, two cats and four parrots. Winston, the youngest bird, was also the most talented – he could sing 'I Left My Heart in San Francisco' in E flat. Each pet had its own personality. They gave me nothing but love; they were like devoted children, although one day one of the parrots, Captain Ned, tried to give me a kiss and bit a big chunk out of my lip.

Then in January I headed for Cannes to sell the *Lovin' Feelings* album at Midem, the music industry's biggest marketplace. The idea was that I would perform some of the songs for potential buyers but I was pulled from the show without any explanation and the record was quietly canned. It was a lost endeavour and I returned to Los Angeles disappointed.

I was wondering whether anything else could go wrong when the phone rang and Buddy McCormack said, 'There's a girl wants to have lunch with you.'

'No way – I'm going through my Ernest Hemingway period.'

'She's from Europe and she's your biggest fan.'

'I really don't want to see anybody.'

'Don't break her heart. Just have lunch with her.'

At Buddy's insistence, I invited the girl over to my house in Sherman Oaks. After lunch, I let her drive the Trans Am go-kart that the cast and crew of *Knight Rider* had given me. She drove it around the back lawn and smashed into a rock-pile, completely annihilating the nose. I thought: 'Well, that's perfect.' To change the subject, she said brightly: 'Are you still singing?'

My *Night Rocker* album had sold about seven copies in the USA.

'My parents bought three copies,' I said, 'and I bought three and some idiot bought one.'

'It's Number One in my country,' she said.

'Where did you say you were from?'

'Austria.'

'Austria – cool. Where's Austria?'

We found Austria on a map. It was about the size of Rhode Island. The only other thing on the horizon at that time was an American tour with the road company of *Grease* for which I had been taking dancing lessons on my basketball court from Patrick Swayze's mother, Patsy. My Austrian fan had got me thinking about another possibility, such is the power of positive thinking.

I tracked down the phone number of a Viennese rock-'n'-roll promoter named Herbie Fecther, who ran a company called Profil Promotions. If you want it done, do it yourself.

'Hi, my name is David Schwartz. I represent David Hasselhoff. I understand his record *Night Rocker* is Number One in your country.'

'*Ja, ja* – that is so.'

'He'd like to come over there with the Knight Rider Tour.'

'Will he bring the car?'

'Absolutely.'

'I'll get back to you.'

He rang back. 'I have an opening.'

When I informed Jan McCormack about my plans, she wasn't enthusiastic.

'You can't go on tour,' she said, 'you've got to be back in time for the new pilot season in five weeks' time.'

'What if I can organise the show and complete the tour in four weeks?'

Jan smiled. 'You never give up, do you?'

So Jan contacted Herbie Fecther and negotiated a fee of $100,000 for me to make a fourteen-day tour of Europe.

Then I called my best friend, Marcus Barone, who had arranged the *Night Rocker* album, and told him about the tour. 'Bring your bags – you're staying here,' I said. 'We're going to prerecord the whole show.' I hired guitarist Danny McBride and three other musicians, and under the watchful eye of our mascot Wiener we arranged and rehearsed all the music.

I also called Patsy Swayze: '*Grease* is out, Austria is in.'

'I'll come right over.'

Patsy choreographed the dance routines with me and two dancers on my basketball court and then we recorded the whole thing on video. Patsy wrote the moves down and sent them and the video to a choreographer in Austria who would work with me when I got there.

Then I called Dad: 'I need two black Trans Ams. We're booked in Austria.'

'Okay – I'm on it.'

Two days later he showed up with them. Neither car was registered, but Marcus and I drove them illegally down the 405 Freeway and shipped them over to Austria by Hapag Lloyd Shipping in exchange for a few autographed photographs. I arrived at Vienna Airport with Dad, Buddy McCormack, Marcus Barone, the musicians and a set of audio and videotapes. When we reached Graz, I rehearsed the whole concert with the band and two new backing singers, Bettina and Sabrina. We blacked out one of the windows of the Trans Am and placed a German-speaking driver inside with a microphone.

Two weeks after I'd made the phone call to Herbie Fecther, the Night Rocker Tour opened in a huge marquee in an Austrian town. Herbie came into the dressing-room. 'This is unbelievable,' he said. 'You're drawing more people than the Rolling Stones.'

Dad was in charge of merchandise. 'I've got good news and bad news,' he said. 'There 10,000 people out there but the bad news is that we've sold out of merchandising.'

The Austrian youth magazine *Bravo* reported our first performance:

With bombastic sound and heavy fog, suddenly the door of a pyramidal tent, made of white satin, opens up. Slowly KITT rolls on stage and David is standing on his roof in a black leather outfit and playing a red guitar. He starts to sing the first song from his first LP, *Night Rocker*. Then he slowly slides down to the ground and asks, 'Would you please say hi to my friend?'

The whole hall was raging. The red light in front of KITT starts to blink, a sign that he wants to say something. The crowd is screaming '*We love you, KITT*', and KITT answers '*I love you, too*'. Then KITT starts reporting about their trip to Austria in German. He even teases David, 'Hey David, why don't you speak German?'

With the backing of Bettina and Sabrina, I belted out all of the songs from the *Night Rocker* album. It was corny, it was hysterical but it worked. After that first night, Dad, Buddy and I embarked on *The Sound of Music* tour with the musicians, the road crew and the beautiful Bettina and Sabrina. Every time our bus went around a corner in the Alps we'd all sing, 'The hills are alive with the sound of music . . .'

I kept chuckling, 'Where's Austria? I *love* Austria.'

And you *had* to love Austria. Everywhere we went the girls would strip off and get into the showers and saunas naked. It was only polite to join them – that was Austrian etiquette. We sometimes took two or three saunas a day; it was important for our health. Sabrina was blonde and cute and we had a brief fling. Bettina was hot for Marcus but he was pining for a Jewish-American princess back home and could not be tempted.

In a small town outside Vienna, the crowd were chanting 'Da-vid, Da-vid, Da-vid' as I walked on to the stage with the band. As I was warming up, a paramedic came over and said, 'There's a dying boy coming to see you.' I remembered Randy Armstrong's words, 'Please help other children.' My brain went into slow motion as I saw, out of the corner of my eye, a little human bundle being rolled into the hall on a hospital gurney.

The boy's face was unmarked but he had suffered third-degree burns to 90 per cent of his body in a terrible accident and, although he was in no pain, the paramedic said that he would not live through the night due to infection. His last wish was to meet me. 'I've got a ticket to David Hasselhoff's concert,' he told the doctor. 'Do you think I could see it?' I walked over to the little boy and, holding his hand, told him that I would dedicate this concert to him. He stayed awake all through the performance. I went over to check on him several times. To this boy I was his hero Michael Knight but I couldn't save him – he died the next day.

In Innsbruck, I visited a hospital where Martina, a young girl suffering from cystic fibrosis, was lying in bed. She seemed to have given up hope, the doctor said, and hadn't spoken a word in six weeks. They feared she was going to die. I held Martina's hand. She looked at me and mouthed the word, 'Danke.' The doctor looked at me in amazement as if a miracle had occurred. We were witnessing the power of love. Later, I phoned Martina for a chat and the doctor told me that she was well enough to return home. Martina and I exchanged letters and I visited her every time I went to Austria. She lived for another six years.

My last concert was on 17 April. Afterwards, an enthusiastic kid who had had a few too many drinks decided to test KITT's amazing powers by driving through the brick wall of a disco. Fortunately, the car crumpled on impact; otherwise there would have been carnage. The driver wasn't hurt – stupid but not hurt – although the car was a write-off.

I was about to leave my hotel room and go downstairs to the disco when Buddy dashed in and said, 'Quick – get in the bathroom.' There was a policeman outside my room who was going to arrest me for having made disparaging remarks that cast doubt on the provenance of another Trans Am whose owner claimed it was the original KITT car from the Knight Rider series. In Austria, defamation was a criminal offence.

Dad, unfazed as usual, went out to chat to the cop. Having ascertained that he was a fan of mine, Dad gave him some autographed photos. The cop said, 'I'll just stand outside the door and if I don't see Mr Hasselhoff then I can't arrest him.' Dad came into the bathroom and said, 'Don't worry – I've got it covered.' He arranged for a large van to be pulled up outside my hotel window and I climbed out on to its roof. Later that night, we crossed the border into Germany and escaped the clutches of the law.

Herbie Fecther said, 'The real market is in Germany – this is where we can make a lot of money.' I was about to head back to the USA when I was booked to sing two songs on German television. The first episode of Knight Rider had appeared in Germany on 28 August 1985 and the series was still running, so I was well-known there. I took the Lovin'

Feelings album with me and sang two songs from it, 'You've Lost that Loving Feeling' and 'Historia De Un Amor', the latter in Spanish.

By one of those twists of fate, the mother-in-law of a successful music producer named Jack White was watching the show and, knowing that Jack was always on the lookout for American singers who might appeal to the European market, telephoned him. 'There's quite a handsome American actor on TV,' she said, 'and he's singing in Spanish.'

Jack switched on his TV set and saw me. After the show, he rang Herbie. 'I believe I can make David a huge star in Germany,' he said. Jack White turned out to be a charming German whose real name was Horst Nussbaum; he had anglicised his name to make it easier to deal with English-speaking stars and their managers. 'I'm well connected with radio and TV stations,' he told me, 'and I've already done this with Pia Zadora and Engelbert Humperdinck.'

For the next year, on and off, I toured Europe with the Night Rockers while Jack figured out a way to put me on top of the German charts. I was now a familiar figure in Austria, Germany, Switzerland, Greece, Sweden, Portugal and the Benelux countries (Belgium, Holland and Luxembourg). In Amsterdam, a journalist from *Rolling Stone* magazine reported that he couldn't leave his hotel because it was besieged by a horde of squealing girls. 'I said, "What's going on?" and the clerk said, "Hasselhoff". I thought that was a Dutch word for something exciting. It turned out that David Hasselhoff was staying at the same hotel.'

When I wasn't touring with my band, I was doing movie work. In Las Palmas, I made a film with Austrians, Germans and Italians called *Zärtliche Chaoten II* (*Lovable Zanies II*), a steal from *Back to the Future* in which two down-trodden office workers, Frank (Thomas Gottschalk) and Xaver (Helmut Fischer), get hold of a time machine and travel back to the 1930s to prevent the conception of their bullying boss. Nobody spoke much English and filming was chaotic. I retreated to my hotel, where I started hanging out with a beautiful Egyptian actress. This looked promising, although any chance of a relationship evaporated when dozens of Italian holidaymakers invaded the hotel and hassled me for autographs. One girl followed me around, saying, 'Thank you for existing.'

Las Palmas was a bizarre place, the destination of planeloads of people who wanted to get violently and dramatically drunk. Dozens of Finnish tourists headed for Puerto Rica bay, where they drank so heavily that they passed out on the beach. In the morning, I'd look out of my hotel window and see thirty bloated bodies scattered over the sand. It was a surreal sight. To get away from this saturnalia of sin and sunburn, I decided to go to Casablanca with Buddy on my weekend off. It was a bad choice.

Everything was fine on the flight going over to Morocco but on arrival my visions of a cold beer in Rick's Place or some similarly exotic watering-hole were soon dispelled. Casablanca was one of the hellholes of the world, a filthy, disgusting dump. When we got back to the airport to catch the plane to Las Palmas, we found that the police officers checking passports were all drunk and insisted that I pay them a huge fee for two exit visas. I refused. After an hour's argument, they finally said that I could leave but Buddy would have to stay until the money was paid. The Curse of Buddy had struck again – it was always Buddy.

I went to the news kiosk and bought a magazine that had my picture on the cover. I showed this to the constabulary and said, 'Look, I'm famous.' All of a sudden, they wanted my autograph. There were apologies all round but, they explained, we had missed our flight and would have to take another one. We were ushered out of the airport terminal to find a plane sitting on the runway, very much in the style of the last scene in *Casablanca*.

After boarding the plane, we realised that something was seriously wrong when a couple of dozen fully armed troops marched up the stairway and stowed their backpacks and machineguns in the overhead lockers. The plane took off but instead of heading for Las Palmas we flew due south. All efforts to engage our fellow passengers in conversation about our destination proved futile. I thought about offering them an autographed photo but decided against it; if looks could kill Buddy and I would both have been dead. This was a military aircraft and the soldiers clearly didn't appreciate giving a lift to a couple of civilians.

After several hours, we landed somewhere in south-west Africa. From one of the crew, we learned that we were in Luanda, delivering mercenaries to the war in Angola. Later that day we reached Las Palmas by a roundabout route. I was never more pleased to see a bunch of Italian autograph hunters.

A few months later I checked into a big hotel in Johannesburg to make another film. This establishment was having trouble with one particular guest. People had complained to the management that a naked man was disturbing their sleep by swinging from balcony to balcony late at night. The culprit turned out to be Oliver Reed, the British actor, who was getting drunk and then doing a death-defying Tarzan impersonation high above the street. I had loved Reed's performance in *Women in Love* and wanted to meet him, but he was caught in the act by security staff and kicked out of the hotel.

Since my previous visit, Soweto had become a battleground. The onslaught of armed police and troops on the townships had ignited fresh riots and strikes, which had plunged the country's economy into freefall. The regime was wavering and it seemed it would be only a matter of time before it collapsed.

I was sitting in the lobby being interviewed by an Afrikaner journalist who was asking questions about my drinking habits and the break-up of my marriage. Then he asked me what I thought of South Africa.

'It's a beautiful country,' I replied. 'But it's frightening and sad how black people are treated here.'

The reporter said, 'There really is no apartheid: it's a myth exploited by the foreign press.'

As he said that, I heard 'Bap! Bap! Bap!' I swung around and saw an elderly black man fall to the ground in a pool of blood a few yards away inside the lobby. Three beefy white security guards, armed with handguns, were standing over him. There was panic; women screamed and were ushered out of the way. A squad of paramedics dashed in and carried the dead man away. Everything was soon quietened down.

I went over to find out what had happened. One of the security guards told me that the dead man, a hotel employee, had come in to make a protest about his working conditions. He had been carrying a screwdriver and when the guards confronted him and told him to drop it he had replied, 'I will not work on holidays unless you pay us time and a half.' Instead of tackling him to remove this fairly harmless weapon, the guards had shot him dead.

'He was a troublemaker,' the guard said.

I turned to the Afrikaner reporter and said, 'End of interview. I'm outta here.'

I went upstairs, packed my bags and checked out of the hotel. I felt sick in my stomach and very angry. I moved into an apartment across town.

The film, *The Final Alliance*, later released as *Tigerman*, was a blood-soaked thriller with Bo Hopkins, Jeanie Moore and John Saxon. It was all very silly but I had fallen for a beautiful twenty-year-old South African girl and didn't care. I had met Patricia Lewis when I was invited to a modelling show at my hotel and she was one of the models. Patricia, the daughter of a former mayor of Johannesburg, was a champion gymnast and a terrific singer. It was a great time to be in love with a twenty-year-old who was appreciative, sweet and kind. Buddy McCormack said, 'This is the first time I've seen you look happy since your divorce.'

Patricia and I spent our first romantic night together at the Heia Safari Ranch outside Johannesburg in an African-decor bungalow. That first night in camp one of the guides mimicked the mating cry of a wildebeest. Next day, we drove around the safari park in a little hire car. When we saw two wildebeest, I couldn't resist trying out the mating cry. Patricia roared with laughter but one of the animals looked up and headed straight for us.

'Wow – this mating stuff really works!' I said.

We wound the windows up and I frantically tried to start the diesel engine, but before I could get the car in gear the wildebeest had rammed his head into the bodywork again and again. We made it to the park's entrance and while the gatekeeper was letting us out a passing ostrich ripped off the radio antenna.

I said, 'They'll never believe this.'

Back at the rental agency, I sheepishly handed over the car.

'What happened?' the guy asked.

'I was attacked by a wildebeest and an ostrich ripped off the aerial.'

He didn't flinch. 'Happens all the time,' he said.

Only in Africa …

During another break in filming, we drove to a Zulu village in Natal to watch a tribal dance.

'Why are they staring at me?' I asked Patricia.

'They know who you are,' she whispered.

'How can they possibly know who I am?'

'Because they watch TV. This is where they made a film about Shaka Zulu, king of the Zulu nation. The chief has a satellite TV in his kraal and they all watch it. See, they keep looking at you.'

As a gag, I looked down at my watch and shouted, 'Hey KITT, come pick me up.' In the middle of the dance, every Zulu head swivelled to the right to see if the Knight Rider car was coming. I laughed and laughed. We were invited back to the chief's kraal where everyone partied on some very powerful Zulu beer.

Back in Los Angeles, my old buddy Brandon Tartikoff was still head of entertainment at NBC.

'You know what, David?' he said when I bumped into him in a shopping mall. 'You're ready to come back.'

Brandon called Grant Tinker, former chairman and CEO of NBC, who had left the network in 1986 to develop his own shows. Grant, a handsome silver-haired man in his early sixties, had been married to Mary Tyler Moore when he had formed MTM Enterprises in 1970 to produce the highly successful *Mary Tyler Moore Show* on CBS. MTM went on to produce *Lou Grant*, *Hill Street Blues* and *St Elsewhere*, but Grant had left MTM in 1981 to join NBC. With no shows in the top ten and only two in the top twenty, Tinker had worked with Brandon Tartikoff to revitalise NBC's prime-time schedule. It rose to first place in the ratings with its famed Thursday night line-up of *The Cosby Show*, *Family Ties*, *Cheers*, *Night Court* and *Hill Street Blues*.

Grant had always been associated with literate, sophisticated programming usually referred to as 'quality television'. Trying to emulate his success with MTM Enterprises, he had formed GTG Entertainment after teaming up with Gannett, the giant media conglomerate. One of the shows they were developing was called *Baywatch*.

Brandon Tartikoff told his old boss: 'You hire Hasselhoff and I'll buy the show.'

In the fall of 1988 Jan McCormack handed me the script for the *Baywatch* pilot episode. I read it and told her, 'This is basically *Knight Rider* in a bathing suit. I really don't want to do a show like this.'

Jan sometimes knew me better than I knew myself. She said, 'Just look in and see the presentation video.'

Then Grant Tinker called me in. He said, 'You were at NBC when they were Number Three and when you left they were Number One. I was there, too. This is my first shot back at producing. Come in and take a look at this.'

So I met with the producers, Greg Bonann, Doug Schwartz and Michael Berk, and watched their video of gorgeous girls romping around on beautiful beaches to the beat of Don Henley's hit song, 'Boys of Summer'. Greg had shot it in a very cool way and the lifeguards looked like bronzed Adonises. The 'Baywatch' name had been taken from the nickname for beach patrol boats in Santa Monica Bay.

'Look, guys,' I said, 'I think it's great but I really don't want to wear a bathing suit to work. Imagine it with my skinny legs. I'm happy with my music career, so good luck and I'll see you later.'

I got in my car and called Jan. 'I just told them I don't want to do it, but get me the part – it's a hit.'

'I guess they didn't believe you,' she said. 'They've already called me and we're negotiating.'

In October 1988, *Baywatch* bought me, and NBC bought *Baywatch* from Grant Tinker's production company, GTG Entertainment. I was signed to play Lieutenant Mitch Buchannon, the head lifeguard on Baywatch Beach, in reality the Will Rogers State Beach beneath the high, muddy cliffs of Santa Monica Bay. The credit for a TV series based on surf, sand and sea rescue belongs to Greg Bonann, a Los Angeles lifeguard and Medal of Valour winner who had come up with the idea while sitting on a beach in 1980. It had taken him eight years to get it on to the small screen with the help of his brother-in-law, Doug Schwartz, and Doug's first cousin, Michael Berk.

Even before we'd shot a single frame, sex was a hot issue with the network. I knew from my experiences on *Knight Rider* that it was essential we got the chemistry between the lifeguards absolutely right. We needed actors with charisma – ones you couldn't take your eyes off. The original cast hit a home run on that score by casting three beautiful people: Parker Stevenson of the *Hardy Boys* as Craig Pomeroy, Billy Warlock from *Days of Our Lives* as Eddie Kramer, and nineteen-year-old Erika Eleniak, a gorgeous blonde with riveting blue eyes, as Shauni McClain.

Billy Warlock looked like a perennial teenager. 'I'm not short,' he'd say to Parker Stevenson and me. 'I'm normal to me – you guys are the weird ones.'

Erika had grown up a lot since she played the little girl who kissed ET in Steven Spielberg's sci-fi movie. She was the perfect *Baywatch* girl, although she nearly didn't make it into the cast when NBC chiefs discovered that she had shot a *Playboy* nude centrefold. The timing couldn't have been more unfortunate; the pictures were due to be published in July 1989, just as *Baywatch* would be selling itself to the TV critics if everything went according to plan. NBC wanted us to fire

Erika 'to maintain the cast's integrity' but she was such a sweet girl that we talked them into letting her stay. It was an important decision because her Shauni McClain character was *Baywatch's* original female attraction. The love affair between Shauni and Billy's Eddie Kramer developed into the highlight of the first season.

We also hired beauty queen Shawn Weatherly to play lifeguard Jill Riley. 'My job is not the exhibition of my body,' Shawn had announced after winning the Miss Universe contest in 1980. With a pay packet of $17,500 per episode, the *Baywatch* scriptwriters soon changed that. Shawn was a quiet, reserved girl but when she ran down the beach she was poetry in motion.

Michael Newman, a lifeguard and fire-fighter, was hired as the veteran wise-cracking 'Newmie'. Behind the scenes, he was the guy who showed us how to run with the rescue can, use a wave-runner in the surf and dive from a boat going 30 m.p.h. He saved our butt in the water more than a few times; he really is a legendary lifeguard. Finally, two fine actors, Monte Markham (Captain Don Thorpe of the Lifeguard Service) and Gregory-Alan Williams (Sergeant Garner Ellerbee of the LAPD) came on board to give the cast extra depth and experience.

Filming of the two-hour pilot of *Baywatch* started under the direction of Richard Compton on 4 January 1989 with a generous budget of $4 million. It was 49°F in the water off the beach at Malibu and the whole crew turned up in wet suits to film the first scene in which Parker Stevenson's character drives the Baywatch lifeguard truck under Malibu Pier and gets trapped by the rising tide.

Elegantly dressed in jeans, T-shirt and sunglasses, Richard Compton strolled on the beach to find himself cut off from the action by fifty yards of water. And the water was filthy. There were faeces, hypodermic syringes, trash – all of the detritus of a big city was pouring into Santa Monica Bay. When we got sick from a stomach virus, GTG decided to transfer the whole project to Hawaii.

Brandon Tartikoff, who had script approval, called us there and said, 'I don't care where you film it – I want the word "panic" and I want the word "Malibu" in the title.' Henceforth, the pilot episode was known as 'Baywatch: Panic at Malibu Pier'.

Hawaii was an ideal location for filming the water work that was to be at the heart of every *Baywatch* story; the weather was mostly fine and we could get a full day's work in. We were shooting all the water scenes around a barge which contained the make-up department, a dressing-room and a place to eat lunch. What nature hadn't intended, the make-up artists could provide; anyone who didn't have an olive complexion was painted with dark body-coloured make-up. It had to be waterproof and it was an absolute nightmare to get off.

On the first day, I came up for lunch after shooting in the water all morning and noticed that a bunch of divers, carrying spear guns armed with shotgun charges, had followed me on board. I asked around and discovered that this was the shark patrol; there were a large number of people-eaters in these waters and the divers were making sure we didn't get eaten. Nobody had told us – after all, we were only actors and I guess they didn't want to scare us.

Part of the idea behind *Baywatch* was that all of the cast would do as much of their own stunt work as possible. In one scene, the script called for me to swim over to a boat, climb on board and put on some scuba gear and then dive back into the water. The oxygen tank, however, was loose on my back and when I dived in it slammed me on the head, dislodging my mouthpiece and knocking me senseless. I regained consciousness a few seconds later to find I was underwater looking up at the surface and sucking in water instead of air. I started choking. I thought 'Boy, the ratings are going to go through the roof if I don't make it.'

By this time, the camera crew who had filmed the shot had climbed back on the boat without realising that I was missing. Several professional lifeguards had been hired to watch each scene and they dived in and found me. They dragged me up on to the boat, where I gasped and wheezed for several minutes but was otherwise all right.

For professional stunt work, I had two doubles at different times, Alex Daniels and David Haas. I met David when I went to see Michael Frayn's play *Noises Off* in Kansas City. As I walked out of the theatre, a big guy walked up and said, 'Hi, I'm David Haas. One day I'm going to be your double.'

I said, 'I like your attitude – you sound like me.'

First day on *Baywatch*, a guy walks up and says, 'Remember me?' It was David Haas. We hired him on the spot. He stayed for eleven years. Had he read *The Power of Positive Thinking*?

The pilot, however, was bedevilled by production problems of one sort or another, including the exorbitant cost of relocating the entire cast and crew to Hawaii. GTG's line producer Robert Hargrove allowed the shoot to go $2 million over budget, a bad start to our relationship with the network, even though GTG would have to pick up the tab. But despite all these difficulties 'Panic at Malibu Pier' was scheduled to be aired by NBC and its affiliates on Sunday 23 April 1989.

Meanwhile, Jack White had worked out a marketing strategy for me to take the German record market by storm. 'I want you to record one song,' he said. 'It was released in the 1970s and it was a big hit. It's time for it to come back.' The song was entitled 'Auf Der Strasse Nach Suden.' Jack renamed it 'Looking for Freedom' and I recorded it in English as a single which was released on the BMG Ariola label in Germany in March 1989, just as a wave of revolt began sweeping through the Communist countries of Eastern Europe.

'Looking for Freedom' entered the charts at the bottom and showed every sign of staying there until Jack White hired Eugen Joeckel, a big Santa Claus of a man whose job was to place acts on television. Eugen's attitude, I quickly discovered, could be summed up in eight words: 'Let's drink schnapps, have fun and be happy.' He was always laughing and smoking and drinking schnapps but he pulled some strings with his TV contacts and got me a booking on a variety show. 'Looking for Freedom' was the perfect song for the time and place – the audience went wild for this guy from America singing about freedom: the singing Knight Rider.

Synchronicity again.

Tom Jones (the singer, not the composer) performed on the same show and afterwards we took twenty dancing girls back to our hotel and headed for the rooftop swimming pool. Eugen, meanwhile, had engaged in a wager with a columnist from *Bildzeitung* newspaper.

'I'll drink you under the table,' Eugen told the journalist. 'If I win, you put my boy on the front page.'

The journalist, a big drinker, agreed to take the bet and the drinking contest got underway, while Tom Jones and I were swimming with the dancing girls. Swimming and kissing, swimming and kissing. I *liked* being a star. I came down once or twice to check on Eugen. He was in the bar, drinking away, but when I went back at 3 a.m. I found him asleep at the table. The journalist staggered to his feet.

'Your friend has lost the bet,' he said. He swayed towards me. 'But I still put you on the front page.'

The following day there was a front-page item saying, 'Who is this David Hasselhoff? Not since the Beatles have I seen such a reaction in Germany.' The day after the article appeared, we sold 17,000 copies of 'Looking for Freedom'; the next day I did another TV show and we shifted a further 27,000 records.

Eugen said: 'We're moving up the charts – from Number 220.'

When I left Germany two weeks later, 'Looking for Freedom' was Number One. There was an immediate problem in that we had no follow-up record to release to capitalise on the success of 'Looking for Freedom'. Jack White said: 'Go to Austria and hole up in my house in the Alps. I'm going to gather some songs. We need to record an album.'

Jack's house was in Kitzbühel and Patricia Lewis joined me there. We romped in the snow and, of course, followed the Austrian etiquette of taking many saunas together. We looked the essence of happiness when a photographer shot us for the cover of the German magazine *Bunte*. Things were going so well that I had to ask myself whether Patricia was in love with me or whether, like some of my previous girlfriends, she was in love with my celebrity and the possibility of becoming a star herself. It was very hard to know. In the past, I had been devastated to catch a look in a girl's eye that told me she was hooked on fame and had become more attracted to the camera and to stardom than to being my partner. I don't think any of them had even been aware of it.

On 23 April 1989 the great *Baywatch* saga that would captivate a global audience of a billion viewers at its peak opened on the sparkling blue waters of the Pacific Ocean with a shot of an ordinary seagull. After just five seconds, however, the first blonde appears on screen and precisely three seconds later the camera lingers on the first cleavage in a close-up of a sunbathing bikini girl in a straw hat. The pilot could have been more accurately entitled *Fatal Attraction Goes Surfing* because the storyline has Parker Stevenson's character rescuing a homicidal nymphomaniac, played by Madchen '*Twin Peaks*' Amick, who becomes infatuated with him, stalks him and tries to kill his wife Gina Pomeroy (Holly Gagnier) when he rejects her.

And that was only part of the story. The action takes place on Mitch's first day at Baywatch Beach, where he has taken over as lieutenant, making him a 'hard shoes' man among the barefooted lifeguards. It's a difficult day; not only has Craig stuck the Baywatch truck under Malibu Pier, but Mitch has to contend with the arrival of two rookie lifesavers, Eddie and Shauni, and an arrogant Australian, Trevor Cole (Peter Phelps), as well as dealing with his young son Hobie (Brandon Call) and his difficult ex-wife Gayle (Wendie Malick).

Trevor Cole introduces himself to Mitch as 'a shark fighter and virgin converter' and tells him that he's so famous back home in his native Australia that his face is on cereal boxes. Mitch and Trevor fall out when several swimmers are caught in a riptide and Trevor rescues an attractive girl.

Mitch: 'You don't pass up one victim for another one. Not in my water anyway.'

Trevor: 'You're just sore because I out-swam you, mate.'

Mitch: 'Saving lives isn't a competition on my beach. You step out of line one more time on my beach and you've got me to answer to, mate.'

The dialogue, like the plot, left a lot to be desired. Rarely in the long and varied history of American television have the critics had such a perfect target as *Baywatch* to aim their barbs at. The *Variety* critic, 'Tone', wasn't impressed, complaining that writers Michael Berk and Douglas Schwartz 'present a barrage of flesh, characters who've been on the beach too long and tales that lose their lustre before the first wave. Covering lots of bases, "Baywatch: Panic at Malibu Pier" doesn't even get its feet wet.' Another critic called *Baywatch* 'the silliest show of the season'.

I'd heard all of this before when the critics had written off *Knight Rider*. 'We got bad reviews,' I told the cast. 'That means we're going to be around for years.'

Brandon Tartikoff loved the pilot and so did the viewers. The *Baywatch* pilot scored a 17.1 rating with a 34 per cent share. It drew the second highest audience of the week after *60 Minutes*. NBC ordered twelve episodes for the fall schedule, with another nine to follow if these were well-received.

Meanwhile, Jack White had dug up old songs that Engelbert Humperdinck had sung and he had bought others from American songwriters Diane Warren and Mark Spiro. While we were putting the album together in Los Angeles, 'Looking for Freedom' stayed at Number One in Germany for eight weeks and sold over a million copies. I smiled so much that the Germans called me 'the Sunny Boy'.

All that year the Cold War had been heading towards its dramatic conclusion and 'Looking for Freedom' had become an anthem for the

German people on both sides of the Berlin Wall in their struggle for reunification. It was Jack White's genius that he had chosen a song that captured the frustrations of the German people over their years of division between East and West. By the time Berliners started hacking away at the concrete wall that had divided their city for a generation, they were singing in English, 'I've been lookin' for freedom; I've been lookin' so long; I've been lookin' for freedom; still the search goes on.'

The album, *Looking for Freedom*, released just before Christmas, also hit the top of the German charts and stayed there for three months. It went gold and triple platinum in Europe on its way to becoming Germany's Number One selling album. I was named Germany's Most Popular and Best Selling Artist of the Year, with two German newspapers running banner headlines screaming, 'HASSELHOFF: NOT SINCE ELVIS!' and 'HASSELHOFF: NOT SINCE THE BEATLES!' And all because of a little Austrian girl who had won a lunch with me in Los Angeles. Thank you, Buddy. Forty gold and platinum discs later, I owe her my life-long gratitude, but the credit also goes to Buddy because if it wasn't for him I wouldn't have had lunch with her that day.

Baywatch was a different story. The knives were out for us when we assembled in the ballroom of the Century Plaza Hotel in Century City to meet the press. The reporters and TV critics had viewed 'Panic at Malibu Pier' plus a promotional video and seemed determined to crucify us even though we had yet to shoot the opening episode of the first season. We had been warned by Grant Tinker that we would be attacked and he had briefed Greg Bonann on how to handle hostile questions such as 'Why is Grant Tinker doing a tits-and-ass show?' and 'Why have you made a retread like David Hasselhoff the star of *Baywatch*?'

Flanked by Shawn Weatherly, Parker Stevenson and me, Greg said: '*Baywatch* is a serious drama about a group of dedicated men and women who've made a commitment to saving lives. Parker's character is an attorney who is also a lifesaver. He's dealing with how he's perceived at his law firm and the stereotypes that he must dispel.' When someone questioned my casting, Greg pointed out that the last time NBC had won the Friday night slot 'was in 1985 with David Hasselhoff in *Knight Rider*'. 'He is hardly a retread,' he said. 'He's a proven star.'

'Why is Grant Tinker doing a tits-and-ass show?'

'We have Shawn Weatherly, a Miss Universe, and Erika Eleniak, a *Playboy* Playmate,' Greg said. 'They are both beautiful women. We also have Hasselhoff, Stevenson, Billy Warlock, a whole bunch of buff guys. And, yes, everyone is running around in a red bathing suit. However, this show is about lifeguards rescuing people. You cannot perform a rescue wearing street clothes. I've been lifeguarding since 1970, I should know. In order to demonstrate the reality of our profession, we must show fit, healthy men and women wearing the appropriate outfits: bathing suits.'

'There are plenty of beautiful girls in *Baywatch*,' I said, 'because there are plenty of beautiful girls on California's beaches. It may not be art, but it's real life.'

Greg Bonann explained some of the new resuscitation procedures that saved the lives of many swimmers who would otherwise have died. Meanwhile, conditions on the beach had become more dangerous for lifeguards owing to hypodermic needles discarded by drug addicts and the presence of armed gangs. *Baywatch*, he said, would capture all of these important elements.

Mark Dawidziak of the Knight-Ridder News Service commented that very little of this had showed up in the *Baywatch* pilot, which he described as 'a mindless parade of cheesecake and beefcake'. We were determined to prove the critics wrong when we started filming the first *Baywatch* episode, 'In Deep', at Will Rogers State Beach on 1 August 1989. We were soon in trouble. The director, Peter Hunt, a friend of Michael Berk and Douglas Schwartz, had never directed water work before and the eight-day shoot overran by two days, with Greg Bonann's second unit having to film most of the water work. The water was still filthy and to overcome the health hazards we were doused in disinfectant by medics every time we came out of the water.

But it was the script that bothered me most. The series got off on the wrong foot in the very first episode when two drunken jet-skiers run over and kill a female windsurfer. Mitch tracks down the killers and hands them over to the police. If the pilot had been *Fatal Attraction*, this was *Hill Street Blues*. NBC's executives were comfortable with the familiar cops-and-robbers formula and expected high ratings. 'In Deep' finished a credible second in its time slot to ABC's *Full House* and *Family Matters*.

As I saw it, the problem was one of credibility: lifeguards did not apprehend criminals, so it would be difficult for the viewers to believe in us. I was incensed when the network gave us a promo featuring a serial killer in a scary mask and told us to build a show around it. 'We're killing off someone in every episode,' I complained. 'Nobody is going to want to go to Malibu.' The first twelve episodes were saved by two things: viewers loved the scenes between Mitch and his son Hobie, and they were drawn to the love affair that developed between Shauni McClain and Eddie Kramer. All four of us were getting large amounts of fan mail and we were confident that NBC would place an order for another nine shows.

Meanwhile, the success of *Looking for Freedom* had taken me back to Germany, where I had been signed for a tour by Marcel Avram of Mama Concerts. My band consisted of musical director Glen Morrow on keyboards; Jeff Phillips, drums; Danny McBride, guitar; Al Marni, bass; and Koko Kojima, saxophone, keyboards and guitar.

Glen, a six-foot-five-inches-tall Canadian, had previously worked with Jeff Phillips in the Chris de Burgh band and became a dear friend. He came to my house in Sherman Oaks and we put the lyrics of every song up on the wall and jammed together until we were satisfied with the arrangements. Then he went back to Toronto to rehearse the band prior to flying to Germany to meet me.

KITT crashes through the Berlin Wall – an auspicious sign
of things to come

10 Travels with the Hoff (III)

'East Germans thought Knight Rider *was
a Western and turned up in cowboy hats.'*

My first impression of East Germany was that I had gone from colour to black and white. You left your peace of mind at Checkpoint Charlie, the American border crossing on Friedrichstrasse, and entered the uncertain Communist world beyond. The Wall had ringed the Western sectors of Berlin since 1961 and had come to symbolise the Cold War in Europe. This was where it had all started with the Soviet blockade of Berlin in 1948 and where, in a few months' time, it would all come to a shattering end.

The main reason I was in East Berlin was that I hoped to play the part of Dean Jones, an American who had married an East German girl and had been murdered by the Stasi (the East German secret police) for fighting for human rights. I figured the experience of actually visiting East Germany would be useful so I had accepted the invitation of a West German newspaper to do an interview with one of its reporters at the Grand Hotel in East Berlin.

'This,' the reporter said, 'is where diplomats stay when they visit the German Democratic Republic.'

The Grand looked like a relic from Germany's imperial past, all polished brass, ornate furnishings and flowing stairways, but it was in fact a prefabricated East German construction. Over lunch, the reporter asked me for my impressions of life in a Communist country. I looked outside and saw drably dressed passers-by muffled up against the easterly wind. It was a bleak, depressing scene. I told the reporter I wasn't comfortable having lunch in this hotel, which seemed too luxurious, too privileged and too remote from ordinary East Berliners.

'I totally understand, Mr Hasselhoff,' he said. 'Let's go outside and meet some of the people.'

On Friedrichstrasse, military lorries swished through the grey drizzle, and little Trabants, the tiny East German car with tail fins and a two-cylinder, two-stroke engine like a lawn mower, put-putted past in clouds of exhaust smoke. We were heading in the direction of Alexanderplatz when two teenage girls came up to me and said, 'David Hasselhoff.'

'Hi – you know me?'

They had a little English and I figured they must have seen me in *Knight Rider*.

'Do you watch TV? A talking car?'

One of the girls looked at me quizzically. 'A talking car? No – your song.' And she sang, 'I've been looking for freedom.'

'Have you ever been to West Berlin?'

'No, we are too young. Sometimes old people are allowed to go into the West, or people who are very ill, or in special circumstances. Sometimes they try to escape.'

I asked the photographer to take a photograph of me with the girls and arranged to meet them at the same spot the following day. Next morning, the picture appeared in the paper. I went back into East Berlin and gave each girl a copy of the *Looking for Freedom* album, with the comment, 'Here's a little taste of freedom.' They were so overwhelmed that they cried.

Back at the Brandenburg Gate in West Berlin, I asked Eugen Joeckel, 'Do you think the Wall will ever come down?'

He shook his head.

'Not in my lifetime.'

As we looked up, we saw East German soldiers patrolling back and forth on top of the Wall. One of them glared at us so I gave him a V-sign. At that moment, I felt a real animosity towards the Russians; it seemed that the fear and repression of World War II was still as powerful as ever. But the dramatic events that would bring down the Wall had already started with President Mikhail Gorbachev's decision to give up the Soviet Union's military hold over Eastern Europe. On his first official visit to West Germany in May 1989, Gorbachev had informed Helmut Kohl, the West German Chancellor, that Moscow was no longer willing to use force to prevent the democratisation of its satellite states. The rot had set in.

I returned to Germany with my band in the summer of 1989 to do the Freedom Tour, which turned out to be prophetically accurate. Influenced by Eugen Joeckel's 'not in my lifetime' comment, I had come up with the idea of destroying the Wall as a dramatic part of the show. We recreated the Wall out of painted Styrofoam blocks and I drove a Trans Am named 'Freedom' straight through it. The crowd went wild.

Then at 6.53 p.m. on 9 November 1989, a member of the new East German government was asked at a press conference when the promised new East German travel law would come into force. He answered: 'Well, as far as I can see, straightaway – right now.' Thousands of East Berliners surged to the border crossings and demanded to be let through. At 10.30 p.m. that night the border was opened at Bornholmer Strasse; this was the historic moment that signalled the end of the Berlin Wall.

We were now able to perform on both sides of the Wall and thus I became the first American entertainer that many East Germans had ever seen. After doing a concert in Kiel, I fell asleep on the tour bus, only to be shaken awake when we hit a series of potholes. We had reached East Germany. We spent a lot of time in Rostock, Schwerin, Kemnitz and Leipzig, among other places. The only smooth roads were outside the town halls. In Leipzig, the acid rain was so potent we feared it would strip the paint off our bus. In Rostock, the citizens showed their feelings towards their Communist masters by tearing down the statue of Karl Marx.

How had these people survived under Communism? It took years to get a telephone or a car, and people informed on their neighbours to the Stasi. The East German economy had collapsed, so we lowered our admission prices to enable as many people as possible to see the show. We played ice hockey rinks, basketball gymnasiums, school halls, and it was an honour to be there.

Schwerin, one of the oldest cities in East Germany, looked as though it hadn't changed since World War II. Our hotel was an army barracks, with little single beds and the most rudimentary fittings. Most of the population of Schwerin had never seen an American performer and queued in the rain to buy tickets. When we went on stage, we saw that the audience was dotted with cowboy hats. We were blown away. They had come to see 'the American singer' and had a perception of Americans as cowboys.

After the concert, the crowd was so enthusiastic to see us that we were trapped in the hall. It was 4 a.m. before the fans finally went home and we were able to get back to our 'hotel'. So 1989 was the year everything turned around for me, and that night I really felt like the star who came in from the cold. Maybe *Looking for Freedom* did have some influence on the Wall coming down.

There was an unexpected postscript in 2006 when Dirk Nowitzki, the seven-foot-tall German-born star of the Dallas Mavericks basketball team, was questioned about his astonishing 90 per cent success rate with free throws in the NBA league. Asked how he maintained his concentration to shoot so accurately, Dirk replied, 'I sing David Hasselhoff's *Looking for Freedom* in my head.'

Jack White with his wife Janine, the record producer
who set me on the path to gold (and platinum)

Meet Captain Mitch Buchannon . . . my alter ego for eleven long
and happy years on *Baywatch*

11 Birth of *Baywatch*

'You know what? I'm ready for fatherhood.
I want to get married.'

Back in Los Angeles, I caught up with Sammy Davis Jr when Mom, Dad and I attended his concert at the Greek Theatre, where he was appearing with Frank Sinatra and Liza Minnelli. Backstage, Sammy welcomed us with open arms. He said to Mom: 'One of the greatest regrets of my life is that I never got to sing with your son.'

Cranky Frankie was having a tantrum. 'It's too damn cold to sing,' he said. 'Let's get out of here and find a bar.' Liza talked him into staying, although he cut his act short, much to the disappointment of the paying customers.

The last time I saw Sammy was in Las Vegas when John Ritter, now a big TV star, asked me to host a telethon in aid of a cerebral palsy charity. We had every major star in Vegas on the show, including Engelbert Humperdinck, Wayne Newton and Sammy Davis Jr. It was just a few months since Sammy had been fitted with an artificial hip and he walked in leaning on a cane. 'Hang on to this for me, Snapper,' he said, handing me the cane. His first song was a new one, 'This is the Moment', and then he sang his trademark 'Mr Bojangles' and walked off to a standing ovation. He collapsed in my arms.

'This is killing me,' he said.

Soon afterwards, Sammy was diagnosed with throat cancer. He told his doctor that if he couldn't sing he didn't want to live. 'We could have performed an operation on his voice box,' his doctor told me, 'but it would have ended his singing career and he wasn't prepared to make that sacrifice.' Sammy succumbed to throat cancer on 16 May 1990. 'This is the Moment', the song he had sung in Vegas, was one of the ballads from a new Leslie Bricusse show called *Jekyll and Hyde: The Musical*. It was an omen for the greatest experience of my professional life.

Meanwhile, I had fallen in love. Pamela Bach, a beautiful blonde with green eyes, had been a guest star in 'Knight Racer', Episode 71 of the *Knight Rider* series. We didn't have any scenes together, but I had seen her on the set and, as a joke, a crew member had sent her an invitation to join me in my trailer. Pamela, however, had a boyfriend, a well-known comedian, and she politely ignored the invitation. Some time later I met her in Las Vegas when I went to see the comedian's show. I was then married to Catherine and Pamela was still involved with the comedian.

Things changed in December 1988 when I went to the opening of a club called the Last Tango in Studio City, Sherman Oaks. Pamela was there.

'Are you still with the comedian?'

'No. Are you still married?'

'No.'

That night, we talked and talked. I rang Pamela early next morning and we talked some more. We talked every day for a week. On Friday night I asked her out for a date. We decided to hang out. We jogged together and became friends. The last thing I wanted was to get into another long-term relationship but she was beautiful and, as she liked to say, 'all girl'.

Pamela was the middle of three sisters who had been raised in Tulsa, Oklahoma, in Will Rogers' old ranch-house. It was a big family; over the years her mother and stepfather had raised thrity-seven foster children. Like me, Pamela had been performing since the age of nine when she had sung 'Raindrops Keep Falling on My Head' and realised that she loved the stage. But she was good at maths at high school and had studied engineering at Northeastern Oklahoma Junior College for two years before heading for the West Coast, where she hoped to make a more creative career as a broadcaster. While living in Los Angeles she had acted in plays largely as a way of meeting new people and had worked as a page at the TV station KTLA, when she was approached by an agent offering to represent her, she decided to make a career in acting.

On our second date, I invited Pamela to fly to Hawaii while I was filming the *Baywatch* pilot. My plan was to declare my love for her in a suite of the Hilton Hotel on the shores of Waikiki Beach. But she said no. I thought that was cool. She wasn't in a hurry to jump into bed with me and I respected that.

In the summer of 1989 I flew to South Africa to end my relationship with Patricia Lewis. My feelings for Pamela were growing stronger and I had realised that the Patricia thing was not going to happen; she was determined to pursue a singing career in South Africa, while all of my hopes and dreams were in America and Europe.

When I got to Germany for the second leg of the Freedom Tour, I called Pamela and asked her to join me. She flew across the Atlantic and checked into my hotel in Munich on a 'strictly separate bedrooms' basis. It was an ideal set-up for a romantic interlude but I blew it by working too hard and spending too little time with her. One morning, I left Pamela a note saying, 'See you at 1700', but she saw some beer bottles outside my room and mistakenly thought they were mine. She packed her bags and checked out of the hotel, saying, 'Tell him I'm leaving.'

I spent the day searching Munich for her. When I finally found her, she said: 'I wouldn't have come if I'd known you were going to be so busy.' Not wishing to complicate matters, I hadn't told Pamela anything about Patricia Lewis, but Pamela had seen a picture of Patricia and me on the cover of a German magazine. She had asked the maid to explain what it meant in English. I didn't know she had seen this – I was hiding every article I could find – but she said, 'You know what? I don't think this is for me.'

'I did lie to you,' I said. 'I did go down to South Africa to see a girl to say goodbye. And I did say goodbye.'

'I'm leaving.'

'No, you're not. I want to make our relationship work. I love you and I want to give you my heart.'

Over the next week, we spent every day together and became very close. Pamela accompanied me to London while I cut a new record. The same problem occurred again, however, when I spent too much time at work.

'I'm still leaving.'

'No, you're not.'

'Yes, I am.'

But when Pamela looked for her passport it had mysteriously disappeared. She was forced to stay in London for another week and all that time her passport was in the back pocket of my jeans. Then we went to Bruges, where we made passionate love for ten days. We returned to Los Angeles very much a couple.

A few weeks later we were in Carmel while I recorded 'On the Wings of Tenderness'. When I saw a man holding a little child, I said to Pamela, 'You know what? I'm ready for that.' In the next few days, I proposed and she accepted.

Meanwhile, *Baywatch* had received a mixed reaction from just about everybody. Our critics saw it as a tits-and-ass show with little dramatic merit, while many viewers loved it despite its off-putting 'cops-and-robbers' storylines. Brandon Tartikoff told us that NBC would order the remaining nine shows of the first season on condition that we brought in former soap star John Allen Nelson to add some mayhem to the show as John D. Cort, a former Baywatch lifeguard with a reputation for incorrigibility. When Cort roars up on a stolen motorcycle, Mitch and Craig are surprised to see him, but they aren't surprised when he is soon fighting with Eddie Kramer, chasing girls, breaking the rules and getting involved in smuggling and gambling. Being a Baywatch lifeguard, however, he turns out to have a heart of gold.

Baywatch's first cast problem arose when Shawn Weatherly announced that she was leaving because she felt that her character, Jill Riley, had been marginalised in favour of Erika Eleniak and the numerous guest stars who were invited on to the show. 'I've read the upcoming scripts,' she said. 'It's all bullshit. My character has nothing to do.' When we were unable to persuade her to stay, we wrote an episode in which her character is attacked and killed by a great white shark while she is rescuing some children. Jill and Mitch were in the water together. We had to shout 'Shark!' but it was so cold we could hardly speak. When I climbed out of the water, it took me an hour to stop shivering.

'Shark Derby' was Greg Bonann's first directing gig and Jill's death added a touch of realism to *Baywatch* by showing one of the real hazards of a lifeguard's work. It turned out to be the highest-rated show of the first season. We sorely missed Shawn, however – she was a real pro.

On 9 December 1989 Pamela and I both wore white and exchanged rings at our wedding in the Little Brown Church at Studio City (the same church, incidentally, in which Ronnie Reagan had married Nancy). My father Joe acted as my best man. There was no time for a honeymoon. A few days later I received an invitation to appear on the popular Sylvester Show in Berlin on New Year's Eve. They wanted to shoot me performing three songs at a gala in the Berlin Hilton. I said, 'Sure I'll come, but I want to sing on the Berlin Wall.'

I never figured they would agree, but they called back and said, 'Okay.' So I left the beach and, with Pamela and a couple of buddies, headed for the most amazing night of my life. The temperature was two degrees below zero and falling when we checked into the Berlin Hilton. Just before we set off for the Wall, I realised that we didn't have a video tape to record this amazing experience. The show was being broadcast live on television and there was a video cassette recorder in our hotel room. The problem was, it had no tape. 'No one in Los Angeles is going to believe this,' I told reception. 'I've got to find a video tape.' Enquiries and entreaties proved fruitless until there was a knock on the door and a bellman was standing there holding a videotape in his hand. 'I went home and got mine,' he said. 'You're welcome to use it.' He wouldn't take any payment. I put the tape in, hit 'record' and off I went.

Police cars with wailing sirens escorted us down the Unter den Linden to the Brandenburg Gate, where one million Berliners had gathered on either side of the wall to see in the country's most joyous New Year in five decades. I was placed in the bucket of a crane and hoisted a hundred feet above the Wall. Even before I'd sung a note, the crowd erupted into wild cheering.

As I started to sing 'Looking for Freedom', the people joined in. Thousands of young Berliners, swathed in scarves and overcoats, sang the words of my song in English, clapped their hands and swayed from side to side to the beat. Everyone was singing my song and I was singing, crying and freezing all at once. As the great chorus rose up in the night sky above the Brandenburg Gate, you didn't have to be German to find it emotional. All I could think was, 'What an honour to be part of history.' When I was lowered to the ground I grabbed a bottle of schnapps and took several swigs. Then I started chopping chunks out of the wall with a hammer and putting the pieces in my pockets. I took them home and gave them to the *Baywatch* crew on a little plaque saying 'A little piece of freedom'. When I got back to the hotel, the tape was still running in the VCR. I pressed 'rewind' and 'play' and there it was – I had that whole unforgettable night on tape. Since then, that tape has been shown around the world on television many times. If you want it done, do it yourself.

I had been home in Sherman Oaks for a few days when there was a knock on the door and a man introduced himself as the new neighbour who had just moved into the house next door.

'I understand you're famous in Germany,' he said.

'Well, yes – how did you know?'

'There are Germans in my trees.'

We walked up the driveway and there were shouts from the trees on his side of the fence.

'Hello, David!'

'Hi, David, this is Fritz!'

The neighbour was right; there were Germans in his trees. I invited them to come down on to my side of the fence to meet me. It was quite common for fans from Germany or Austria to trek all the way out to Sherman Oaks to pay me a visit and talk about my popularity in their country.

In 2004, I visited a museum in Berlin and told Germany's *TV Spielfilm* magazine that I was a bit sad there was no photo of me singing at the Berlin Wall among the museum's extensive photographic collection. By the time this remark had been translated into English and published in the West, I was accused of taking the credit for bringing down the Wall, for reunifying the two Germanys and for ending the Cold War in Europe. Under the headline 'DID DAVID HASSELHOFF REALLY HELP END THE COLD WAR?', the BBC – the British Broadcasting Corporation, no less – reported on 6 February 2004: '*Baywatch* star David Hasselhoff is griping that his role in reuniting East and West Germany has been overlooked.'

The Press Association, under the headline, 'HASSELHOFF CLAIMS HE HAD HAND IN BERLIN WALL FALLING', wrote that

David Hasselhoff has complained to museum curators after finding his photo absent in a collection of memorabilia about the fall of the Berlin Wall. The actor and producer claims he is partly responsible for the fall of the concrete divide. Speaking to German magazine *TV Spielfilm*, Hasselhoff said in 1989, the year the Wall fell, he had helped reunite the country by singing his song 'Looking for Freedom' among millions of German fans at the Brandenburg Gate in Berlin.

The *National Enquirer's* utterly false report, headlined, 'NO THANKS TO WALLOWING *BAYWATCH* STAR', began: 'Maybe you thought the collapse of communism in Russia ended the Cold War and reunited East and West Germany. Well, you're wrong – it was David Hasselhoff.' Through one branch of the media or another, millions of people around the world read these stories and believed what they read. I've been living it down ever since.

Back then at the beginning of 1990, I was in a good space. I was happily married, my wife was pregnant with our first child; I had a successful music career in Europe and *Baywatch* was showing on American television. *Cosmopolitan's* editor Helen Gurley Brown had also chosen me to pose as the (almost) nude centrefold for her magazine's twenty-fifth anniversary issue in May.

I'd drive over the hill in the morning and see the beach and go, 'Ahhh – thank you, God, what a job!' When the first season came to an end in April 1990, *Baywatch* seemed to be a good bet for renewal. We had made it into the top thirty programmes of the year and NBC had achieved their best Friday-night ratings since *Knight Rider* in the same time slot five years earlier.

Pamela and I went to look at a new house in Topanga Canyon with Ron Armstrong, a great friend who also sold real estate. We were high up in the mountains when Pamela suddenly started to have a miscarriage. With only minutes to save the baby, Ron drove us down the mountain at high speed while I sat in the back seat holding Pamela in my arms. We made it to hospital just in time for the doctors to save the baby. It had been a close call and we were grateful to Ron for his cool nerves. Later, he would play a life-saving role in my own life.

I started touring Europe full time with the Freedom Tour, with Pamela accompanying me from country to country. There was a cut-off point when she would have to fly home to have the baby, but in Germany she suddenly decided to go back to Los Angeles. The airline asked her why she was flying home early and she replied, 'I don't think that really matters. I need a doctor. I'm in labour.' Luckily, she made it home or our daughter Taylor-Ann would have been born Canadian. Instead, she was born in Los Angeles on 5 May 1990 while I was on stage in Frankfurt. It was one of the happiest nights of my life – and one of the saddest because I was 10,000 miles away from the delivery room.

I completed my engagements in Germany and Switzerland and then flew home. At the hospital, Pamela handed me the baby and said, 'Here's your daughter.' Taylor-Ann immediately took priority over everything, even the bad news from Grant Tinker that he could no longer finance *Baywatch*.

NBC had been paying GTG Entertainment a licence fee of $865,000 per episode to broadcast *Baywatch* in the USA. With NBC's cash and foreign rights payments of $75,000, GTG received a total of $940,000 for each episode but, as each episode cost $1.2 million to produce, GTG had to cover the $260,000 shortfall themselves. At the end of the first season, Grant Tinker and Gannett had dropped $5.4 million on the twenty-one episodes of *Baywatch* made for the first season, plus a $2 million overspend on the pilot. The *Baywatch* balance sheet was nearly $8 million in the red.

I wasn't surprised that we were cancelled. *Baywatch* had been taking completely the wrong direction and I told Greg Bonann so. Ironically, the final episode had been entitled 'The End?', in which a massive earthquake hits Southern California.

I was sorry about *Baywatch*'s demise, particularly for the young members of the cast like Erika Eleniak and Billy Warlock, but I wasn't too concerned about my own future. When I celebrated my thirty-eighth birthday in July 1990, I had plenty of money in the bank, a successful music career to fall back on and, best of all, I had achieved my ambition to have a family.

I'd bounced back before – why not again?

Part II: BEACHED

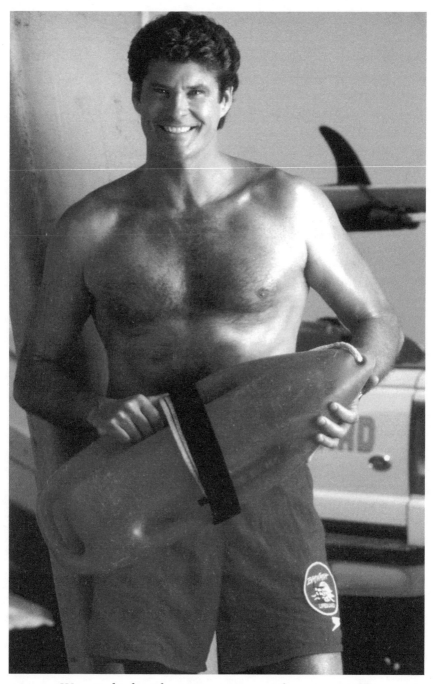

We were back with a vengeance . . . and now we could
do *Baywatch* our way

12 Turning the Tide

'No one made more fun of Baywatch *than us. We were laughing all the way to the plastic surgeon.'*

*B*aywatch was missing from the airwaves when the new American television season started in mid-September 1990; to all intents and purposes, the happy band of lifeguards was finished, kaput, dead in the water. No one was more upset than Greg Bonann. He had worked so hard to make his dream come true that his disappointment was palpable. Greg, however, was a fighter who wasn't prepared to see *Baywatch* end up as flotsam on the beach after just twenty-two episodes.

Nevertheless, the problems he faced in resuscitating the show would have tested the most experienced of producers, whereas Greg was the first to admit he was a novice in the business. His task was to raise millions of dollars from private sources to fund the relaunch, while at the same time retaining the services of the most important members of the cast, namely Billy Warlock, Erika Eleniak, Parker Stevenson, Brandon Call and myself. As the studios were circling with tempting offers, it was only natural that some of the cast would take their talents elsewhere.

Greg's first move was to approach Grant Tinker to ask for the rights back from GTG Entertainment. Grant, being a gentleman, sold his share to him for the princely sum of just $10. Tinker's partner, Gannett, weren't so obliging; they demanded $5,000 per episode if *Baywatch* was successfully revived.

Greg then worked out a new budget which slashed GTG's figure of $1.2 million for each *Baywatch* episode to $800,000, meaning that he had to find a grand total of $18 million to film twenty-two new episodes for the 1991–2 season. Greg told Jan McCormack that he had secured the rights to syndicate *Baywatch* – and wanted to know if I was interested. I had other irons in the fire and said I wasn't interested, so Greg, Doug Schwartz and Michael Berk shopped the project around without me but were unable to sell it.

Jan then agreed to meet the partners again at their request at Adriano's Restaurant in Westwood to listen to what they had to offer. 'They offered 10 per cent of their 100 per cent,' she says, 'but before I left the meeting I had 25 per cent for David – each one equal on the back-end. I told them that was the only way I could convince him to reconsider.'

Having become an executive producer of *Baywatch* and an equal partner with Bonann, Schwartz and Berk in terms of profit-sharing and control over the show's content, co-stars and guest stars, I flew back to Germany to promote my new album, *Crazy for You*. My Mr Fixit, Eugen Joeckel, had arranged for me to appear on *Wetten, dass . . . ?* a hugely popular show with an audience of more than 13 million. Translated as '*Wanna Bet That . . . ?*', the show was broadcast at prime time six or seven times a year in Germany, Switzerland and Austria. Its compère, Thomas Gottschalk, a legend in Germany, asks celebrities to lay wagers on whether contestants can perform certain feats. One man successfully claimed he could name every street corner in Berlin and describe what was on that corner. In between bets, top international artists such as Elton John, Paul McCartney or the Bee Gees would perform.

Thomas Gottschalk said, 'Mr Hasselhoff, we have four bus-drivers who say they can balance trays of champagne on the wing mirrors of their buses and drive down a course without spilling a drop.'

I said, 'That's impossible – if they can do it I'll buy everybody a glass of champagne.'

The bus-drivers successfully completed their stunt and, after the show, there was a huge party when I bought champagne for everybody in the audience. To this day, I owe a lot to Thomas Gottschalk; since then, I have appeared on his show several times and each appearance has seriously boosted my record sales.

The first series of *Baywatch* had been huge in Germany and my concerts were attracting up to 35,000 people a time. 'It's positive rock-'n'-roll,' I told *Entertainment Tonight*. 'They don't throw beer bottles, they're not smoking joints, they're not doing drugs – you know what they're throwing? They're throwing teddy bears and flowers.'

The Munich concert was held in driving rain, but that didn't stop 20,000 people from showing up and singing my songs in English. At the end of the show, the stage was covered in flowers. The work I'd put into my singing career now paid off in the resurrection of *Baywatch* in the USA. The combination of four platinum records (with sales of more than five million discs) and *Knight Rider* had tremendous pulling power in Germany. Paul Talbot, head of the Fremantle Corporation, arranged for me to meet some German TV moguls.

'Can you bring us more *Knight Riders*?' they asked.

'No, but I can bring back *Baywatch*.'

'Does it have a car?'

'No.'

'Are you in it?'

'Yes.'

'We buy it anyway.'

To clinch the deal that would bring back *Baywatch* for at least one more season, they insisted that I appear in all twenty-two episodes. Paul Talbot, a gentleman of the old school and one of the heroic figures of American television, was the man responsible for stitching the whole foreign deal together. Paul had founded the Fremantle Corporation in 1952 to export American television shows such as *All My Children*, *The Price Is Right*, *Romper Room* and *The Galloping Gourmet*. During the NBC season, he had licensed *Baywatch* to TV outlets in several foreign countries, mostly in Europe. Two of those companies – Beta Taurus, part of the Kirsch Group in Germany, and ITV in the United Kingdom – were now offering to pay $425,000 per episode for the rights to the new *Baywatch*, the largest episodic fee ever offered for a syndicated show.

ITV had previously paid just $25,000 per episode for the first season, but it was prepared to increase that sum to $75,000 per episode as a licence fee, with another $75,000 as an equity fee from which they would profit if *Baywatch* was successful. Their $150,000 was included in the $425,000 total.

ITV had shown the first season of *Baywatch* after the 9 p.m. watershed in Britain which meant that scenes of violence, sex and drug-taking could be included. London Weekend Television, however, wanted to make *Baywatch* available to a younger audience before 9 p.m. – at the peak British viewing time of 5.45 p.m. on Sunday – and that, according to Warren Beach, our point man at ITV, meant we would have to cut right back on stories that included violence and sex, particularly anything relating to women and children.

ITV had thus given us the key to *Baywatch*'s international success – the new series would be a family show that could be aired at any time of the day or night in Britain, China, Spain, Brazil, Russia, Japan, Iceland, South Africa, South America – in fact, just about any country in the world outside of Iran and North Korea.

With half of the required $18 million now guaranteed by Fremantle, we set out to sell *Baywatch* to local TV stations across America. Approaches to ABC, CBS and Fox brought zero interest, so we took *Baywatch* to the hundreds of independent stations dotted throughout the States and offered them what is called 'first-run syndication'. We started with Channel 13 in Los Angeles, which was owned by United/Chris Craft, the boat-building people.

In order to sell *Baywatch* to Chris Craft, we teamed up with Lexington Broadcast Services (LBS), a small distribution company run by identical twins Henry and Paul Siegel. Chris Craft was very important because it not only owned a channel in Los Angeles but also had stations in six other major US markets: New York, Chicago, Portland, Phoenix, San Francisco and Minneapolis. Evan Thompson, the Chris Craft boss, shrewdly came on board for a 6 per cent share of the show. Altogether, there were 212 markets of varying size and importance across the nation. After achieving the breakthrough with Chris Craft, LBS agreed to distribute *Baywatch* in as many of those markets as possible, as well as helping us find a guarantor for the missing $9 million.

While they were seeking the additional funding, the Siegels paid Jan McCormack a 'holding fee' to ensure my services. Time was running out on that arrangement when Henry Siegel called and said he believed he was close to closing a deal and could he have an additional ten days without further payment? Jan and I spoke to my attorney Eric Weissler and we agreed to give him an extension. We knew that without a US deal there would be no *Baywatch* and we were confident that the Siegels could pull it off because they had had great success with syndications in the past.

Three days later, Henry called with the news. He had sold the show to Scotti Brothers Records, whose small TV division produced *America's Top 10*. This was only the second time that a failed network show had ever become a syndicated sale. The first time was when Henry and Paul Siegel had syndicated *Fame*, a cancelled network show that they turned into a syndicated success. Syndication history was about to be made again . . . but on an even greater scale. Scotti Brothers, which merged with All American Television in February 1991 to form All American Communications, signed on with us as guarantor for a $9 million loan from the Chemical Bank.

When all the paperwork had been completed, I shared 50 per cent ownership of *Baywatch* with Bonann, Schwartz and Berk, while Scotti Brothers/All American received 25 per cent and the remaining 25 per cent was divided between LBS, Chris Craft, Fremantle and ITV. We then took *Baywatch* to the National Association of Television Programming Executives (NATPE) convention in New Orleans in January 1991 to promote a cancelled show that none of America's networks would touch.

We had beautiful blonde models in bathing suits to lure the heads of the country's local stations into the elaborate exhibition booth that LBS had set up in the convention centre. Potential customers could watch a promotional video, talk to Greg Bonann and me about the show, have their photograph taken with Erika Eleniak and discuss business with Henry and Paul Siegel of LBS and Syd Vinnedge of Scotti Brothers. Guys came in from all over the USA.

'Hi, I'm from New York, what's going on here?'

'This is *Baywatch*. If you put this show on, I'll come to New York and do publicity to promote it.'

'Will you come to our bowling alley party?'

'How many stations have you got?'

'Nine.'

'Let's go bowling.'

And I would. I'd show up. I'd do anything, anywhere to get this show on the air. It didn't hurt that many of the buyers were women. As an actor, you're lucky if a hit prime-time show comes your way once in a lifetime; twice is highly unusual and I wasn't going to let this chance slip through my fingers, especially to own the show, produce it and retain creative power. What a dream: no more network to screw it up. I went around the country nickel-and-diming our way up to $800,000 per episode. In the end, we booked twenty-two episodes of the new *Baywatch* on nearly 200 American stations for its second season.

As well as developing the foreign sales of American TV programmes, Paul Talbot had also pioneered the barter syndication business under which a TV show would be given to the stations free of charge in exchange for six and a half minutes of advertising time. With *Baywatch*, LBS's barter division, TV Horizons, then sold these minutes to big advertisers, such as Coca-Cola and Procter & Gamble, at the rate of $50,000 per thirty-second unit, based on a guaranteed 7.0 household rating.

As our costs were so much lower than those incurred by GTG, *Baywatch* needed only a 4.0 rating to break even, while a 5.0 rating would make a handsome profit and a 6.0 or 7.0 rating would be worth millions to our guarantor and ourselves. Principal photography on the new series was scheduled to begin on 8 July 1991.

Meanwhile, I had gone back in front of the cameras at Universal Studios to reprise the role of Michael Knight in *Knight Rider 2000*, a ninety-minute futuristic thriller, featuring my old buddies Edward Mulhare as Devon Miles and William Daniels as the voice of KITT. NBC wanted to use the film as a back-door pilot for a new *Knight Rider* series. 'Wherever I go, people ask me three questions,' I told an interviewer. 'How come you're so tall? Where's the car? And when is *Knight Rider* coming back?' The answer to all three questions was the same: 'I don't know.'

I was committed to *Baywatch* and wouldn't be available to play Michael Knight even if the series returned. As an alternative, I suggested to Brandon Tartikoff that I do four *Knight Rider* movies-of-the-week. He agreed and ordered a new script; yet when it was delivered to my house I couldn't believe it. I threw it across the kitchen.

Pamela said, 'What's wrong?'

'You're not going to believe this – Michael Knight is washed up and living in the woods because he can't cope with life anymore. They've killed off Devon and handed the Foundation over to a girl – and the car is now red.'

'What are you going to do?'

'What choice do I have? I either play the part or they'll do it without me and say I'm dead.'

So I did it. Susan Norman was cast as Michael Knight's partner Shawn McCormick. Susan seemed to think the film was stupid and she was right. *Knight Rider 2000* missed the point of the original TV series and had taken off in the wrong direction with a story about a former cop turned psychotic killer who brings terror to the city of Seattle in the year 2000.

When the film was shown on 19 May 1990, the ratings were excellent, although when NBC tested audience reaction to Susan with the prospect of her fronting a new *Knight Rider* series the following year she was given the thumbs-down. Secretly, I was ecstatic that my audience still loved me. NBC said to me, 'Okay, Mr Hasselhoff, we're going to do it your way with movies-of-the-week.' But instead of asking Universal to make four movies-of-the-week, as I had suggested, they ordered just one. The studio replied, 'We can't figure out how to make money unless we make at least two films and shoot them back to back.' NBC refused to order more than one movie and that was the end of the *Knight Rider* revival.

Back at *Baywatch*, our immediate concern was to create a suitable home environment in which the Baywatch Production Company could operate. Greg found an old chainsaw factory in Beethoven Street, Marina del Rey, which we rented for $17,000 a month (compared with the $200,000 that GTG had been paying for production facilities at Culver City). We built a fully equipped sound stage, editing-rooms, art department, writers' offices and, later, a huge water tank.

Having everything in one building would save huge amounts of cash and hours of production time. Then we went to Los Angeles County's Department of Beaches and Harbors and said to the Lifeguard Division: 'You've got a lifeguard station at Will Rogers State Beach. We'll build an extra floor on top as a set if you let us use it as Baywatch Lifeguard Headquarters. We'll build it to code and when we are all done with the show you can keep it if you want as part of your headquarters.' The Lifeguard bosses agreed and Will Rogers State Beach on Santa Monica Bay became our main outdoor location.

How do you make a hit show for $800,000 when the network was spending $1.2 million? For a start, we cut our overheads to the bone; then we wrote shorter scripts, with fewer action sequences that required stunt men and elaborate rehearsals; and finally we negotiated a 25 per cent reduction in labour costs with the acting guilds and the tradecraft unions.

ITV's request for a show that could be watched by all members of the family coincided with my own vision of what *Baywatch* should be about. I scrawled 'Heart, Humour, Action' in big bold letters across the first script, 'Nightmare Bay'. I told the writers that NBC had cancelled *Baywatch* because it had become focused on taking lives instead of saving them, whereas it needed to be more positive, with the same theme as *Knight Rider*: one man can make a difference.

'I want something a four-year-old can watch with an eighty-four-year-old,' I said. 'Put something in it for everybody – that's the formula.' We'd go over every script and if there wasn't anything in there for a four-year-old and an eighty-four-year-old I'd send it back and say: 'Heart, humour, action.' When *Baywatch* had become the highest rated syndicated show in the world, a young girl perfectly summed up the phenomenon, 'I like the love stories and the show is exciting and scary, but everything turns out okay.' Wouldn't it be nice if life was like that?

I'd got the four-to-eighty-four age span during a trip to London when a retired major type stepped into my elevator. 'You're in that show *Baywatch*, aren't you?' he said. 'My four-year-old granddaughter loves that show. She loves the rescue stories ...' Then as the elevator door was closing behind him he leered, 'But I watch it for the birds.'

I was the front man. I would do publicity and star in the show, while my three partners would take care of all the producing and directing, and shoot all the montages of beautiful young men and women running across the beach in slow motion to the sound of rock music. They'd say to the second unit crew: 'We're five minutes short – go shoot another montage. Grab the most beautiful extra you can see and shoot her running down the beach in slow motion.'

Greg Bonann had borrowed the idea of slow motion montages from *Chariots of Fire* when he was filming the Winter Olympics. These clips became a signature of *Baywatch*, but they were expensive; you used four times as much film shooting in slow motion and we also had to pay upwards of $25,000 for world rights to each of the songs.

There were some significant cast changes before we could start filming the second series. Parker Stevenson left the show over what he described as 'creative differences', although money – or rather lack of it – was the main issue. Parker was a man I could count on and I was extremely sorry to see him go. To this day, he is a close friend. Peter Phelps, who had played the big-headed Australian Trevor Cole, opted out, while Brandon Call (Mitch's son Hobie) left to join the sitcom *Step by Step*.

When we were looking for a replacement for Brandon, our casting people, Fern Orenstein and Susie Glicksman, told me, 'There's one kid who is a fabulous actor but he is a little older than the others. Could we turn Hobie into a teenager?' I rejected the idea because I wanted a young boy in the cast to attract young viewers. So we chose eleven-year-old Jeremy Jackson as Hobie's replacement and Fern and Susie's favoured candidate, Leonardo DiCaprio, had to wait a while for his inevitable stardom. (When I saw Leo at the Golden Globes in 2004, he was flying high with *The Aviator*. He said: 'Thanks a lot for not casting me in *Baywatch*.')

Jeremy Jackson got the part because of his every-boy innocence and because he was like the son I never had. We bleached his hair blonde so he would look more like the original Hobie. Veteran actor Richard Jaeckel was also added to the cast as Captain Ben Edwards and my wife Pamela was signed to play a recurring role as reporter Kaye Morgan.

We'd been paying huge amounts for music in every NBC episode, so we decided to produce our own theme song. The Scotti Brothers flew one of their top recording artists, Jimi Jamison, to Los Angeles and paired him with Cory Lerios of Pablo Cruise to co-write 'I'm Always Here', which Jimi recorded in his powerful, raucous, rocker's voice. It gave the opening credits of *Baywatch* a tremendous boost when the syndicated series kicked off with 'Nightmare Bay', a two-parter, on 29 September 1991.

In this episode, Pamela and I acted together for the first time when Mitch Buchannon meets her character Kaye Morgan, at Baywatch Headquarters. It had been difficult working with my first wife on *Knight Rider* and I swore I'd never work with Pamela. It worked for a while but, unfortunately, we could not figure out a way to retain her character and she was phased out. As a team player, I had to go along with the decision, even though she was my wife.

We were shooting the new series by the seat of our pants. Without a network to tell us what we could or couldn't do, we took a lot of liberties. We drove our Scarab powerboat at 40 m.p.h. with a helicopter filming so close on top of us that its rotor blades chopped off our aerial. It was wild stuff and we felt like outlaws.

At 6 a.m. on the way to a shoot I would sit in the front of the Scarab, setting up concert deals in Germany on my cellphone with my manager. Buddy McCormack and I would then leave Los Angeles at three o'clock on Friday afternoon when *Baywatch* wrapped for the week, arrive in Germany at nine o'clock on Saturday morning, check into our hotel, freshen up, go to rehearsals, do the show that night, get back on the plane on Sunday at 9 a.m. and get back in Los Angeles at one o'clock that same day. I would be on the set of *Baywatch* the next morning. We did this almost every weekend for two and a half years – it was exhausting but what a ride.

Our biggest publicity boost came from the tabloids. It suited them to regard *Baywatch* as 'soft-core jiggle vision that appealed to pubescent boys, prison inmates and NBA stars'. I told them,

> If you want to blame someone, blame the Beach Boys – they're the ones who made surfing cool. They started the whole beach culture with their music – great music that is still being played today. All we did was shoot it like MTV and make it hip and cool. It was like one big music video. Turn on MTV and you'll see true garbage – *Baywatch* is kindergarten stuff compared with today's music videos. Look at Madonna – she makes videos about getting laid in hotels and these are shown to twelve-year-old girls.

When *Baywatch* was censored in Ireland, I went on television and said, 'You guys are killing each other on the streets of Belfast over who's Catholic and who's Protestant and you're censoring *Baywatch*? If you don't like it, turn it off.'

There was justification for some of the complaints. I told my partners, 'If I see another gratuitous shot of a girl's crotch, I'm out of here. We don't need that – there's a way to shoot women without exploiting them.' It was also a constant battle between me and the writers to make the show more acceptable to family viewers. In retrospect, there were times when I was completely right and there were times when I was completely wrong. One time, I said to the writers, 'This story is so stupid and trivial whether Eddie Kramer and Shauni McClain are going to live on this boat together.' Then I visited a high school where all these kids ran up to me and said, 'Are Eddie and Shauni going to get back together again?'

I called in next day and told the writers: 'Remember that story about Eddie and Shauni? Put it back in. I'm an idiot. There's an audience for it out there.' It was the love affair between Eddie and Shauni that really captured the audience's interest in our second season.

Halfway through season two, LBS went bankrupt and All American Communications acquired its equity in *Baywatch*, with Henry Siegel of LBS becoming president of All American Television. This coincided with a big shift in emphasis when my efforts to introduce emotional storylines with heroes started to pay off. We cut back on the music montages, introduced new characters and focused on social issues such as chemical spills in the bay, returning injured sea animals to their natural habitats, homelessness and inner-city gangs. There were emotional dramas about a fat girl on the beach, Eddie Kramer's schizophrenic brother and a teenage girl who faked her own death.

Our demographic research showed that 66 per cent of our audience in the USA were women aged eighteen to forty-nine. Women loved the scenes between Mitch and Hobie because he was a single father raising his boy and trying to find a suitable partner for himself. The father–son interaction gave *Baywatch* its essential 'heart' ingredient. Jeremy Jackson was a hit from the start. His fan mail increased fourfold from the beginning of the season to the end. He was then twelve years old and literally grew to manhood on the *Baywatch* set over the next eight years.

Considering that we'd had only a two-month period to write scripts and prep the early episodes for a production start of 8 July, we were proud of what we had achieved in our first season in charge of *Baywatch*. We had completed twenty-two hours of television time in twenty and a half weeks, on budget and without deficit. The show was substantially better than the original NBC season and Jimmy Pergola, our director of photography, maintained the high-quality look of the original series. *Baywatch* ended up as the highest-rated, new, one-hour weekly series in syndication and the Number One US import around the world. We reached an amazing 47 per cent share of the English audience and maintained almost 11 million viewers there weekly. We were able to dissect the content of each show according to its Nielsen rating to see which ones had been most popular with viewers.

When ITV presented us with their comments, 'Nightmare Bay' was deemed to have had the best balance of 'heart, humour and action'. However, Warren Beach, controller of programme planning, presentation and promotion at London Weekend Television, warned that several episodes had drawn criticism for stories about drugs, gang warfare and threats against women; there were also accusations of voyeurism and claims that we had included too many dream sequences.

In a letter to the *Baywatch* distributors, Beach said that the season's success among four- to fifteen-year-olds in the United Kingdom was based on sun, sea and surf. In the main, these viewers wanted identifiable characters 'who are attractive, who relate well to each other in a "romantic" sense, rather than in an adult warts-'n'-all way'. 'You have these characters but some of the situations they have been involved in for Series Two have been too adult,' Beach said. 'They want to see how the characters live on and off the beach. Most of all, they want storylines which involve rescue and a race against time and tide. The episode when two boys are trapped in a storm outfall and the incoming tide is threatening them is an ideal example.'

Beach named episodes that had caused problems as 'The One that Got Away' for including knife attacks and threats to women, 'Reunion' for a sadistic beach burial and nudity in a love scene, and 'Point of Attack' for a gang rape and dope-smoking. 'If we are to go to Series Three, and I hope we do, we must address the storylines,' Beach said. 'We cannot risk having a third series that causes as many problems with our censor as Series Two has, or with the BSC (Broadcasting Standards Council), or that the series becomes emasculated by going the fantasy route. You must tread a very careful line – I don't envy you but you've proved it can be done.'

Being married to Pamela enabled me to enjoy the beauty of women on the set, to respect them and to let them know it wasn't okay to come by and throw themselves at me. This happened a lot and it was sad to see girls use their sexuality to try to further their careers. It was blatant and it was also scary. I knew one of these young actresses could close the show with a lawsuit and shut down my marriage. There were many occasions when girls would sashay past my motor home. It would have been easy to invite them in but I thought, 'If I jump at that, my marriage is over.' Parker Stevenson, who was married to *Cheers* star Kirstie Alley, said to me, 'Either you're married or you're not.' His words stuck in my head. Greg Bonann had met a lovely girl, Tai Collins, during the first season and was still with her fourteen years later. 'She trusts me,' he said. 'It's a matter of honour.'

To protect everybody, the partners introduced an anti-discrimination and sexual harassment clause that would be signed by every *Baywatch* employee. This would limit the Baywatch Production Company's liability in any legal action, and also send a clear message to the crew and office staff that sexual harassment would not be tolerated. An internal memorandum on the subject said:

> Keep in mind there were a number of complaints on the set this year. Without a harassment policy we are extremely liable. A disgruntled extra or someone who has been the brunt of a crude joke can turn what someone thought was 'good fun' into a million-dollar lawsuit that could shut us down. Far from being a political issue, the adoption of a harassment policy is common sense. The very nature of the show makes us a likely target for a lawsuit. We must be overly cautious and unafraid to dismiss someone who crosses the line.

We adopted the anti-harassment policy drafted for MCR/Universal by Lew Wasserman and Sid Sheinberg. This stated:

> Sexual harassment is defined as unwelcome sexual advances, requests for sexual favours, and other verbal, physical or visual conduct of a sexual nature when (1) submission to such conduct is made, either explicitly or implicitly, as a term or condition of the individual's employment. Or (2) submission to or rejection of such conduct by an individual is used as the basis for employment decisions affecting such individual.

Despite all of our precautions, Baywatch Productions still ended up with a suit for harassment. This case was settled out of court.

When you're in a show as big as *Baywatch*, the predators come out looking for grounds to launch a lawsuit because they know the company will do just about anything to avoid the publicity of a sensational trial. Our insurers also wanted us to settle claims to avoid astronomical legal fees. Nor were our problems confined to sexual harassment – a crew member might say, 'Would you take a look at my script?' and if we later used a scene about an airplane crashing he would accuse us of ripping off his idea. They were constantly winning on these ridiculous issues, once even about the inappropriate hiring of a make-up artist. We would settle these cases and then discover that we couldn't fire the litigant because it would look like victimisation and wrongful dismissal.

Nevertheless, *Baywatch* had emerged from season two with an expanding share of both the domestic and international markets. We planned season three at a retreat at the Two Bunch Palms resort at Desert Hot Springs, east of Los Angeles, in early March 1992. We had a full four months to develop and write the first twelve scripts prior to the first day of photography on 6 July 1992. I was contracted to appear in all twenty-two episodes of the new series. 'We want to continue to centre *Baywatch* around David Hasselhoff's Mitch Buchannon character,' Doug Schwartz told us. 'His relationship with his son Hobie is of paramount importance. Our show appeals to a strong family audience first and foremost.'

They say if you want to give God a laugh, tell him your plans. Even with the best will in the world, things often don't work out as planned. In the case of *Baywatch*, they turned out even better than anyone had expected.

President Bill Clinton took me jogging . . . and talked about *Baywatch*

Pamela Anderson was every boy's dream girl and my great friend

13 Venus in Spandex

'We hired Pamela Anderson and the rest,
as Vanity Fair *once said, was hysteria.'*

Life started to imitate art when Billy Warlock fell head over heels in love with Erika Eleniak. He had also fallen out of love with *Baywatch*. He didn't like the slo-mo montages and the other fluff, and he didn't like the fact that his salary had been cut for budget reasons. He quit the show over a contract dispute. Then Erika decided she couldn't live with the prospect of being regarded as a '*Baywatch* bimbo' for the rest of her life and followed Billy into feature films. We suddenly found ourselves with a crisis on our hands requiring a major recast.

In place of the brash, cocky Billy we hired male model David Charvet, who was cast as spoiled rich kid Matt Brody. David had been born in France and had moved to the USA when he was nine years old. After graduating from high school, he had been spotted by a photographer and his modelling career had taken off. By age eighteen, he had landed national print campaign ads for Bugle Boy casual wear, Levi's, Miller's Outpost and Coca-Cola. David had an extremely sensitive nature and the audience picked up on that and liked it. He worked hard and became a huge star.

Alexandra Paul was hired as senior lifeguard Stephanie Holden, who is assigned to Baywatch Headquarters despite Mitch's misgivings.

Stephanie is one of his previous lovers and her ambition is to be the first female captain in the Lifeguard Service. 'We want to play the sexual tension between Mitch and Stephanie,' Doug Schwartz said, 'and by doing this we will keep her feminine side alive so that when she plays the authority figure she doesn't become butch.'

Nicole Eggert, an experienced nineteen-year-old television actress, was signed as rookie lifeguard Summer Quinn, with Susan Anton as her mother Jackie, who is fleeing from an abusive relationship. Alicia Silverstone and Denise Richards were turned down for parts as being not quite right for the customised red swimsuit. Kelly Slater, the Number One teenaged surfer in the world, was added to the cast as Jimmy Slade.

The line-up for 'River of No Return', the pilot episode in *Baywatch*'s make-or-break third season, was complete except for Erika Eleniak's replacement. We had tested Paula Abdul, Sandra Bullock and forty other hopefuls without success when David Charvet suggested his Canadian girlfriend for the role of C. J. Parker. Annoyingly, she cancelled her audition eleven times and was going to have an uphill battle to convince Fern Orenstein and Susie Glicksman that she was a serious contender. Finally, when they had almost given up hope, a blonde with a friendly smile sashayed into their office and said, 'Hi, I'm Pamela Anderson.'

We had heard so much about Pamela Denise Anderson that all four executive producers turned up to see her. Pamela already had a job as Lisa the tool-time girl on ABC's popular sitcom *Home Improvement*, so she wasn't in a hurry to find a new one. The thing that bothered me was that she had been a *Playboy* Playmate in 1989 and I didn't want any more Playmates on *Baywatch*. We had crossed the line once with Erika Eleniak and I didn't want to do it again.

I told my partners: 'You know, guys, I don't really want anybody else from *Playboy* in the show because, frankly, *Playboy* sends the wrong message.' I was completely opposed to telling girls that if they took their clothes off, they could get a job in television. Somewhere along the line somebody was going to get raped and they were going to blame *Baywatch*.

Pamela was wearing a halter top and a skirt. When we asked her to read a page of the script, she stood up, stripped off her top and skirt to reveal a swimsuit underneath. The guys couldn't take their eyes off her breasts because they were beautiful and they were real.

I said, 'Put a camera on her.'

Pamela proceeded to read her lines and was so charming and funny – and so absurdly beautiful – that it was no contest. Everybody wanted her, so I said, 'Okay – she's in.'

The camera photographs your aura and you've either got it or you haven't. Actors like Robert De Niro have got auras to play bad guys – you put a camera on him and he just has to walk around and he's menacing. Pamela had a big aura – a sweet, adorable, Marilyn Monroe quality, plus a terrific amount of charisma.

To shoot Pamela's *Baywatch* debut, we left the beach and headed for northern California. Written by Michael Berk and Douglas Schwartz, 'River of No Return' was carefully contrived as a launch vehicle for Pamela Anderson to cash in on the Marilyn Monroe movie of the same name. With Doug Schwartz directing, we filmed it on the south fork of the American River, near Sacramento.

Mitch Buchannon, his son Hobie and lifeguards Eddie Kramer and Shauni McClain travel to California's rugged gold country to investigate the mysterious death of Mitch's prospector uncle. Their guide is Casey Jean (C. J.) Parker, a former lifeguard known to Mitch. They first catch sight of C. J., eye-catching in a lilac helmet and denim shorts, paddling a kayak down the raging river.

Mitch sighs, 'Beautiful, beautiful – I'm talking about the river.'

He catches up with C. J. when he sees her on the riverbank, practising on her saxophone.

'Any lovesick moose around?' he asks.

C. J. swings around and accidentally knocks him into the water.

'Oh my golly, Mitch, I'm so sorry,' she says. 'I was just so surprised to see you standing there.'

Mitch persuades C. J. to come back to Los Angeles as a lifeguard at Baywatch Beach, while Eddie and Shauni fade out of *Baywatch* by getting married in a beach ceremony and moving to Australia. By cutting back and forth from the goings-on at Baywatch Beach, 'River of No Return' had also introduced David Charvet's Matt Brody and Nicole Eggert's Summer Quinn. The coast was now clear for the writers to introduce new romantic entanglements involving Matt and Summer as a substitute for Eddie and Shauni, a changeover that worked so well that none of the viewers complained.

My wife Pamela was due to give birth to our second child in

September and I promised that nothing would stop me from being in the delivery room. As well as filming *Baywatch*, I was supposed to be singing at a concert in Prague, but having missed Taylor-Ann's birth, I cancelled that trip and stayed in Los Angeles. It was just as well because, as with Taylor-Ann, Pamela went into labour six weeks early.

When she was admitted to Cedars-Sinai Medical Centre, the doctors were concerned that the baby's lungs might not be fully developed, so they carried out some tests. Since we wouldn't get the results until later that day, I went off to work as usual. I got a call on the set in the afternoon saying the baby's lungs were fine and that Pam would give birth after midnight on 26 August. I dashed to the hospital and was shown to the waiting-room, where Kurt Cobain, leader of the grunge band Nirvana, was waiting to see his wife, Courtney Love, and his daughter, Frances Bean Cobain. I was at the hospital when Hayley Amber was born – I even held her head as she was coming out of the womb and cut the umbilical cord. With two daughters, I felt twice blessed.

Heavily promoted on hundreds of channels, Pamela Anderson was introduced to the *Baywatch* audience in the first episode of the third season in September 1992. The rest, as *Vanity Fair* later noted, was hysteria. Pamela was different from anybody we'd ever had in *Baywatch* – or ever would have. She added a lot to the show, mostly a sensational amount of exploitable publicity via the paparazzi and television chat shows. It seemed David Letterman and Jay Leno had just been waiting for her to materialise to make *Baywatch* one of the staples of their shows. Their wisecracks about Pamela introduced *Baywatch* to a sophisticated late-night audience and people were tuning in to see what all the hoopla was about. The tabloid press, tabloid TV shows like *Hard Copy* and shock jock Howard Stern promoted *Baywatch* almost non-stop. ('My favourite *Baywatch* episode,' Howard said, 'is the one when you operated on someone with a pencil.')

Thousands of people arrived at Will Rogers State Beach to watch *Baywatch* being filmed. We had crime tape around the set to keep the crowd at bay and bodyguards to escort us from the trailers to the set. Pamela was Venus in Spandex. By virtue of being able to say her lines and run down the beach in a red swimsuit while carrying a rescue can, she had suddenly become one of the most famous people in the world. She found the whole idea of *Baywatch* hysterical and grabbed the opportunity to make her mark in show business by going completely over the top with big lips, big eyes, big hair and an all-over Malibu tan. Her own hair and make-up artist would arrive at her home at 3 a.m. and she would turn up on the set at 5 a.m. ready for action. 'You have to take these things into your own hands,' she would say, 'otherwise people just walk all over you.'

Pamela was born on Vancouver Island, Canada, on 1 July 1967. Despite her mother's warnings about the dangers of big-city life, she moved to Vancouver, where she worked as a fitness instructor at a gym until she was 'discovered' wearing a Labatt's Beer T-shirt in 1988 at a British Columbia Lions football game in the city stadium.

When a TV cameraman flashed a picture of Pamela, then a brunette, on to the stadium's giant screen, a huge roar of approval went up from the crowd. The roar was repeated every time the camera focused on her. Labatt's Beer signed her up to do a commercial and with her earnings she had her breasts enlarged. With a new figure and her hair dyed blonde, she attracted the attention of *Playboy* magazine, which put her on the cover of its October 1989 issue.

Playing the ditzy blonde bimbo for all it was worth, Pamela soon had the press eating out of her hand. 'I'll melt if you put me too near the radiator,' she giggled. 'I think I've got Tourette's syndrome, I love to talk about sex so much.' The real Pamela was a clever little self-promoter. 'A lot of people seem to think I'm just two boobs walking around,' she said, 'but I know what I'm doing.' In her spare time, she meditated and read Carl Jung. She kept crystals in her trailer as a means of producing good karma and brought her golden retriever Star on to the set for good luck. She was a free spirit, part rock chick, part earth mother.

Pamela and David Charvet had been living together until her sudden stardom threatened their relationship. David wasn't envious of her success – they just ran out of things to say to one another. They were both on the same show and that, as in the case of Billy Warlock and Erika Eleniak, simply didn't work.

'How was your day at work?'

'Oh, I guess the same as yours.'

Baywatch was breaking them up.

Alexandra Paul made her debut in the second episode of the third season, 'Tequila Bay', when her character Stephanie Holden reports for duty at Baywatch Beach. Alexandra to me was the perfect *Baywatch* girl.

Built like a tall gazelle, she was an eco-warrior and an American triathlete. In a world of double-D cups, she was proud of her athleticism and the fact that she had small breasts.

During season three, as well as introducing Pamela Anderson, Nicole Eggert and Alexandra Paul, we featured episodes on bulimia, blindness and Alzheimer's disease. We had developed a conscience and made a point of getting a social message across. In later episodes, we tackled manic depression, teenage suicide and skin cancer. One of our biggest assets was Michael 'Newmie' Newman, the only authentic lifeguard in the cast. Many of our storylines were taken from actual lifeguard reports about incidents that had happened on the beach. Newmie advised the writers how to recreate rescue scenes to ensure they were accurate in every detail, particularly on methods of resuscitation.

Our fan mail contained letters from all over the world saying that someone's life had been saved using cardiopulmonary resuscitation (CPR) techniques seen on *Baywatch*. As an antidote to all the negative publicity about the show's sexual content, the Santa Monica Red Cross presented us with an award when our lifesaving scenes helped a youngster save a life. At the Lifeguard Championships, lifeguards came up to me and said, 'Hey, man, thanks. Everybody respects our profession now and knows we aren't just guys who are checking out babes on the beach.'

On the set, I constantly rewrote scripts to fit the new actors' personas, then watched the dailies on a VCR in my trailer. Getting people in the water was a challenge. If it was cold, and the girls didn't want to go in, I jumped in. Staying in shape was a challenge. The guys had a thing called 'the Rolling Six-Pack' – when someone would shout 'Rolling!' everybody would breathe in so you'd see a muscular six-pack on our chests. Our economies of time and space, with a smaller crew, fewer takes and shorter scripts, had made *Baywatch* the fastest-produced programme on television. In 1993, we took only five months to film the twenty-two episodes of season four, ranging in subject matter from Mitch rescuing Hobie and ex-wife Gayle from a submerged airplane to Matt Brody and Summer Quinn falling in love, and John D. Cort returning to Baywatch Beach and winning C. J. Parker's heart. In 1993–4, ratings hit their highest point ever at 6.8.

One of the strongest episodes in season four was 'The Child Inside', written by Doug Schwartz's wife, Deborah Bonann Schwartz, in which the lifeguards host a special Olympics for Down's syndrome children. The kids were innocent and loving, always ready to go to work and always enthusiastic. Every time one boy saw me, he said into his watch, 'Hey, KITT, can you pick me up?' And then he'd laugh delightedly. The competition was to win gold medals but the children weren't acting – they took it all very seriously. They were some of the finest human beings I've ever worked with.

The guest star was Mary Lou Retton, who became the first American woman to win a gold medal in Olympic gymnastics when she won the All-Around Gold Medal at the 1984 Olympic Games in Los Angeles. After her first scene with me, the entire crew held up signs that gave her a '10', while I scored a '2'. 'The Child Inside' was a fitting tribute to Baywatch, which had just been acknowledged in the television industry as the most-watched TV series in history.

In October 1993, the magazine Entertainment Weekly featured Pamela Anderson, Nicole Eggert and me on the cover, with a story on 'How David Hasselhoff turned the frothy, washed-up Baywatch into the most popular TV show in the universe'. Baywatch had become the top-rated series in Britain, France, Germany, Ireland, New Zealand and Australia. Rupert Murdoch's satellite network Star TV beamed us all over Asia. We were being watched in seventy-two countries worldwide, including Outer Mongolia and the Lebanon.

We were a gift to headline writers. Mad Magazine christened us Babewatch, while I was 'the Sultan of Surf' and the other lifeguards became 'the Bod Squad'. Our audience were branded 'mammophiles' and 'trash-enthusiasts'. David Letterman, Jay Leno, Howard Stern, The Larry Sanders Show and Saturday Night Live kept up a steady stream of anti-Baywatch gags, while two new syndicated shows, Paradise Beach and Acapulco H.E.A.T., attempted to duplicate our winning formula. For many people, Baywatch was a guilty pleasure and very few would admit to actually watching it. Then the news came in from London that Princess Diana was a Baywatch fan and I felt we'd really made it!

Princess Diana and I had such fun when we met
in London in November 1993

14 **A Date with Diana**

'The Princess looked me up and down. "You look good with your clothes on," she said.'

Simon Cowell, the 'Mr Mean' of *Pop Idol*, *American Idol* and *The X-Factor*, approached me with a smile on his face. 'I make massive hits,' he said, 'and I absolutely believe in you.' He was bright, funny, sweet and supportive (nothing like the character you see on television), and as Artists and Repertoire Consultant for the powerful BMG record company in London, he was perfectly placed to give my music career a huge push.

Simon invited me to work with Stock, Aitken and Waterman, Britain's biggest hit-makers of the 1980s whose work favoured a high-spirited blend of pop music and Hi-NRG, a high-tech version of Euro-disco. I checked into the Piccadilly Hotel (now Le Meredien) and, on the first morning, a car picked me up and took me to the studio. Pete Waterman was in the process of leaving the merry band of songsters, so I dealt mainly with Mike Stock, their resident song-writing genius and creator of such numbers as 'I Should Be So Lucky', 'Too Many Broken Hearts' and 'the Fast Food Song'.

In the studio, Mike said, 'Sing.'

'Sing what?'

'Just sing.'

They didn't have a song. They'd play a few bars and say, 'Sing.'

On the second day, it was the same.

I said, 'Give me a line.'

They said, 'This is the way we do it. You sing a little bit and we play it.'

'I don't know what's going on here,' I said, 'but I'm not a writer. I just can't make up stuff.'

On the third day, I said to Simon Cowell, 'Listen – these guys don't know what they're doing.'

Simon said, 'Don't be precious.'

'Precious? Nobody has ever called me precious in my life. You're the one who's being precious.'

He laughed. 'Don't worry – I'll sort it out.'

The fourth day, the car didn't show up at my hotel.

Simon Cowell came in and said, 'On behalf of BMG, I apologise, but they've pulled out of the deal. They say they can't work with you.'

The feeling was mutual. Mike Stock is in the *Guinness Book of Records* as the most successful songwriter of all time, with seventeen Number One hits to his credit but, unlike Kylie Minogue, Rick Astley and Bananarama, I was never destined to enjoy the benefit of his talents.

Then Simon Cowell found a song called 'If I Could Only Say Goodbye', written by two guys from Brighton, so I went down to Brighton and recorded it. On 28 October 1993, I performed 'If I Could Only Say Goodbye' on the BBC's *Top of the Pops*. Pamela had joined me in London and a few days later we were mobbed in Leicester Square by people who had recognised me from television. With the help of a couple of London bobbies, we fought our way through the crowd and hopped into a taxi which was then surrounded by hysterical fans. Back at our hotel, I got a call asking whether I would like to host a fund-raising show with Princess Diana and say a few words.

'What on?'

'The wellness of women.'

The show was in aid of one of Diana's charities, Birthright, which raised funds for research into maternal deaths and how to take care of babies in the womb. The purpose of this particular function was that Birthright was being renamed WellBeing (and later changed its name again to WellBeing of Women). Since I had two daughters who had been born six weeks premature, I had something to say.

The glittering room at the Savoy was packed with chattering people when the decibel level suddenly dropped and all eyes turned to the tall woman who had just entered. She spotted us and walked over. I remember thinking, 'God, she's tall.' She had high heels on and was almost as tall as me. She was strikingly beautiful, with the face of an angel. We shook hands.

'You look good with your clothes on,' she said to me.

'And so do you,' I replied.

Diana laughed, blushed and then looked coy. It wasn't my imagination – she was flirting with me. Pamela elbowed me. She and Diana were both wearing almost identical Escarda dresses, so perhaps that had something to do with it.

On television, Diana always seemed humble and shy, averting her eyes and keeping her head bowed; that was the image I had of her – 'Shy Di'. I knew she was separated from Prince Charles but I didn't know anything about her private life or her attitude towards men.

Diana said: 'What are we talking about?'

'I have no idea.'

'Good – because neither have I!'

An elderly gentleman with a ruddy face was standing next to us. 'What do you do?' he asked me in a broad Scots accent. 'Are you one of the charity organisers?'

'I am a TV actor,' I said. 'I do shows like *Knight Rider* and *Baywatch* and I also sing a little.'

He seemed none the wiser. He hadn't heard of *Knight Rider* or *Baywatch* and he certainly hadn't heard me sing. He focused his attention on Pamela, who discovered he was 'quite a character and quite a flirt'. He turned out to be Sir John Junor, a well-known news-paperman who wrote an item about us in his column in the *Mail on Sunday*. ('Their name didn't mean a thing to me. In fact, I was not sure I had heard it properly.')

When the event started, Diana went up to the microphone and made a speech in which she said, 'The press would probably rather have me with my head down the loo than doing a charity event today.'

Then she introduced me and I walked on stage.

'Do I curtsy or kiss you?'

'Do whatever you want.'

So I gave her a big kiss. She smiled and blushed and sat to one side with her hands on her knees and a pert look on her face.

After I'd finished speaking about the premature births of Taylor-Ann and Hayley, one of the organisers took over the microphone.

I asked Diana, 'Where do I sit?'

'Anywhere you like.'

So I sat down with my hands in my lap and looked down and then looked up. She laughed. She turned beet red. She knew I was mimicking her.

Afterwards, at a reception we talked about her sons. She told me they were big fans of *Baywatch*. I gave her a couple of *Baywatch* hats for Prince William and Prince Harry and a couple of autographed cards.

'I'm going to keep these hats,' she joked, 'because I'm afraid my deputy will pinch them.'

Her 'deputy' was her butler, Paul Burrell.

Diana didn't seem to have a lot of people around her; in fact, I got the impression that no one was there for her at all. She seemed to be alone and a bit lonely. It was a nice reception and it was rather sad to leave her there. We gave her a big hug and said goodbye. I didn't know at the time that Diana had been devastated a short time earlier when her brother, Earl Spencer, had reneged on an offer to let her rent a house in the grounds of Althorp, the Spencer family's estate in Northamptonshire. She had been looking forward to spending time with her sons William and Harry away from prying eyes at her ancestral home. I guess a bit of flirting was just her way of taking her mind off things.

That morning, I had been in Liverpool doing a TV talk show and afterwards I went to see the Beatles Museum. After Diana's fund-raiser, Pamela and I went to the British Music Industry Awards, where Paul and Linda McCartney made a beeline for us.

'Linda and I want to get on *Baywatch*,' Paul said.

'You're talking to the right man. I can make that happen.'

'I want to ride a horse,' Linda said, 'and get Paul to rescue me.'

I said, 'I just came from Liverpool where there's a Beatles Museum.'

'Well, I just came from Germany,' Paul said, 'and there ought to be a Hasselhoff Museum in Munich.'

Linda took Pamela by the arm. 'We need to talk about what it's like being married to two living legends,' she said.

At the awards ceremony, Paul was presented with the trophy for the most played record of all time: 'Yesterday'.

I said, 'Wow, what a dream.'

'Yes it was,' he said. 'It came to me in a dream and I wrote it all down.'

On the way back to the hotel, the driver said: 'You know, Fergie's having a party tonight.' Pamela wanted to meet her and I was up for it. As we walked in, Fergie announced: 'Here's our surprise guest, Mr Hasselhoff. We're auctioning things for my charity, Children in Crisis – what would you like to offer?'

'$25,000 from anyone who wants to be on *Baywatch*.'

A hand shot up.

'I'll buy that.'

It was Richard Branson. A year later, he appeared in a *Baywatch* episode entitled 'The Runaways' in which he sets a world record for water-skiing while being towed behind a blimp.

Pamela sat next to Fergie. 'She was kind of what you expected,' Pamela says, 'but she was even more so – more out there and great fun. Her biggest thing was telling me when to smoke and when not to smoke. She was giving me cues rather like a mother hen. I said, "I've lived this long without you. Calm down!" I really liked her.'

Princess Diana had invited us to work out at her gym the next day, but I had another appointment and couldn't make it. She went by herself to the LA Fitness Centre at Isleworth, London, where the proprietor Bryce Taylor had planted a hidden camera in the ceiling. He photographed her working out in a leotard and sold the photographs to the *Sunday Mirror*. This betrayal of her privacy led Diana to announce a few days later that she was giving up her charity work and retiring from public life. It was all desperately sad and it confirmed my impression that no one was looking after her.

Meanwhile, 'If I Could Only Say Goodbye' had reached Number Thirty-five in the UK charts, where it stayed, despite the best promotional efforts of Simon Cowell.

Back on *Baywatch*, Nicole Eggert hung up her red swimsuit, telling the press that 'the water was too cold'. The real reason was that she thought she could act and the other cast members couldn't – that's why she left. Nicole had been a teenage star on the series *Charles in Charge* but, she told me, she had never had a real childhood. Beneath her sweet, lovable exterior there was a rebel just waiting to break out – and break out she did after she had left *Baywatch*.

With Summer Quinn gone, her screen mother Susan Anton was also let go. We brought in Yasmine Bleeth, a former star of the soap *One Life to Live*, as Stephanie's young sister Caroline Holden. Yasmine, a brunette like her screen sister, was the sweetest, kindest angel ever to grace our set; she never said a bad word about anyone. She added a touch of class to *Baywatch* and was probably the best actress of them all.

I developed more challenging stories – stuff from the Michael Landon school of television that made people cry. We still had sex but the sex was never about getting laid because, on *Baywatch*, nobody ever went to bed with anybody else. We had a reputation for being sexist because we shot girls' cleavages or beautiful butts, yet our Number One audience in the USA was women. Women liked to watch women – what were they wearing? What were their figures like? It was not a sexual thing but natural curiosity and we tapped into that.

On NBC's *Today Show* in April 1994, Katie Couric took a marker pen and coloured a giant map of the world in red to indicate the number of countries showing *Baywatch*. When she added them up, the total had risen to 145. One billion people were watching us every week, more than had ever viewed any previous television series. In Spain, we were known as *Los Vigilantes de la Playa* (*Vigilantes on the Beach*), in France, the show was called *Alert à Malibu* (*Malibu Alert*), in Portugal *Mares Vivas* (*Sea Lives*), and in Brazil *SOS Malibu*.

At the MIPTV convention in Cannes, Henry Siegel, president of All American Television, told a packed press conference that *Baywatch* was 'perhaps the most valuable television franchise of our time'. He announced that I had signed a new contract to continue with the show beyond the 1995–6 season. I would also develop another drama series as star and executive producer. The new series would have action, romance and beautiful women; some fifty potential storylines were being looked at.

Despite my television workload, I was determined to get my singing career off the ground in the USA. The chance came when Jan McCormack received a call from an executive producer in New York offering me a concert on Pay-per-view to be televised at the Trump Plaza. It would, I thought, establish me as a mainstream singer in front of a huge American audience. The point I wanted to make was that I was a singer who had become a TV star, not a TV star who wanted to be a singer.

The concert, 'David Hasselhoff and His Friends, Live', directed by Robert Mackintosh, was televised from Trump Plaza, Atlantic City, on 17 June, with a big band and a bevy of *Baywatch* stars making guest appearances. Donald Trump made only one request: he wanted his wife Marla Maples in the show. No problem – I liked Marla and we sang a duet together. The other guests included Pamela Anderson, Greg-Alan Williams, Jeremy Jackson and David Charvet. Everything went well and, after an encore, I bounded backstage to find Donald in my dressing-room, watching television. I'd done a great show and wanted to hear the good news.

'How did we do?'

Donald pointed to the TV set. 'Take a look at our buddy.'

'Huh?'

'It's O. J. – he's running from the police.'

I couldn't believe what I was seeing. O. J. Simpson was tooling along the 405 Freeway in his white Ford Bronco with LAPD patrol cars and every TV news helicopter for company.

'Tell me that isn't live!'

Donald's expression told me that it was. The slow-speed chase was the most widely watched event in American television history, bigger even than the Moon landing. O. J. got 90 million viewers. I got 30,000. I had paid and nobody viewed. It cost us $1.5 million.

Meanwhile, nothing could stop *Baywatch*. In December 1994, we passed the hundredth-episode mark and celebrated with a party at the Ritz Carlton Hotel in Marina del Rey. With the cast elegantly dressed in evening wear, we roared into the hotel's dock in the *Baywatch* Scarab. The press went wild. NBC had the good grace to take a full-page advertisement saying 'Oops – Congratulations' in the *Hollywood Reporter* to acknowledge their mistake in cancelling the show.

Then Pamela Anderson showed up in *Playboy* magazine again with a new bustline. The press went wild again. Most of the girls on the show became insecure about the size of their breasts and visited the plastic surgeon for breast enhancement. Some of the implants were so heavy that the girls couldn't stand up straight.

One of our stars had become so body-conscious after having her breasts enlarged that she insisted on wearing a jacket in her scenes, which rather cancelled out the effect. After Nicole Eggert quit the show, she told Howard Stern she hadn't had a breast job on *Baywatch*, but admitted she had had one *after* she left the show.

'You quit *Baywatch* and had a breast job?' he said. 'What, are you crazy – you quit the Number One show in the world? What did you do – take some of your brain out and put it in your breast?'

Pamela's relationship with David Charvet had come to an end, but the script now called for their characters to fall in love. Greg Bonann celebrated the romance by filming the sexiest music-video montage of all time, a take-off on the famous Burt Lancaster–Deborah Kerr clinch on the wet sands in *From Here to Eternity*. After the break-up, David had said gallantly, 'It's important that we don't ruin the chemistry of the show.' It must have been very difficult for him to keep his real feelings in check.

We were prepared for shocks with Pamela, but she exceeded all our fears – and the tabloids' wildest dreams – when she started dating Tommy Lee, the self-confessed 'Rock Pig' drummer of Motley Crue. Tommy pursued her to Mexico and, after a torrid four-day courtship, married her in a beachside ceremony at Cancun on 19 February 1995, with the bride looking dazed in a white bikini.

While Pamela and Tommy were on honeymoon, my wife and I flew to Washington to attend a gala for the American Red Cross, where I spoke on water safety programmes. Then we went to the White House with a lot of other Red Cross people to meet President Bill Clinton. Security was so tight that you practically had to have your DNA checked to get in. It took three hours to get inside. Pamela was tired and had to use the bathroom.

She said, 'You remember in *Forest Gump* when he meets Nixon and he says, "I think I've got to pee?"'

By the time we reached Clinton, Pamela was desperate. She said to the President, 'Hi, have you seen the movie *Forest Gump*?'

'Why yes, Pamela,' he said. 'Why is that?' He had a little Elvis smile and his eyebrows were raised, like he was thinking, 'What's she going to say next?'

Pamela got all red-faced. 'Never mind.'

He says, 'Tell me.'

Pamela said the first thing that came into her head. 'I was trying to find you this morning to go running with you.'

Bill Clinton's eyebrows raised again. He said, 'Is that so? Okay, come here at six thirty in the morning.'

Next morning, we got to a particular entrance at the White House at six fifteen and our names were at the gate. We went through security again and walked across the lawn and the President came down in his sweats, carrying a bottle of water. He offered us coffee and after we'd had a cup we got in his limo. He sat Pamela opposite him, knees touching.

'I'm sorry, Bill,' she said, '. . . I mean Mr President. What do I call you?'

He just laughed. Then he said: 'The American people just don't understand what the press is trying to get them to believe about the deficit.'

This went right over our heads. There were fifteen police cars escorting us to the park to go jogging. Pamela took out her Walkman – she couldn't run without music – but Clinton looked a bit insulted and made her hand it over to one of his secret service guys. He talked when he ran and he wanted everybody to listen. He ran a fast pace, an eight-mile minute, and he talked the whole way. I had a hangover and a newly repaired knee, but we spurred each other on. I wouldn't call it a competition, but the male ego was definitely involved.

Clinton was warm and personable and asked questions about *Baywatch*. He had more charisma than almost anyone – forget politician; he would have excelled in whatever field he had chosen. After five miles, we stopped for a rest. When we'd caught our breath, he said, 'Okay, let's go', and we were off again. As we started running, several photographers popped out from behind a tree and snapped our picture.

Finally, Clinton had had enough and we drove back with him to the White House, where he took us into the Oval office for a guided tour. He seemed quite taken with Pamela and showed her Kennedy's desk (which he had rescued from storage) and his favourite mementoes. That night, we were back in the White House for dinner. Bon Jovi and Natalie Cole sang and Clinton brought Hillary and Chelsea over to meet us.

So what did the President say to me while we were jogging in that park? He said, 'Did you ever think *Baywatch* would be as big as this?'

I replied, 'I never thought a President of the United States would utter the two syllables *Baywatch*.'

Bill Clinton liked *Baywatch*. Wonder why?

My band could blow up a storm . . . one night the earth actually moved

15 Whole Lotta Shakin'

'I knew I was going to need a flashlight . . .
I just didn't know what for.'

At 4.31 a.m. on 17 January 1994, I was asleep in our house in Sherman Oaks when there was a rumbling like a train going through the living-room. The walls started shaking and I heard the shattering of glass, the breaking of china plates. The whole neighbourhood was being shaken to pieces. I shouted to Pamela, 'Get Hayley!'

I leaped out of bed. The lights weren't working. I stumbled into Taylor-Ann's bedroom to get her. The door was jammed shut, I forced it open. Her room was in darkness and there was no sign of her. I was searching among the bedclothes when I remembered that she had come into our room and was asleep in our bed. I dashed back to our bedroom and there she was, standing on our bed doing what we later called 'the earthquake dance', while the walls swayed and the floor heaved up and down.

Bam! Bam! Windows were popping and glass was flying everywhere. We picked up the children and ran through the kitchen to get outside into the backyard. We made it; nobody had been hurt. The whole house had jumped up in the air and come down four inches away from its original position.

I had had a premonition that an earthquake was coming, although this was worse than anything I had imagined. Registering a magnitude 6.7 on the Richter Scale, the quake's epicentre was located under Northridge, just a mile north of us in the San Fernando Valley. It was the biggest earthquake to hit a suburban area of Los Angeles for sixty years. The neighbours came over. One of them said, 'Have you turned off your gas?' I had a lighter and was about to flick it on.

The guy said, 'There's gas everywhere – you'll be blown to bits.'

'Oh, okay, I'm sorry – I'm an actor.'

He helped me to turn off the supply.

'Thank you very much,' I said. 'I've never seen you before – are you new around here?'

'No, we've been here for ten years.'

'Oh yeah – LA.'

'Yeah, LA.'

I went to the front yard. Oz Scott's house next door had lost its outer wall and I could see his son playing the piano. You could hear the notes of the piano echoing through the neighbourhood. He was trying to calm everyone down. It looked like a bomb had gone off.

It was cold. I told Pamela, 'I'll get some blankets.' I went back inside the house and found a flashlight that worked. The kitchen had been destroyed. Every cabinet was open, the refrigerator's contents were all over the floor, every glass, cup and plate had been smashed. In the bedroom, I was picking up a bundle of blankets when the rumbling started again. I thought, 'Here it comes again – I'm going to be buried alive.' The aftershock was quite severe but didn't cause any further damage and I rejoined Pamela and the children in the backyard.

I suddenly remembered that the producer Robert Mackintosh had arrived from London that day and was staying at the Radisson Hotel on Ventura Boulevard. I had met Robert, elder brother of Sir Cameron Mackintosh, in London the previous year when, at Simon Cowell's instigation, we had discussed possible roles for me in *Seven Brides for Seven Brothers* and *The Rocky Horror Show*. Robert was a lovely man and we had become firm friends. We had had dinner together a few hours earlier to discuss future projects. Also in the hotel were Glen Morrow and a Canadian sound engineer named Mick Sturgeon, with whom I'd spent the last two weeks recording a new show for our next European tour.

The phones were dead, so I decided to drive over there. Ventura Boulevard was like a vision of hell. Damage was widespread and everybody was out on the street; hundreds of people roamed around like zombies. Numerous apartment buildings and houses had been severely damaged; some were ablaze. Elsewhere, sections of the Santa Monica freeway had collapsed, plunging vehicles into the abyss.

Outside the Radisson, Glen, Robert and Mick were standing in a carpark near some houses. Glen was in short pants and tennis shoes; Mick Sturgeon was in a state of shock, just clutching his suitcase and saying nothing.

'I was watching television in my room on the fifth floor at 3.30 a.m.,' Robert Mackintosh recalls.

I'd just called my wife Jane in London and the other guys were asleep in their rooms. Within a split second, the television set flew past me and hit the wall next to my ear. I'd seen many American disaster movies and there is always a build-up, but this earthquake hit like a sixteen-ton truck. Next thing, my ceiling fell in around me, pipes were coming down and the cistern broke and started spouting water. I went and stood under the door frame, which is supposed to be the safest place, then I thought, 'This is ridiculous. King Kong is outside shaking this building to pieces – I've got to get out of here.'

I opened the door and took six paces. I had noticed where the fire escape was when I'd come up to my room. The whole corridor was shaking. I was thinking, 'This is not a good move. I know my life is at stake but am I really going to go outside naked?'

At this point a guy of about seventy in the next room stuck his head out of the door and out came an eighteen-year-old girl. He said, 'She's my niece.' Then off they dashed the other way. I grabbed my jeans and a jacket from my room and ran down the fire escape. The metal door at the bottom had jammed but I forced it open with the help of another guest. I went to the carpark opposite the hotel and saw that the building had been split open from the top like a big piece of fruit. This whole episode had lasted for forty-one seconds but they were very long seconds. On the street next to the carpark, a fire hydrant had burst and water was shooting in the air. Sirens were sounding. Then a group of people next to me said, 'Look – there's the Knight Rider.'

I had joined them in the carpark. Glen said, 'I can't believe it. In the middle of all this crap, here comes Hasselhoff in his black car to save the day. You really are the Knight Rider.'

'Who's got the tapes?' I asked.

Glen: 'They're in the hotel.'

Robert and I climbed the fire escape up the hotel's cracked façade. People were coming down with crying babies in their arms. It was a very Persian neighbourhood and a lot of the hotel's guests were immigrants. A chicken dashed past on its way down to ground level. We reached Glen's room, which had really been trashed, but we found the tapes. Robert's room was under nine inches of water. We grabbed his bags and dashed down the fire escape and drove back to Sutton Place. As dawn broke over Sherman Oaks, we took some meat out of the kitchen and cooked it on the barbecue in the backyard. The repairs to my house cost $270,000, but the show went on. A week later we were at the Robinson Club in Switzerland. The deal was that for a week's free hospitality and all the skiing we could do, we would put on one show. It was a sellout.

When we returned to the States, Glen Morrow told us he had been diagnosed with cancer. We had been ribbing him about his hair loss, not knowing that he had secretly been having chemotherapy. Glen was ill and depressed when I visited him in a Toronto hospital.

'Get well,' I said. 'We're going to Taiwan.'

'Taiwan?'

'Yeah, I need you.'

There was no date booked in Taiwan but we arranged one at the Hard Rock Café in Taipei to get Glen out of bed and back on the road. The concert was shown live on V Channel, a local Asian station that was divided into a Mandarin-dominated music video service for northern Asia and a Hindi-dominated music video service for western Asia.

Glen lived for another two years.

My *Baywatch* buddies in 1989 (left to right): Billy Warlock, Erika Eleniak,
Parker Stevenson, Shawn Weatherly and Peter Phelps

Surrounded by children at Camp Baywatch, a charity created by
Greg Bonann's girlfriend, Tai. Greg is on the right

We were laughing all the
way to the beach

Baywatch 1994:
Back row: David Charvet
and Alexandra Paul.
Front: Yasmine Bleeth,
Jaason Simmons and
Pamela Anderson

Learning the ropes

SHIPSHAPE 1995:
Top: Gena Lee Nolin,
David Chokachi,
Alexandra Paul,
Jaason Simmons.
Front: Yasmine Bleeth,
Pamela Anderson and
Jeremy Jackson

BAYWATCH NIGHTS 1996: Greg Alan-Williams,
Lisa Stahl, Lou Rawls and Angie Harmon

On a diving trip with my stunt double and good buddy Alex Daniels.
Great fun, but we almost drowned

Chuck Russell, a terrific director

Ron Armstrong, one of the angels

Lou Rawls… our last meeting

Eugen Joeckel, the incorrigible joker

Robert Mackintosh, producer extraordinaire

Mark Holden, the 'Song Doctor'

Hayley Amber, born 1992: the doctor turned his back for a moment and I was the first person to touch her

Taylor-Ann, born 1990: she was six weeks early and unfortunately I was performing in Europe at the time

Jan McCormack and Jonni Hartman, my manager of thirty two years and my former press agent

Michael Cuccione… unbelievably courageous

Lana Turner, blonde and beautiful

Nancy Reagan, every inch a First Lady

With Dolores and Liberace... 'Lee' was a good friend and a great showman

Mohammed Ali... 'You're pretty Knight Rider, but you're not as pretty as me'

At the White House with Bill, Chelsea, Hillary Clinton and Pamela

Simon Cowell, my good friend and former A&R guy at BMG, on the set of *America's Got Talent*.

Princess Diana… beautiful but so alone

My parents with *Tonight Show* host Jay Leno

The David Hasselhoff Band (left to right) Glen Morrow, Danny McBride, Koko Kojima, Jeff Phillips and Al Marni

Performing with Danny McBride and Koko Kojima.

My room of gold and platinum discs

Rehearsing with Danny McBride, Koko Kojima, Al Marni and Glen Morrow

As the evil Edward Hyde, and (inset)
my Broadway poster 2000

In *Chicago* with Rebecca Thornhill and
Anita Louise Combe 2004

In Morocco with director Joshua Sinclair
and some of the cast of *Shaka Zula*

My high-powered SpongeBob double – an
animatronic replica 12-foot long and
weighing 750lb – and (inset) with my real
SpongeBob double Alex Daniels

'Click'…ing on the set with Adam Sandler

Still wrestling with sharks, even on
vacation, 2006

Miracles do happen . . . my buddy Wade Hubbard after
surviving serious brain surgery

My *Baywatch* buddies (from left) Pamela Anderson, Alexandra Paul, Greg Alan Williams, David Charvet, Nicole Eggert and Jeremy Jackson

16 Planet *Baywatch*

'No one watched us . . . all one billion
viewers were just channel surfing.'

*B*aywatch might not have been the show Shakespeare would have
written if he'd lived in Malibu, but we covered a third of the world's
surface – and the rest was water. On New Year's Eve, Princess Soraya,
second wife of the Shah of Iran, came over to me at the Caribou Club
in Aspen. 'Did you know your show is beamed into Iran by satellite?'
she said, 'People sell tickets to *Baywatch* parties and women have dyed
blonde hair underneath their burcas.'

Los Angeles Weekly also published an article headlined 'Baywatch v. the
Ayatollah', based on interviews in Teheran, which showed that Western
TV shows like *Baywatch* had stirred a huge current of dissension
among young people. It was heartening to know that we were bringing
a little American culture to the land of the mullahs.

In the USA, the *Baywatch* logo of the sun setting behind a lifeguard
tower had become one of the motifs of Generation X, while our theme
song, 'I'm Always Here', was a universal hit. The *Baywatch* name was
licensed to products ranging from Barbie dolls and pinball machines to
air fresheners.

What was the secret of *Baywatch*'s appeal? Sociologists speculated that
it captured a popular international view of America: beautiful people

performing heroic deeds in a land of buffed, fat-free bodies, perfect teeth, Walkmans, frozen yogurt and rollerblades. 'It was this obsession with anything that goes on in California,' Mark Schwed of *TV Guide* said, 'combined with the fact that it had the most incredible eye candy.' Another commentator saw *Baywatch* as the show 'where every story has a happy ending and there is no evil on the planet that cannot be conquered with a mix of schmaltzy scriptwriting and plastic surgery'.

It was all an illusion. *Baywatch*'s sole black character, Garner Ellerbee, played by Greg-Alan Williams, complained that we hired only blond, blue-eyed Aryans so that European viewers would identify with the show. Alexandra Paul agreed with him. '*Baywatch* is too Caucasian,' she said. 'Apparently, Europe wants a Caucasian show but I see all those ethnic divisions in Europe and I think we need to see shows with more colour and diversity.' Even though we added José Solano, a Latino, to the cast and, later, Traci Bingham as the first black lifeguard, the show remained basically Caucasian.

In my early forties, I was in better condition than I had been in my twenties. Every morning at 4.45 a.m., while Pamela, Taylor-Ann and Hayley were still asleep, I headed for the gym for aerobics and weight training. Throughout the day, I would do 300 sit-ups. I stuck to a fruit-laden diet, with the nutritional supplement Met-Rx, and drank lots of water. I saw fame as a responsibility to my family. It kept me in check.

My whole family were extremely proud when I was awarded a star on the Hollywood Walk of Fame. Professionally, however, I felt as though I would be running down a beach in slow motion for the rest of my life. My music career hadn't taken off in the USA as I had hoped. My fourth album, *Is Everybody Happy?*, had been released in Europe to big sales, but the American market was still out of reach. My movie career had stalled. I said to Jan McCormack, 'The only way I'm going to get a good review is if I play a bad guy.' She found me a role as a murderer in *Avalanche*, a TV thriller filmed in Canada. I had internalised all of the bad reviews of *Baywatch* and used them in my character. It felt so good to let it out in a positive way.

We were filming twenty-two episodes of *Baywatch* in four or five months of the year, which left the cast and crew idle until we were ready to start prepping the next series. The answer seemed to be a spin-off series from *Baywatch*. I discussed several concepts with Greg Bonann, Doug Schwartz and Michael Berk and came down in favour of one in which Mitch Buchannon would moonlight as a private eye. We had pitched the idea to All American Television and in December 1994 they agreed to put up the money. This was the project that Henry Siegel had announced in Cannes. It sprang from our desire to make a second series using the facilities and experience of the Baywatch Production Company. It was a big mistake.

The premise of the new show that was sold to independent distributors at the NATPE convention was that Garner Ellerbee (Greg-Alan Williams), resident police officer at Baywatch Beach since the beginning of the series, suffers a mid-life crisis. Finding himself in a dead-end job, he punches his supervisor and then quits the LAPD. He has always wanted to open a detective agency, so he persuades long-time pal Mitch Buchannon to join him. I hated the title of the new series, *Baywatch Nights*; it left me cold. I wanted to call the show *Santa Monica Nights*, but the buyers insisted on a visual link with *Baywatch*.

When the new television season kicked off in September 1995, I was the lead in two prime-time shows that were running in tandem in the belief that many *Baywatch* fans would also want to watch *Baywatch Nights*. The sixth *Baywatch* series opened with Mitch revealing that one of his dreams is to work as a private investigator. The first episode of *Baywatch Nights* then picks up the story, with Mitch and Garner Ellerbee taking over a bankrupt private investigation agency.

Lou Rawls and I went into a studio to record the show's theme song, 'The City of Angels'. I sang the first line and then Lou sang the second. I stopped and said. 'You do the whole thing, Lou.' I was in awe. So he sang the whole song in his incomparable, smokey, deep-soul baritone. Lou Rawls was another angel in my life. Years later, I saw his billboard while driving through Reno and we sang a duet on stage. The gentleman that he was, he attended our Christmas parties and my father's seventieth birthday party.

Baywatch Nights was filmed in a specially-built set at Paradise Cove, Malibu. In the first series (1995–6), Lou plays Lou Raymond, owner of a blues club called Nights, which shares the same building as the detective agency. Mitch walks into the club and says to Lou, 'This is infinitely more exciting – these girls have clothes on.' For the agency's third partner, attorney Ryan McBride, I recruited Angie Harmon after she walked past me on an airplane. I was blown away by her beauty. She *was* Ryan. Angie was a top fashion model and I had a little trouble convincing her that I wasn't trying to pick her up; that I seriously wanted to audition her for a part in a new television series.

The storylines for *Baywatch Nights* were edgier than *Baywatch* and were aimed at an older, late-night audience. We ended each episode with a performance by a top blues artist such as B. B. King or the Jeff Healey Band. Ratings, however, were poor from the start. It was obvious that *Baywatch* fans did not accept Mitch in his new role. They saw his proper place as a lifeguard on the beach and did not want him driving around at night in a flash red sports car solving cases like Magnum, Jim Rockford or Matt Helm. *Baywatch Nights* was panned by one reviewer as 'syndicated lite-crime hour, no strain, no pain'.

In the spring of 1995 Tony Scotti said to me, 'We're not getting the ratings we want. We're losing money. We're bringing in David Gerber as president of All American Television.' Gerber was a seasoned producer but he tried to fashion *Baywatch Nights* into one of the most successful shows of the 1970s. One of the casualties was Greg-Alan Williams. I was upset to see him dropped; we had great camaraderie and I respected him.

Donna Marco (Donna D'Errico, a stunning blonde from Las Vegas) took over from Lou as the owner of Nights, while Griff Walker (Eddie Cibrian) came in as a professional photographer who helps the detectives with their cases. The changes failed to halt the drift. At the end of the first season, our Los Angeles and New York stations passed on buying any more episodes. Fearful that this would reflect badly on *Baywatch* itself, All American renewed *Nights* for a second season and bought airtime in LA and New York at great expense to themselves.

Meanwhile, nothing could stop *Baywatch*'s winning run. David Charvet had gone off to star in *Melrose Place* after completing the filming of season five, but his replacement, David Chokachi, as clean-cut Cody Madison, proved just as popular with viewers. We had ended season five with the introduction of Gena Lee Nolin as bad girl Neely Capshaw, a cold and calculating lifeguard who begins her *Baywatch* career by making a pass at Cody, getting drunk and falsely accusing him of sexual harassment.

Neely is a liar, a cheat and a thief who never hesitates to use her body to get her own way. Gena Lee Nolin, on the other hand, was the ultimate *Fargo* girl from Minnesota – blonde and Nordic and wholesome as a tall glass of milk. She was extraordinarily naïve, which considering the role she was playing, was so unbelievable that you thought it must be phoney. Season six kicked off with C. J. Parker blaming Neely for Matt's departure from Baywatch Beach and they come to blows. This gave the press the idea of conjuring up on-set fights between Gena Lee Nolin and Pamela Anderson, which simply didn't exist.

But stories in the tabloid papers were getting under Pamela's skin.

'They make stuff up – it makes me mad,' she said.

'Katharine Hepburn said, "I don't care what they print about me as long as it's not the truth." '

'Really? Well, they've got that right.'

I had a saying: 'If you pout, you're out.' Pamela knew I wouldn't take bad behaviour from anybody because it showed a lack of respect for the show. There was never trouble with Tommy Lee when I was around the set, but on other occasions he turned up and tried to break into Pamela's trailer after they'd had an argument. Tommy was jealous and hot-tempered. If she had to kiss David Chokachi in a scene, he would go ballistic – bash her door down, break a window, yell and scream. The director had to get security to escort him off the set.

Pamela was working five days a week on *Baywatch* and weekends on her first feature film, *Barb Wire*. On 25 June 1995 she collapsed at her Malibu home and was rushed to hospital, where it was discovered she was pregnant. She took time off from *Baywatch* to give birth to her son Brandon and we started building the show around Gena Lee Nolin. Pamela was devastated when *Barb Wire*, in which she plays a crime-buster in black leather, was released to bad reviews in May 1996. The film was about as successful as *Baywatch Nights*; the public wanted Pamela on the beach in her red swimsuit, not in a sex-and-violence thriller. The demand for pictures of Pamela, however, was higher than ever and the paparazzi went after her like mad dogs. She told me: 'I was in my car and people with cameras around their necks were following me. They tried to run me off the road.'

Pamela demanded twenty-four-hour security to protect her and her baby son, but although we appreciated her difficulties we could not agree to foot the bill. So Pamela Anderson Lee turned in her red swimsuit and quit *Baywatch* after five years in December 1996. I think she'd had enough and just wanted to be a mum. I respected that. Someone leaked the story to the *Los Angeles Times* and that was the first indication we had that she was quitting. 'Giving birth to my son Brandon has opened my mind to explore many new personal and professional opportunities,' she said. 'I have no expectations about becoming a big movie star. I just want to continue working in all areas of the entertainment business and continue to be involved with high-quality projects.'

To explain Pamela's sudden departure, we had C. J. Parker run away to Mexico to marry a rock star, hoping that the viewers would enjoy the joke. We were the Number One show when Pamela joined the cast; we stayed Number One while Pamela was in the show and we were still Number One after she had left.

After less than two years of marriage, Pamela filed for divorce from Tommy Lee, citing irreconcilable differences and seeking joint custody of five-month-old Brandon. The couple were reconciled before the divorce was finalised and, with the birth of a second son, Dylan, in 1997, it seemed Pamela's wild private life might settle down. It was her greatest wish to create a happy family life, but when the violence continued in 1998, Pamela filed for divorce again. Pamela is a great mother, a great friend and a sweet girl. Everything about her comes from a good place. If you saw her with her two sons, you would never imagine she had lived such a frenzied life.

Pamela is also smart. She took my advice and got a piece of *VIP*, her new *Charlie's Angels* tongue-in-cheek show. It ran for six seasons and made her a fortune. And she has a great sense of humour: her claim (in the TV programme *Life after Baywatch*) that she had sex with all of her fellow cast members at least once during her time on the show was just one of her little jokes.

Then Gena Lee Nolin wanted to leave, blaming a sudden fear of the camera. This seemed irrational, so I spoke to her about it and it emerged that she was actually frightened of me. I had the reputation of being one of the greatest improvisers on TV. I would look at a scene and realise that it wasn't good enough, so I would improvise. This completely threw Gena. It would scare her whenever she saw me toss the script away. She said: 'This isn't for me. I'm not cut out for it. I'm a nervous wreck before every scene. I quit.' We made a deal that I would never change a scene that Gena was in. We slowly built her confidence back up and she stayed on the show.

But we did lose Alexandra Paul, who was fed up with the whole

Baywatch scene and begged to be written out of the series. 'It isn't good for young girls to watch our show,' she said. 'It probably makes them insecure. I want to go – kill me off.' We'd killed off Jill Riley in the first season and the viewers were still traumatised, but we reluctantly agreed to do so. In 'Chance of a Lifetime' in season seven, Stephanie Holden is struck by a falling mast during a thunderstorm. She dies in the arms of the two men she loved most, Mitch and her new husband Tom.

Baywatch Nights returned for its second season with a cast reshuffle and a new direction in which we switched to a science-fiction format in the manner of *The X-Files*. Ryan McBride suddenly turns into a scientist and Garner Ellerbee disappears altogether without any explanation – no wonder the viewers were confused. Garner was replaced by Diamont Teague (Dorian Gregory), a paranormal expert who joins Mitch in solving a confusing mixture of cases involving vampires, spectres, psychics and psychos.

Baywatch fans found it even more unacceptable that Mitch Buchannon would leave Hobie at home while he went out at night to fight the forces of darkness. Despite episodes starring Yasmine Bleeth in a crossover role as Caroline Holden and my old *Knight Rider* collaborator Edward Mulhare as Dr Lancaster, a scientist who helps revive two frozen Vikings, the new format did not help the series and it was cancelled after just forty-four episodes. Doing two shows at the same time had drained me mentally and physically and I hadn't had time to give *Baywatch* the attention it deserved. Critics noted that while the second season of *Baywatch Nights* was in production, *Baywatch* had suffered a fall in both script quality and characterisation.

Shortly afterwards, I heard that Edward Mulhare was seriously ill with cancer and took Taylor-Ann to see him at his home in Van Nuys. Edward was very frail and his lanky frame was wasted, but his spirit was as strong as ever. With great effort, he sat up in bed and proposed a toast, 'Here's to us. Where is the likes of us? Damn few left – and they're all dead.' Then he lay down. 'Murder them for both of us, David,' he whispered. The following day – 24 May 1997 – he passed away. The role of Dr Lancaster in *Baywatch Nights* had been this great actor's last performance. I owed him an enormous debt, both for his superb example as a professional actor and for his unflinching loyalty.

Two days later I was in Vancouver to film *Nick Fury, Agent of*

S.H.I.E.L.D., a TV thriller based on the *Marvel Comics* character Colonel Nicholas Joseph Fury. Nick Fury was the opposite of clean-cut Mitch Buchannon. My *Baywatch* curls were closely cropped, my face was covered in designer stubble, I had a cigar butt clamped between my teeth and I wore a black leather jacket, leather trousers, biker gloves and an eye-patch. It was hoped that this film would be the first of four Nick Fury adventures, but it failed to create sufficient excitement among the viewers and the other three were shelved.

Back at *Baywatch*, we had lost Yasmine Bleeth, who quit after four years during season seven. 'I didn't want to get comfortable doing the same thing,' she said. She returned to film an episode in which Caroline Holden wins a part in the fictional TV soap *Shannon's Hope* and moves to New York. In reality, Yasmine donned a business suit and a badge to play internal affairs officer Caitlin Cross on *Nash Bridges* with Don Johnson.

To replace Pamela Anderson, Alexandra Paul and Yasmine Bleeth, three new female cast members had been introduced during season seven: Nancy Valen (Captain Samantha Thomas), Donna D'Errico (Donna Marco from *Baywatch Nights*) and Traci Bingham (as African-American lifeguard Jordan Tate). ITV had dropped *Baywatch* in mid-season after viewing figures had dropped from 11 million to fewer than six million. They were also unhappy about receiving episodes from America at the very last minute, which created scheduling difficulties. However, they picked *Baywatch* up again in the eighth season and I flew to London to promote it. 'We have gone overboard on the babes this season,' I told the press, 'but we will have family stories and plenty of action. The request for more girls came from Fremantle – I would rather have stories with a moral side to them.' We did tests that showed the Number One reason people watched the show was the relationship between Mitch and Hobie. I know it sounds far-fetched, but that was the test result.

My partners had hired so many new girls for season eight that I wondered what was going on. The strategy wasn't so much to replace Pamela Anderson as to make the audience forget she had ever existed by filling with screen with sensational 'eye candy' in the shape of Kelly Packard, Carmen Electra, Angelica Bridges and Marliece Andrada.

One after another, a blonde ingénue would ask me: 'What about me – where's my storyline?'

'You're absolutely right,' I'd say. 'Something's gone wrong . . . By the way, who are you?'

I'd go to the other producers and say, 'Why are we hiring so many girls?' I told them, 'Guys, it's not babes, it's stories with babes.'

To even things up, we brought in male model Michael Bergin as Jack 'J. D.' Darius, an old friend of Mitch and Newmie's. Michael got more publicity than he bargained for when he had an affair with John F. Kennedy Jr's wife Carolyn Bessette, both before and after her marriage. Carolyn was a publicist for Calvin Klein and Michael was the designer brand's super-fit 'Spokesbody'. He was the first to admit, 'Acting is not my strongest suit', but he worked hard and when he smiled he lit up the show.

We probably got closest to my idea of the perfect *Baywatch* script with 'Charlie', an episode based on the story of a little boy suffering from a rare form of cancer who came to visit us on the set of *Baywatch*. Everybody fell in love with Charlie and he became our mascot. Greg Bonann arranged for him to stay with his mother in an apartment close to the beach during the last months of his life. It was a gracious act from a kind and giving man. Charlie dedicated his body to research to find the gene that causes this type of cancer.

When we decided to do Charlie's story on *Baywatch*, I contacted a remarkable young Canadian boy named Michael Cuccione, who had been sent to us three months earlier by the Children's Wish Foundation of Canada. Michael was a very outgoing twelve-year-old, with an irresistible twinkle in his eye. I fell in love with him. Michael had been born on 5 January 1985 at Burnaby, British Columbia, and had been raised with his brother and sister at Coquitlam, near Vancouver. He was an actor, dancer, singer, songwriter and crusader in the fight against cancer after twice beating Hodgkin's lymphoma, the same kind of cancer that had killed Brandon Tartikoff.

I gave Michael a CD and he said, 'I've got a CD for you. I write music about my life. It's called *Together We Can Make a Difference*. I also have a charity because I'd like to help other kids beat cancer.' The revenues from the CD sales had been used to set up the Michael Cuccione Foundation and fund cancer research in Canada.

I rang Michael and said, 'You're the only guy who can play Charlie.'
He said, 'I'd love to.'

Michael came down to the *Baywatch* set and met Charlie's mother to learn about the boy he would be playing. In our version of the story, Charlie lives with his sister April (Kelly Packard) and mother Paige (Judith Ledford) in an apartment near Baywatch Beach. Everyone has been told that Charlie has a rare form of cancer and that he is being treated at UCLA. April tells Mitch, however, that Charlie isn't being treated at all but used for research into his type of cancer. He doesn't have long to live . . .

After the episode had been filmed, Michael went back to Canada where, in 2000, he joined four other child actors to form a group called 2ge+her, created by MTV as a spoof boy band. When they appeared on MTV, however, they became an overnight sensation with such novelty songs as 'U + Me = Us (Calculus)', 'Say It (Don't Spray It)' and 'The Hardest Thing About Breaking Up (Is Getting Your Stuff Back)'.

The fictional band went on the road, playing dates on Britney Spears' summer tour. Then in December 2000 Michael was injured in an automobile accident in which his chest was crushed against the steering wheel. He was admitted to hospital, where it was discovered that, owing to his operations for cancer, his chest had never developed; he had the diaphragm of an eight-year-old boy.

Michael called me from his bed and said, 'Don't worry – I'm going to beat this', but just days after his sixteenth birthday he died of pneumonia on 13 January 2001. His last words to his mother were, 'I'm sorry, Mom.' I was devastated. I travelled to Canada with my new keyboard player Wade Hubbard and sang 'God Bless a Brand New Angel' at his memorial service – the song written for the death of Stephanie Holden in *Baywatch*. To this day, whenever I've been self-indulgent, I think back to when my daughter Hayley was five years old and Michael Cuccione was her date at a fund-raising party for his charity. Instead of joining the other teenagers, he stayed with Hayley and made sure she had a good time.

With two daughters (and the possibility of more children), the time had come for Pamela and me to go house hunting again. I was determined to sell the Sherman Oaks house that I'd bought with my earnings from *Knight Rider* prior to our marriage. We were directed to a property in Louise Avenue, Encino, which you entered down a driveway lined with pepper trees. It reminded me so much of the South that in my mind I'd bought the house before we had reached the end of the drive. When I saw the house, it was three-storeys high with six white pillars in front and set in two acres of grounds with a pool, tennis court and guesthouse.

John Goodman the actor opened the door.

'How are you doing, Hasselhoff?'

'Pretty good, Goodman. Are you selling?'

'Yes. The price is $2 million.'

'Okay, let's take a look.'

After I'd been over the house from top to bottom, I said, 'Thanks a lot – I'll take it.'

'I'm not going to negotiate.'

'You don't have to negotiate – I'll take it.'

I got back into the car and Pamela said, 'What do you think?'

I said, 'I just bought it.'

I sold my house in Sherman Oaks the same day to Michael Chikles (*The Shield*). After the earthquake in 1994, we had rebuilt the house on twenty-five-feet-deep pylons. It is now one of the most quake-proof houses in Los Angeles.

Our neighbours in Louise Avenue included Parker Stevenson and Kirstie Alley, who had bought the old Al Jolson estate. Parker and I had remained friends after he had quit *Baywatch* and taken up directing. When I heard that his marriage had broken up, I called around to see him. Parker was struggling to look after his two adopted children, plus about thirty exotic animals that he and Kirstie had collected during their marriage.

Next day, I asked the director of 'Out of the Blue', the current episode of *Baywatch*, to drop out in exchange for two episodes later on. Then I called Parker Stevenson.

'You're not going to believe this – the director just pulled out.'

'You're kidding me.'

'I need you.'

'I'm in the middle of a divorce.'

'We'll take care of everything – bring the kids to the set; just get down here and direct.'

'You know, man, I could use a job right now.'

Parker showed up on the set and did a thoroughly competent job despite the turmoil in his private life. He directed four episodes of *Baywatch* in season eight and we also brought back his character, Craig Pomeroy, in another three. Parker found out later that the other director had dropped out as a favour and said that going back to work was the best thing that could have happened to him. He's since been there for me during my troubles.

To end the season with a flourish, the scriptwriters decided that Neely Capshaw should marry Mitch in a shipboard ceremony. This was filmed in July aboard the liner *Dawn Princess* during a cruise in Alaskan waters. My partners enjoyed doing product endorsement deals for every brand name from Coca-Cola to Mercedes-Benz. In this episode, I say to my son Hobie that the De Beers engagement ring cost me a month's salary. Doug Schwartz had made a good deal – we think to get that ring for his wife – so when I showed it to Gena on the boat and asked her to marry me, I accidentally dropped it into the water – or pretended to.

'Hey Doug, I'm *so* sorry. I've lost the ring!'

Doug nearly had a heart attack. He kept staring down into the water hoping he might see it. Then I took it out of my pocket and said: 'Are you looking for this?'

We both had a good laugh and Doug gave a huge sigh of relief.

During season eight it was announced that Donna D'Errico, Angelica Bridges, Traci Bingham and Marliece Andrada would not be returning to Baywatch Beach, while Carmen Electra decided to leave of her own accord (framing her red swimsuit as a memento to her time on the show). Only Gena Lee Nolin and Kelly Packard were invited back. Part of me was relieved – I now had only two names to remember. The press called it the 'Baywatch Bloodbath'.

Suddenly, we had a new partner when Pearson Television, a subsidiary of international media group Pearson plc, publishers of the *Financial Times*, bought All American Television and its wholly owned subsidiary Fremantle, an acquisition that brought *Baywatch* under the control of Pearson Television. The good news was that we had a new parent company that had money to invest in the show. The bad news was that some of the Pearson executives had little idea about how to do a series like *Baywatch*. It was disconcerting and there were some memorable creative disagreements.

Back in Los Angeles, I was working with Wade Hubbard to figure out my new album, *Hooked on a Feeling*. In the back of my mind, I had the tune for a worldwide hit. It had been composed by Glen Morrow just before he became ill. 'I don't know what the words are,' he said. 'I've just got the hook.' He played it for me; it was beautiful. I wanted to put Glen's song on the new album, so Wade and I started throwing around lyrics like Lennon and McCartney, or maybe Mike Stock.

Around four o'clock in the morning, Wade sang, "Cause I need you, baby . . .'

And I added, 'More than words can say . . .'

We wrote the song in half an hour.

I called up Glen. 'We've got it.'

'You've got what?'

'The lyrics to your song – "More Than Words Can Say".'

When I sang it, Glen started to cry.

'Make it a hit, will you,' he said, 'my family needs the royalties.'

I recorded 'More Than Words Can Say' in Los Angeles and then, for the video, I shot it as a duet in the Philippines with the top Filipino artist Regine Velasquez. We sent the track over to Hamburg to be included on the *Hooked on a Feeling* album. The Germans thought it was going to be a massive hit; it was what they called 'an earworm' – a tune that gets into your ear and you can't get it out. But *Hooked on a Feeling* dropped like an egg from a tall chicken. 'More Than Words Can Say' went down with it. It was 1997 and most David Hasselhoff fans were now grown up and were listening to gangsta rap. They were too cool to be into me anymore.

Speculation was rife about the future of *Baywatch* and I added to it during a European tour to promote my new album. In Prague, I said I thought it was time I moved on after eight years on the beach, possibly into musicals such as *Phantom of the Opera*. When I got back to Los Angeles, Jan McCormack and Eric Weissler presented me with a brand new three-year contract in which they had negotiated the most lucrative terms per episode that had ever been paid to an actor for a syndicated TV show. After I'd read the contract, I sighed, 'Three more years on *Baywatch* . . . I guess Broadway will have to wait.' I was on my way to becoming a very rich man. I asked Jan, 'Where's the pen?'

In January 1998 I was back in the Philippines to star in the feature film *Legacy* with Rod Steiger. I play Jack Scott, a photojournalist who runs foul of Steiger's panama-hatted villain Sadler in the hunt for a massive treasure. Steiger was the looniest, wildest guy I'd ever met. At seventy-two years old, he was going through a divorce and it was destroying him. Clearly concerned about money, his opening line to me was, 'I don't know how good an actor you are, but you're one hell of a businessman.'

On the first day of filming, my character chases one of Sadler's gang through a fish market. The director, T. J. Scott, had placed a camera two storeys high for long shots and one behind baskets of seafood for close-ups. As we were getting ready to shoot, a mother washing her little girl in the street looked at me and said: '*Baywatch!*' Then an old guy shuffled over and said 'No, *Knight Rider!*'

People were milling around everywhere, most of whom did not realise they were on a film set. When the cameras rolled, I tackled the baddie, he punched me, grabbed my camera and ran off. The local Neighbourhood Watch took this seriously. Word went out, 'A thief has stolen the Knight Rider's camera.' The crowd gave chase and caught up with the bad guy and started beating him up. I looked at the cameras and motioned them to keep rolling, then I dragged the vigilantes, mostly elderly women, off the bad guy and said to him, 'Throw a right and then take off.' We dashed through the market fighting all the way to my trailer. The director came in beaming. 'I got it!' he said.

One evening we went to a cock fight, a barbaric but strangely fascinating 'sporting' event in which two birds rip one another to pieces using razor-sharp talons. Around the ring, people started waving at me, so I waved back.

Our guide said, 'Ah, David, I don't wish to embarrass you, but they're not waving at you, they're betting.'

'What?'

'You just bet about $500.'

'No, I didn't bet anything – they're just waving.'

'If they wave money and you wave back, it means you're accepting their bet.'

Our cock died in the ring and I paid up. Outside, people were sewing up wounded cocks so they could fight again. I didn't go back.

Rod Steiger was a solitary figure; he would take his lines and go off on his own. Eventually, the director would get fed up with waiting for him to reappear. He'd say: 'There's only one person who can control him and it's you.'

So I would find Steiger and say, 'Are you ready, Mr Steiger?'

He would scream, 'Who the f— are you to f——— come in here and f——— tell me what to f——— do!'

I'd say, 'Are you finished, Mr Steiger? I'm going to give you my line and then we want one line from you.'

He didn't give a hoot about the director, but he was fond of me and always complied. He was on a short fuse and found it hard to take the noise in Manila. 'I can't concentrate, it's so f———— loud. Hasselhoff, you're a f————- hero – stop the traffic!' But although representations were made to the city authorities, the traffic would not stop, even for Rod Steiger. Nevertheless, he stole every scene he was in. The last time I saw him I was on a pedestrian crossing in Malibu. He almost knocked me down in his car. I shouted at him to be more careful and he shouted back and drove off. He hadn't even recognised me.

I got back to Los Angeles in March 1998 to the news that the wedding episode of *Baywatch* had run into trouble with our test audience. They did not like the fact that Mitch had got married. Then Gena Lee Nolin announced she was quitting the show to look after her young baby. It's amazing how scriptwriters can rearrange the world to suit the viewing public. They decided that the marriage was invalid because the ship's captain had not been qualified to conduct the ceremony. At a stroke, Mitch was single again.

When season nine went on air in September 1998, however, the old *Baywatch* magic was no longer working. The scripts had become so repetitive that we were plagiarising ourselves. The arrival of three new faces – Brooke Burns (*Ally McBeal*), Mitzi Kapture (*Silk Stalkings*) and Erin Gray (*Buck Rogers*) – failed to halt the slide. In desperation, the writers devised stories that sacrificed characterisation and everything else for the sake of excitement.

Mitch drives racing cars, goes skydiving. *Baywatch* got to be so crazy that I saw a truck containing a twenty-five-feet-long eel driving on to the set. The idea was that Mitch would fight the monster in an underwater cave to save Hobie's life. I said, 'Are you kidding me?' One of my fellow producers tried to persuade me that this episode was based on a true story when an eel had escaped from an aquarium and had grown to a huge length in the Malibu sewers.

I had never expected *Baywatch* to last for so long. By the fourth season, we had achieved an impressive 6.5 rating week after week. In 1994–5, we were in the Top Twenty in syndicated programming with a seasonal average of 6.0, while for the past three seasons the show had scored ratings of 4.1, 3.4 and 3.2. *Baywatch* had launched the acting careers of Pamela Anderson Lee (*VIP*), David Charvet (*Melrose Place*), Billy Warlock (*General Hospital*), and Greg-Alan Williams (feature films). The end, however, seemed to be in sight. The budget had climbed to $2 million per episode and the show was now becoming unprofitable. In November 1998, our great allies the Germans threatened to cancel. It was only when we promised to introduce a complete change of scenery that we gained a stay of execution. We decided to take *Baywatch* down under to Australia.

Everything happens to Buddy . . . Buddy McCormack
with Taylor-Ann as a baby

Hitting the highs at Princess Diana's memorial concert,
Althorp, June 1998

17 Goodbye, Princess

'Some people are too beautiful for this life.'

After finishing the Alaskan cruise episode of *Baywatch*, I was in the gym of a hotel in Anchorage on the night of Saturday 30 August 1997 when a picture of Princess Diana appeared on the TV screen. I was wearing a headset and had no idea what was happening when Pamela dashed in and told me that the Princess had been injured in a car crash in Paris. Our hearts were pounding as we hurried back to our room where we followed the drama on television. Then, an hour or so later, it was announced that Diana had died; we were completely dumbstruck – just two of the billions of hearts that were deeply touched by the tragedy.

We remembered the day we had met her in London and I recalled our impression that she had been alone and unprotected. It seemed that feeling had been confirmed in the cruellest possible way just as Diana had re-emerged into public life from her self-imposed exile to carry out great humanitarian work among AIDS patients, lepers, the homeless and the victims of landmines.

Diana had been in Paris as the guest of Dodi al-Fayed, whom she had met six weeks earlier through her stepmother Raine Spencer. They had left the Ritz Hotel at 12.15 a.m. in a Mercedes driven by Henri Paul, the hotel's deputy security chief. The paparazzi had given chase on motorbikes. By the time Henri Paul and his passengers – Diana, Dodi and bodyguard Trevor Rees-Jones – had entered the Alma Tunnel beside the Seine, the photographers were almost a quarter-mile behind. Swerving to avoid a slower vehicle, the Mercedes had hit the right wall of the tunnel with a loud crash, then rebounded into one of the reinforced concrete pillars that divided the lanes from oncoming traffic. The car ricocheted again, hurtling across the tunnel and spinning around before coming to a halt. Henri Paul and Dodi al-Fayed were dead, while Diana and Trevor Rees-Jones were barely alive. Diana was treated at the scene, and then taken to hospital, where she was pronounced dead at four o'clock that morning.

Within a few days, conspiracy theories abounded. Mohammed al-Fayed, Dodi's father, claimed that the crash had been perpetrated by the British secret service on the orders of the Duke of Edinburgh. Apparently, the motive was to prevent Princess Diana from marrying Dodi, bearing his child and becoming a Muslim. It sounded ridiculous but there were plenty of people who were prepared to believe it. Some even believed that the accident had been faked and that Diana and Dodi were still alive and living on a Middle Eastern island.

I didn't know what to think. Then I heard Diana's brother Charles, Earl Spencer, deliver his eulogy at her funeral and realised the power of some of the anti-Diana forces that had been at work in British society. Describing his sister as 'a standard bearer for the rights of the truly down-trodden, a very British girl who transcended nationality', he said,

She talked endlessly of getting away from England, mainly because of the treatment that she received at the hands of the newspapers. I don't think she ever understood why her genuinely good intentions were sneered at by the media, why there appeared to be a permanent quest on their behalf to bring her down. It is baffling. My own and only explanation is that genuine goodness is threatening to those at the opposite end of the moral spectrum. It is a point to remember that of all the ironies about Diana, perhaps the greatest was this – a girl given the name of the ancient goddess of hunting was, in the end, the most hunted person of the modern age.

In June the following year I got a call at my home in Los Angeles from Charles Spencer to say he was organising a concert at his home, Althorp House, to commemorate Diana's birthday and to raise funds to build a memorial to her. The event was scheduled for Saturday 27 June, four days before what would have been the Princess's thirty-seventh birthday. Duran Duran would be on the show, Chris de Burgh, Cliff Richard and many others she knew and loved. 'She was a fan of yours,' he said, 'and often talked about you. Would you like to perform?'

I said, 'I'm in.'

I called my band and said we had to figure a way of getting to England, rehearsing and getting back for $25,000. Who was in? Everybody was in. I put together two songs, 'God Bless a Brand New Angel' and 'Castles in the Sky'.

After checking into a Northamptonshire country inn, it was pouring with rain when we drove past the winding hedgerows to Althorp. We bumped over the cobblestones to where a purple-and-blue stage and seats for 15,000 people had been set up in the deer park. There we met Charles Spencer, boyish-looking and enthusiastic, and we rehearsed our two songs.

There were hundreds of sheep in the surrounding fields.

'Those sheep,' said Charles, 'have been in our family for four hundred years.'

Then he pointed out Princess Diana's grave on a little knoll in the middle of a small lake. 'She'll never be far away,' he said.

He was upset over criticism of his plans to charge people to visit the gravesite, but added that all of the proceeds would be going to the appeal fund in her name. He was particularly upset that several artists had declined to appear at the concert, including Elton John and Paul McCartney.

Charles then invited us to have lunch with his family at 'the house', this massive castle that loomed in the background. He would join us there after rehearsals, he said, so we walked from the stage to the house; it was bucketing down and the mud was thicker than molasses. Everybody had to take off their muddy shoes and leave them at the front door next to a neat row of little rain boots belonging to Charles's children and the children of other guests, including Chris de Burgh and Duran Duran. There was an immediate sense of family and a sense of home, rather than grandeur and royalty. In our stockinged feet, we tiptoed into the house, while lightning flashed outside.

We had entered a huge Palladian hall decorated with paintings of English hunting scenes and statues of famous statesmen. In the half-light, a woman like Lady Macbeth was descending a huge wooden staircase.

'We just came from rehearsal,' I said. 'His Lordship, Charles – you know, Diana's brother – invited us here for lunch.' We were very nervous. 'Could someone show us where to go?'

The lady smiled. 'Come on – I'll show you around.' She led us down a panelled gallery with huge portraits of the Spencer family lining the walls. 'Charles is quite proud of his house,' she said. She pointed to various Spencer ancestors and gave a short assessment of their character: this one drank too much, this one was a womaniser, this one gambled, and so on. Then she led us up the carpeted staircase, past more members of the Spencer lineage.

At the top of the stairs, Pamela said to our guide, 'You seem to know everything about the family.'

She laughed. 'That's hardly surprising – Charles is my son.'

So this was Frances Shand Kydd, Diana's mother.

After showing us the upstairs picture gallery and library, she took us downstairs for lunch. We walked into a huge saloon like an atrium, lined with books and more paintings of various Spencers. All of the children were there, having lunch. It was plain that Frances doted on her grandkids. There was a wooden stairwell in the saloon and when Charles arrived he sat in it with the children. Over lunch, he talked to me about South Africa and how his wife, Victoria, was still living there. He was humane and sincere, and I liked him very much. I congratulated him on his speech at Diana's funeral. 'They wouldn't leave my sister alone,' he said. 'They hounded her everywhere.'

Then Francis Shand Kydd suddenly started talking about Diana. That dreadful night, she had heard about the car crash in a phone call from Buckingham Palace. She had since made inquiries about what had really happened. It had been an accident, she said, despite the talk of conspiracies and murder. What had shocked her most was that photographers had been at the scene and had taken pictures of her daughter. 'Those bastards photographed her for fifteen minutes and didn't help her while she was dying,' she said. 'She was alive and asked them to help her and they did nothing to help.'

Late that afternoon it was still raining as 15,000 people in Barbours and wellington boots gathered in the deer park to watch the concert. At the last minute, the rain stopped and bright sunshine streamed down.

I went on stage and said, 'Earlier today I prayed to Diana, "Could you do this one last thing and part the skies?" And she did. It was the most amazing thing she did today. Thank you, Diana – this one's for you.'

Chris de Burgh, Jimmy Ruffin, Julian Lloyd Webber, Lesley Garrett, the Soweto String Quartet – everyone performed to great ovations. 'This is our first opportunity to pay tribute to a wonderful compassionate woman,' Sir Cliff Richard told the audience. 'She struck a chord in all our hearts.' At 12.20 a.m. the concert's 'surprise guests' Duran Duran, Diana's favourite band from the 1980s, came on stage and wrapped up the show, while giant clusters of stars exploded in the night skies and laser beams flashed across the façade of Althorp House.

As the red tail-lights of departing cars wove through the oak trees to the exit of Althorp Park, about sixty performers and their families headed back to the house for a late-night supper in one of the dining-rooms. The drinks were flowing and there was a great sense of camaraderie. We went around the table and talked about Diana. At the foot of the staircase was a piano, which Diana used to play when she visited Althorp. Our pianist Wade Hubbard sat down at the keyboard and started playing the Beatles' song 'Martha My Dear'. Chris de Burgh sang along with him and Jimmy Ruffin joined in. Then everybody came out of the dining-room and sat on the massive, polished walnut staircase and we had another concert in that magnificent hall, with everybody making a contribution.

Frances Shand Kydd sat at a little card-table with Pamela and talked about Diana again. She said she did not believe that Dodi was the love of Diana's life, nor was Diana pregnant with his child, as had been suggested, and nor were she and Dodi going to get married. She could not stand Mohammed al-Fayed and thought his talk of conspiracy was nonsense. As tragic as it was, she blamed the crash on the paparazzi. Nor did she like Raine Spencer, who had married her ex-husband. She explained that she had left Earl Spencer and that her children had not been raised by her after she had remarried. She was very open about it, without being maudlin or self-pitying. Diana's death, however, was such a senseless waste of life and could easily have been avoided.

It was 4 a.m. when we arrived back at our little country inn. We looked at each other and said, 'What just happened?'

It had been a very surreal experience.

Everything happens to Buddy . . . here he meets the Gay Roo in Sydney

18 G'day, Australia

'Hello, Knight Rider – you look like you need a drink.'

I was feeding a little wallaby at Koala Park, a magical place outside Sydney, when a huge bird that looked like an ostrich suddenly attacked me. I started to run and the bird gave chase. It could run faster than me and I was petrified of being pecked to death. I climbed up a gum tree and looked down. This fierce creature (actually an indigenous Australian bird called an emu) was watching me with beady eyes.

Buddy McCormack, meanwhile, was getting along famously with a very large marsupial, a male kangaroo. Buddy adored animals and couldn't understand why I was so frightened of a harmless bird. One of the rangers led the emu away and when I climbed down from the tree, everybody was laughing that the Knight Rider was such a wimp.

'Yeah,' the park ranger sympathised, 'they can be a bit aggressive.'

Buddy's problems, however, were just beginning. The kangaroo had taken a fancy to him and before he could duck out of the way, it got up on its hind legs, placed it paws on his shoulders and started making sexual advances to him. I dragged the roo's claws off Buddy, but the beast had got so excited that he sprayed sperm all over him. He became known as 'the Gay Roo' and Buddy turned seven shades of red. The Curse of Buddy strikes again.

You had to be prepared for the unexpected in Australia. When we landed at Mascot Airport a couple of days earlier it was boiling hot and

Allen Payne had taken out a powder puff to mop my brow prior to facing the press. This scene was snapped by a photographer lurking in the airport lounge and appeared in one of the local newspapers under the headline: 'PUFF RIDER ARRIVES!' It was 1983 and that was my introduction to the Australian media. The first newspaper I read had a story about a man who had been arrested for having sex with a porpoise. I thought, 'This is a strange country.'

I was in Sydney to co-host the Most Beautiful Girl in the World pageant with Jayne Kennedy, a former Miss Ohio, *Starksy and Hutch* actress and one of the first women to infiltrate the male world of sports commentating as co-presenter of the prestigious CBS show, *NFL Today*. The beauty contest was being broadcast live to the States so that people could phone in their votes for their favourite contestant. Miss America had a very good chance of winning because the only people who could phone in and vote were Americans.

When the cameras started rolling, however, there was a power failure in the studio. Dick Clark, the compère, came backstage and told Jayne and me there was no videotape playback, so we would have to ad-lib until the supply was restored. Someone handed me a koala bear and I was supposed to cuddle it for a few moments and say how cute it was. I should have known better. The little monster sunk its claws into my arm and refused to let go.

Peter Allen, the Boy from Oz, was one of the acts and, while he was performing, people tried to prise the bear free but its claws were embedded under my skin. It took forty minutes to restore the power supply and longer than that during commercial breaks to get rid of the bear. The whole thing was something of an ordeal and I was relieved when the show wrapped and it was party time.

The organisers had presented me with a complimentary Rolls-Royce which Allen Payne and I filled up with contestants and off we went. After a few cocktails, my companions suddenly changed from sweet little princesses into vixens whose one intention was to party and find men. We ended up in a bar called the Cauldron.

'Hello, Knight Rider,' a voice greeted me. 'You look like you need a drink.'

The guy was taller than me, better built and very good-looking. He was the first man who had ever taken attention away from me. It was disconcerting – the girls were swarming around him.

'I'm not used to this,' I said. 'Who are you?'

'I own this place.'

His name was John Bonnin. We became good friends and later travelled to many unlikely places in search of adventure.

Back at the Sebel Townhouse, our hotel in Kings Cross, the party continued at the pool, where the girls stripped off and swam naked. Later that night I decided to see how many countries I could visit. I visited Canada, then I visited South Africa. I told Miss South Africa that I'd be right back and headed off to see Miss Canada again. Unfortunately, I had some of Miss South Africa's lipstick on my cheek and Miss Canada punched me out.

Those little liaisons were fond memories in 1998 when Greg Bonann proposed filming a two-parter for *Baywatch*'s ninth series in Sydney as a prelude to shifting the entire cast and crew to Australia for our tenth season. I was totally in favour of the move; the question was which one of the dozens of golden beaches would suit our purposes best? Bondi was the most famous beach in Australia – it was right up there with Waikiki and Acapulco – but it was too close to the city centre and too crowded, so we chose Avalon Beach, a small community on the Pacific Ocean just north of Sydney. Avalon, apart from its evocative name, was perfect for our needs. The broad, sandy beach was enclosed between two rocky headlands, with high sand-dunes running along both arms. The beach itself was surrounded by Norfolk pine trees and natural undergrowth, which shielded it from a small village-like shopping centre. With permission, we repainted the Avalon Beach Surf Lifesaving Clubhouse in the Australian colours of green and orange and started filming.

In 'Baywatch Down Under', Mitch Buchannon and a team from California fly to Australia to compete in a gruelling test of stamina against Australian lifesavers. Mitch's team consists of Alex (Mitzi Kapture), Jessie (Brooke Burns), April (Kelly Packard) and Cody (David Chokachi) from Baywatch Beach, plus Jake Barnes (Rib Hillis, formerly a guest star on *Baywatch Nights*) from Zuma Beach.

I was staying at the Star City casino-hotel on Sydney Harbour and travelling up to *Baywatch*'s new location every day. It soon became apparent that we weren't popular with some of the local residents who didn't want their idyllic little beach turned into a Hollywood set. There were complaints that the town's peace and quiet was being disturbed by the rumbling of heavy-duty trucks heading to and from the set. Greg Bonann's argument that we would bring two hundred jobs and $20 million to the area in the immediate future fell on deaf ears; the people of Avalon just wanted to be left in peace. A couple of examples of high-handed behaviour were reported in the local press: a surfer had been frogmarched off the beach by one of our security guards; while skateboarders had been told to keep out of the carpark when the *Baywatch* stars were taking a siesta in their trailers during the hottest part of the afternoon. The Australian media picked up the story and asked, 'Should *Baywatch* be allowed to stay – or told to go?'

Despite the controversy, filming on both parts of 'Baywatch Down Under' was completed without any undue trouble. In fact, the biggest problem was that the Australian accents were too strong to be intelligible to an American audience, so all of the Australian actors had to redo their lines in American accents. The highlight of the shoot actually took part in Sydney Harbour when we rode four abreast on wave-runners under the famous coat-hanger bridge. The water was surprisingly choppy and I had difficulty keeping up with Kelly Packard, the best *Baywatch* performer on a wave-runner.

While Greg Bonann stayed in Sydney to negotiate with the citizens of Avalon about *Baywatch*'s future, I walked off the beach and on to a film set in Morocco. *Shaka Zulu: The Citadel* was an ambitious four-part mini-series with a budget of $20 million starring Omar Sharif, Karen Allen, Grace Jones and James Fox. Starting in 1827, *The Citadel* continues an earlier saga on the legendary African warrior King Shaka of the Zulus, who resisted the British conquest of his lands in the nineteenth century. The director was Joshua Sinclair, the American author of the book *Shaka Zulu*, and writer and co-director of the original, highly successful *Shaka Zulu* mini-series in 1987. King Shaka would again be played by the great South African actor Henry Cele, who had shown tremendous passion for the role in the first series.

Many of the scenes of *Shaka Zulu: The Citadel* were to be shot around Ouarzazate, a village in the High Atlas Mountains on the fringe of sweeping desert plains to the south of Marrakech. Consisting of a main street with hotels on either side, the village was close to Aït Ben Haddou, one of the locations of my all-time favourite film *Lawrence of Arabia*, as well as *The Last Days of Sodom and Gomorrah* and *The Jewel of the Nile*.

When I arrived in Ouarzazate with my stunt double Alex Daniels and my assistant Cary Kwasizur, Joshua Sinclair and his Italian film crew had been shooting for four weeks and were three weeks behind schedule. Joshua turned out to be a charming man with a fascinating history. A medical doctor specialising in tropical diseases, he had worked with Mother Teresa in Calcutta. He was also a professor of comparative theology, a best-selling novelist and a film and television writer, actor, producer and director. His 1979 production of *Just a Gigolo* had the distinction of being Marlene Dietrich's last movie. Joshua, however, was making heavy going of his latest project. He and his Italian crew were turning the film into a work of high art, with slow dissolves, evocative scenery and fiery montages of falcons soaring against the setting sun. It was beautifully filmed, but it was going to take forever to complete.

The crew would spend hours setting up each scene, while hundreds of extras were standing around doing nothing. They weren't getting the first shot of the day until two o'clock in the afternoon. Joshua didn't seem to understand that you can't hold a close-up for three minutes; that you can't shoot inserts when you've got three hundred extras on the set. He was surrounded by all this expensive production equipment while he was focussing on little details. The extras, incidentally, were Senegalese medical students who didn't look much like Zulus; only Henry Cele, magnificent in loincloth, headdress, ivory tusk necklace and leopard-skin cloak, looked like a real warrior.

Realising that Joshua was nowhere near ready to film my scenes, Alex Daniels, Cary Kwasizur and I wrapped ourselves in kashkouls and went camel-riding. When this proved to be an extremely uncomfortable mode of transport, we hired dune buggies, put on goggles and raced each other across the desert sands. We also met the local snake man and danced with his reptiles while he played the flute. He looked a bit concerned when I got too close to the head of a black cobra. After a few days, we'd seen the sights and went back to the set, where Joshua had fallen even further behind schedule. At lunchtime, he would go up the mountain and pray, but what he really needed was some professional assistance. We went up to him and said, 'Hey, Joshua, can we help?'

He responded with gratitude. He asked whether Alex could direct the second unit to film the battle scenes, while he took the first unit and me down to the coast to film my scenes. Alex was delighted and went from stunt double to assistant director. The citadel of the title refers to Shaka's fortress, which is overrun by his enemies in a fierce battle. Shaka is captured and sold in the slave market on the island of Zanzibar, where Omar Sharif is Sultan. Joshua was a great writer, but he had saddled Omar with impossible lines such as, 'It is unlucky to dispense ill-fated kismet without a remedy readily at hand.' No wonder Omar always had the hint of a smile on his face whenever the camera was on him. We had dinner and he told me, 'You know, acting is important to me, but the most important thing is that I'm a grandfather.'

My character, Mungo Prentice, is the bearded, pony-tailed captain of the slave ship *Defiance*, a man who has given up on the world until he meets Karen Allen's Miss Farewell while transporting her to Africa to find her father, Captain Francis Farewell (James Fox). Joshua Sinclair had based Prentice on John Newton, composer of the hymn 'Amazing Grace' and the self-proclaimed 'wretch' of the lyrics. Newton was captain of a slave ship who, on a homeward voyage on 10 May 1748, experienced a 'great deliverance' when his ship was saved from a violent storm as though by divine intervention. Newton became a clergyman, who wrote the Olney Hymns with William Cowper and campaigned against slavery.

We had shot many hours of film when the German investors dropped in to check on the progress on their investment. Joshua Sinclair began his presentation to them with the words, 'There are two tragedies in the world – slavery and the Holocaust.' This wasn't an auspicious start, but we showed the Germans some clips from the film and I said a few words. They agreed to continue funding our endeavours, but things soon went from bad to worse. There was a horrible accident and half a dozen extras were injured when a rowboat overturned in the surf; then a virus swept through the extras' camp and we had to shut down the set for two weeks.

There was very little to do in Ouarzazate. I bought drinks for everybody and ran up a bar bill of $3,000. Alex Daniels and I tried watching DVDs, but the player exploded and Alex was hit in the face by a flying battery. Then we heard that another movie was being filmed nearby and decided to check it out. The film turned out to be *Gladiator*, Ridley Scott's sword-and-sandals drama that won an Academy Award for its star, Russell Crowe.

Back in Sydney, Greg Bonann had decided to take on the citizens of Avalon. 'There were 10,000 miles of other beaches on the Australian coastline,' he says, 'but most of them were similar to the beaches on Santa Monica Bay. Avalon was perfect for our purposes and I was prepared to fight for it.' A public meeting was called to discuss whether *Baywatch* should be allowed to stay. Greg met with his three most outspoken opponents the night before the meeting was scheduled to take place.

It was an unnerving experience. Greg found himself face to face with one of the men who, sweating profusely, veins bulging and face beet red, told him, 'Listen to this carefully. The sand of Avalon Beach is my flesh. The water is my blood. I will do *anything* to keep you from coming here. Anything!' Whatever he may have meant by 'anything', Greg interpreted it as a threat to the safety of his cast and crew.

Next night, he found himself in a room with 1,700 residents, most of them hostile. 'Little seven-year-old kids were marching up and down saying, "No *Baywatch*,"' he said. 'The locals were furious that access to their beach had been blocked while we were filming there the previous year.' The residents were fearful of everything from an invasion of California culture to an environmental disaster.

'We've just about lost all our koalas already,' former world-champion surfer Mark Warren told the meeting. '*Baywatch* will only make matters worse.'

Alex McTaggert, one of Greg's opponents from the previous night, told him, 'Just get out and never come back.'

'We're not going to go where we're not wanted,' Greg replied. 'It's a matter of who wants us to spend a couple of hundred million dollars in six years, and who wants to export to the world the most important television programme.'

'Leave us alone,' angry citizens shouted. 'We don't want you here.'

Greg took off in a helicopter and flew south of Sydney to survey the industrial city of Wollongong, which said it would be delighted to host *Baywatch*. Somehow, *Baywatch Wollongong* didn't sound quite right.

The news that we had been kicked out of Avalon reached me in Morocco when pictures of Greg being shouted down at the public meeting were flashed on to the TV screen in my hotel bedroom: '*Baywatch* has been thrown out of Sydney,' the announcer screamed. 'Avalon doesn't want David Hasselhoff. Meanwhile, he continues to shoot scenes for *Baywatch*.' They then showed film of my stand-in, David Haas, who was still in Sydney. It was an understandable mistake, but it was also typical of the whole Australian fiasco.

Greg Bonann was in a theatre watching a movie when he got a message that the Australian Prime Minister, John Howard, was on the line. 'I had to go to Canberra to see John because he had just left his home in Sydney,' Greg says. 'He said his sons Tim and Richard were *Baywatch* fans and he wanted *Baywatch* to come to Australia. He said, "You've got to stay for the economy, the spirit and the soul of Australia." '

Publicly, Howard stated that the loss of *Baywatch* would be a blow to Australia's chances of attracting international investment. 'We can't simultaneously say an unemployment rate of 7.5 per cent is too high, yet behave in an unwelcoming way towards opportunities that will create jobs,' he said.

I'd seen Russell Crowe in *LA Confidential*, but had never met him. He came up to me in my hotel and introduced himself. He said his favourite show when he was growing up was *Knight Rider*.

'Good show, mate.'

'How's it going?' I asked him.

'It's going real well,' he said. 'I've just done a movie called *The Insider* and I think it's going to be big.'

While we were talking over a couple of drinks, a bus arrived with fifty body-builders on board. Russell explained that the body-builders would be gladiators in his new film. Ridley Scott had assembled a small army of 250 cast and crew in the hotels of Ouarzazate. The town where Russell's general-turned-gladiator Maximus is sold into slavery had been constructed at the village of Aït Ben Haddou by adding a small provincial arena to the existing buildings. That night, 13 March 1999, there was a big fight in New York between Lennox Lewis and Evander Holyfield. Russell held a party in his hotel suite to watch it on TV. He told me with a twinkle in his eye that someone had spiked the brownies. I saw twenty-five very happy body-builders having a great time watching two real gladiators slug it out in the ring and laughing hysterically.

Russell and I hung out for several days and shared many stories about Australia. He thought it would be great if *Baywatch* relocated there – he had a farm at Coffs Harbour on the New South Wales coast and suggested that might be a possibility. Sure enough, Coffs Harbour became one of the contenders. Greg Bonann's gaze, however, had shifted further north to Queensland, where he was being offered $2 million in inducements to move *Baywatch* to one of the Gold Coast's beaches, probably Currumbin. Accompanied by reporters and TV cameras, Greg checked out the Gold Coast and then flew back to Los Angeles, where he was contacted by April Masini, a Honolulu-based producer who put Hawaii forward as a contender for our new home.

Hawaii had the advantage of being only five hours' flying time from Los Angeles, compared with thirteen hours to Queensland. We would also be filming in summer, rather than wintertime on the Gold Coast, an important consideration given the amount of time we spent in the water. With its rugged headlands and tropical backdrop, Hawaii would also give us a very different look from the high mud cliffs of Santa Monica Bay.

Then 'Baywatch Down Under' was aired in the USA and failed to generate much interest among viewers. Ratings were poor, which made the Queensland option somewhat less attractive. On the other hand, labour costs were 30 per cent higher in Hawaii, while the US dollar would give us 40 per cent more purchasing power in Queensland. Greg and Syd Vinnedge, who had joined Pearson Television, flew to Hawaii to inspect the derelict Hawaii Film Studio at Diamond Head, which had been used in the production of *Hawaii Five-0* and *Magnum, PI*. They decided that we could easily rebuild the sound stage, bungalows and offices using much of the existing equipment in our facilities at Beethoven Street.

The point about higher labour costs was solved when the Governor of Hawaii, Ben Cayetano, pleaded with the Teamsters Union to accept our terms and conditions and they relented minutes before Pearson's deadline expired. Production on *Baywatch Hawaii*, as the series would be renamed, would begin in June 1999, with principal outdoor filming at the Haleiwa Alii Beach Park on the North Shore of Oahu. The deal was for at least two years to film a guaranteed forty-four episodes of *Baywatch Hawaii* costing around $38.2 million, or $870,000 an episode.

The Queenslanders were furious. They accused Greg of double-dealing, and claimed that the *Baywatch* producers had used them to force Hawaii into granting tax breaks and other economic concessions.

'Their coming to Queensland was nothing but a deceitful charade designed to panic Hawaii into signing a deal immediately,' the Tourism Minister, Bob Gibbs, said.

On television, I caught the *Jay Leno Show*. 'Last night we told you that David Hasselhoff had been thrown out of Australia,' he said. 'Well, now he's been thrown out of Mexico for smuggling grapes in his Speedos.'

I picked up the phone and called him. 'I heard that thing about grapes.'

He said, 'I was just making a joke.'

I said, 'Jay, it wasn't grapes, it was a banana and two apples.'

Then Oliver Reed, who was playing the gladiators' instructor Proximo, turned up in Ouarzazate. Following his activities in Johannesburg ten years earlier, I left orders with the security guards not to let him anywhere near me. I knew what would happen if we ever met up – there would be heavy drinking and, as Oliver regarded himself as the toughest guy on the block, probably some fighting. Soon after he arrived, I left town for El Judida and stayed there for seven days. It was probably a wise move. A few weeks later, when *Gladiator* had moved to Malta, Oliver was drinking in a bar in Valletta when he suddenly collapsed and died of a heart attack.

By then, I was back in Australia. Since my first trip to Sydney in 1983, John Bonnin and I would meet up somewhere around the world every couple of years. We had gone white-water rafting on the Zambezi River, marlin fishing in Mauritius, and on safari in Botswana and Zimbabwe. On this trip, John called and said, 'I'm taking you for a little ride.' With David Chokachi and my assistant Cary Kwasizur, we set off in John's private plane for the Queensland coast. At Hamilton Island, we took a helicopter 100 miles out to sea to a barge moored on the Outer Barrier Reef. It was used for the transfer of nautical pilots who guided shipping down the Queensland coast. This was about as remote a diving spot as anywhere on the planet and we were looking forward to seeing the exotic sights underwater. What we hadn't bargained on was that we would encounter the biggest tide of the year. When David Chokachi and Cary Kwasizur dived off the pontoon, they were immediately swept away by a ferocious undercurrent. It was so strong that they couldn't get back. We had a rubber dinghy with us, but it wouldn't inflate, so John and I ended up in the water, hanging on to the barge's anchor chain to avoid being swept away while trying to rescue the other two.

At the end of three hours, there were several bruised egos but David and Cary had both reached safety.

The next leg of the trip was a flight from Cairns to Darwin and thence into the Outback. As soon as I stepped out of the plane, I was attacked by thousands of flies. I wrapped a kashkoul around my head and when that didn't stop them I added a towel and a pair of sunglasses, but they still got into my ears and up my nose. At Swim Creek, north of the Kakado National Park, we drove swamp boats to look at the buffalo and bird life, and chased wild pigs over the slippery mudflats on quad bikes.

The flies were still bothering me and I was relieved when we adjourned to an air-conditioned kitchen for dinner. I was enjoying Outback hospitality when I looked over to the cabin where we were spending the night. John had left the light on and the entire room was smothered in thousands of moths and a variety of other winged insects, some of them very weird. We spent most of the night trying to clear them out with pesticide. In the morning, there was a magnificent sunrise and when I looked out of the window I saw dozens of kangaroos asleep on the ground. It was one of the most beautiful things I had ever seen.

Wherever we went, the flies seemed to have advance knowledge that I was coming and great buzzing black clouds would head straight for me. In Arnhemland, John suggested we look at the ancient rock paintings on Mount Borodale, but I'd had had enough of flies by then and decided to stay on board our little boat and do some fishing. What happened next is best described by John Bonnin:

We were up an escarpment looking at aboriginal art when I heard an almighty scream from the boat. I looked down and saw that a large fish that David was in the process of catching was also being hunted by a crocodile. The croc had surfaced and was devouring the fish as David was trying to land it. In his wisdom, David decided to get a closer look at the croc and moved to the front of the boat, which was actually a punt just one foot out of the water. I yelled at him, 'Get into the middle of the boat and stay there', but he couldn't hear me. The crocodile was about fifteen feet long and could easily have leaped out of the water and grabbed him. David was screaming with delight and I had a vision of the hero of *Baywatch* being eaten alive in the Outback. He was very, very lucky.

In June 1999, I walked on to Haleiwa Beach on the North Shore of the island of Oahu to start filming *Baywatch Hawaii*. The wheel had gone full circle – I was back in Hawaii where the *Baywatch* adventure had begun ten years earlier. The *Baywatch Hawaii* studios were only a few minutes drive from the Hilton Hawaiian Village at Waikiki where many of us stayed and less than an hour from the *Baywatch Hawaii* lifeguard headquarters. We shot a new opening sequence along the Na Pali coast of Kauai and updated the theme music with the addition of lot of percussion, Hawaiian chants, drums and conch shells.

Greg Bonann had the last laugh.

Looking for a place to rent, he was shown a fabulous house built around a swimming pool. It had a Steinway grand piano in the living-room and a fully equipped gym. It was perfect for his needs.

Greg asked the agent, 'What is this place?'

'It's the Australian Consulate,' she said.

'I'll take it!'

The tenth season of the rebranded show opened with the two-hundredth episode, 'Aloha Baywatch', which finds Captain Mitch Buchannon visiting Hawaii, where he conceives the idea of leaving Los Angeles and building an international training camp on Oahu Island, a 'top gun' academy to share ideas and techniques with lifeguards from various parts of the world. These included new cast members Jason Brooks, Brandy Ledford, Stacy Kamano and Jason Momoa, who joined existing stars Michael Bergin, Brooke Burns, Michael Newman and Simone Mackinnon. Out of a total of sixty-two actors who had become *Baywatch* regulars over the years, I was the only one who had been with the show from the very beginning.

Baywatch Hawaii represented a rebirth. Michael Berk and Doug Schwartz had dropped out of the show to pursue other projects, which left only Greg Bonann and me of the original partners. The highlight of *Baywatch Hawaii* was the friction between us. 'I love you like a brother,' I told him, 'but we have different tastes.' There were too many shots of beautiful beaches and gorgeous girls for my liking. The opening credits now contained blatant exhibitionism, featuring an athletic water ballet and three girls in yellow swimsuits spelling out the word *Baywatch*.

I appeared in fourteen out of the twenty-two episodes in series eleven, although seven of those were cameo appearances, so I hadn't been riding shotgun over the show's content as closely as I had in the past. One episode, 'Baywatch O'hana' opens with a long sequence of Jenna Avid (Krista Allen) working out in the gym to a suggestive song. The cleavage shots and the storyline in which Sean (Jason Brooks) sets up a dirty weekend with her destroyed any pretence that *Baywatch* was still a kids' show. The cast comprised several impressive young actors, all talented, but the question was whether Greg and the writers could mould them into a group of people that audiences would care about, as they had with previous casts.

In September, just as the first episode of the tenth season was airing, I was undecided about my future on the show. 'This may be my last season on *Baywatch*,' I told one reporter. 'Honestly, I don't know yet.' Greg Bonann had told me that *Baywatch Hawaii* would continue with or without me, but I had always considered that it was my decision as to whether I quit or not and there was no sign in any of the scripts that Mitch was retiring.

For ten years, I had said that I would never walk away from a winner. If there was a way for me to come back to keep the show going, I would find it. I had directed my first episode, 'Come Fly with Me', in the ninth season and would consider directing a few episodes each year, while pursuing my other interests. If I decided to leave, Mitch's heir apparent, Sean Monroe (Jason Brooks), was already in place. I told Greg that I would notify him in December whether I would return for season eleven. Greg, however, had already made up his mind.

The power struggle between us came to a head in 'Killing Machine', the last episode of the series, when Mitch has to defuse a bomb planted underwater by two eco-terrorists (Pamela Bach in a new role and Alex Daniels). The original script, filmed in December 1999, called for Mitch to rescue the bad guys and survive an underwater blast. The film, however, was then edited to make it appear that Mitch had died. Unbeknown to me, Greg had shot additional scenes in which the bomb blows up and only remnants of Mitch's wetsuit float to the surface. 'Killing Machine' was not due to be aired until May 2000, but I learned of Mitch's demise from Alex Daniels months before then. When I challenged Greg about it, he replied, 'I thought you knew.'

Over the years, Greg and I had fought like brothers, but only out of passion for the show. It was never personal. To this day, I greatly respect his ability and regard him as a tremendous friend.

The New York *Daily News* celebrated Mitch's exit with an unexpected tribute. 'Hasselhoff,' it said,

> is one of the most influential figures in small screen history. Say what? It's true. Think about it. He helped propel the television careers of such hotties as Pamela Anderson Lee, Carmen Electra, Erika Eleniak and Yasmine Bleeth. Angie Harmon, now a big star on NBC's *Law & Order*, got her break with Hasselhoff on *Baywatch Nights*, a credit conveniently left out of her NBC bio. For these achievements alone, Hasselhoff should have his own wing in the Museum of Television & Radio.

My advice on Australia: always expect the unexpected

The Maasi had never heard of me . . . so I decided to become one of them

19 Travels with the Hoff (IV)

*'Africa is no place for someone
suffering from fame withdrawal.'*

'**S**o you don't know me, huh? A talking car – on TV?'
The Maasai warrior solemnly shook his head. 'No,' he said. 'We don't get TV.'

I was on safari in Kenya with Pamela. We had a portable bar and restaurant, sleeping quarters and a microlight aircraft for aerial sightseeing. Everything was fine, except that after a week I was suffering from fame withdrawal. So I visited the Masai Mara, hoping the Maasai might have heard of me.

'Are you sure you don't recognise me? *Baywatch*? Running in slow motion down the beach with a rescue can?'

They shook their heads and opened more bottles of beer.

Pamela said she came out there and I was drinking with a bunch of Maasai guys, holding their hands and talking about a talking car. I ended up singing and dancing with them, all of us jumping in the air to try to be the tallest.

I'd given up hope of being recognised when another warrior walked up to me and said, 'Michael Knight!'

'Well,' I said to the others, 'he knows who I am.'

'That's because he works for the chief and the chief has got a TV set.'

I offered them a rescue can in case anyone got into difficulties in the river.

'We don't swim,' they said.

'The Maasai don't like swimming?'

'No,' they said, 'the river is full of crocodiles.'

I flew to Vancouver to film *One True Love*, a tear-jerker for CBS. After eleven years, my *Baywatch* days were over and I was filling in time waiting for the next big thing to show up on the radar. I play Mike Grant, a fireman who rescues a young woman, Dana Boyer (Terry Farrell), from a car crash. Both are engaged to other people but realise that they need to find each other again. The film was based on a harrowing true story and it proved to be one of CBS's most popular movie-of-the-weeks of all time.

In the hotel elevator, I spoke to a mother and her teenaged daughter.

'Nice to see you guys.'

The daughter started freaking out.

'You're her favourite star,' the mother said.

'Why, thank you. I've got to go to work right now, but if you write down your name and address I'll leave you an autographed picture.'

When I got back to Los Angeles, there was a letter from the mother saying,

Thank you very much for the photographs. My daughter had attempted suicide that morning. She said she had nothing to live for. The only person in the world she believed in was you, David, and because you happened to be in that elevator and because you took a moment to say hello, you restored her self-esteem. She said, 'I will never try to kill myself again because I believe that he was sent to me for a reason.'

God does send angels and sometimes we are his angels.

With Greg Bonann on *This Is Your Life* 1993 . . . he killed off
Mitch Buchannon, but we're still buddies today

As the evil Edward Hyde . . . surprisingly, some women liked his character

20 Broadway

'There comes a time in your life when you've got
to stop saving the world and save yourself.'

A few days before I replaced Sebastian Bach as the lead in *Jekyll and Hyde: The Musical*, the longest-running Broadway show ever staged at the Plymouth Theatre, a reporter named Karl Taro Greenfeld interviewed me over lunch at Sardi's Restaurant. He wrote:

> Wearing a Hawaiian shirt, brand-new Levi's, and white sneakers, he looks like a turbocharged, machine-tooled version of the American suburban dad. Nothing is out of place. His features, his Hasselhoffness, are just so there that you can't help but sneak glimpses at him when you think he's not looking, just to see if it all holds together even when he relaxes. It does.
>
> The slabs of tanned, muscled forehead and cheek; the blinding teeth; the cleft, sinewy chin. His looks are so powerful that they seem like another person in the conversation. Like we're all sitting there together: me, Hasselhoff and his looks . . . The Hasselhoff, for all his stereotypical hunkiness, has built the Hasselhoff brand with a single-mindedness that would make the folks at Procter & Gamble proud.

If only he had known . . . Just before I set out for the theatre on my opening night, I was hit by the worst case of nerves in memory. Mom had always believed in me, so I called her.

'I don't know if I can do this – it's too much.'

'David, get out of your apartment, go on the stage and do it. You definitely can do it and you can do it really well. You're made for the stage.'

She was right. I had been raised in the theatre – in a world of wonderful, off-the-peg characters any one of which I could try on for size. 'Dress up and pretend ...'

I could do it again tonight. This show was tailor-made for my talents. *Jekyll and Hyde* had been developed for the theatre by Steve Cuden and Frank Wildhorn from the 1886 novella *The Strange Case of Dr Jekyll and Mr Hyde* by Robert Louis Stevenson. The book and the lyrics had been written by Leslie Bricusse, while Wildhorn had composed the music. Bricusse, a double Oscar winner whose credits included *Stop the World – I Want to Get Off*, *The Roar of the Greasepaint – the Smell of the Crowd* and *Dr Dolittle*, was one of the greatest lyricists of all time, yet he and Frank Wildhorn had been crucified by the critics because *Jekyll and Hyde* was more an operetta than a musical in the style of Andrew Lloyd Webber. People who adored *Phantom of the Opera*, *Cats* and *Les Miserables* put the show down because the score was linear – it was written in a way that people could understand.

It tells the story of Henry Jekyll, a doctor who experiments with drugs on himself in an effort to find a cure for his father's mental illness. During one of his tests, he changes into Edward Hyde, a violent criminal. In time, the dark side takes control and Jekyll is powerless to prevent Hyde from embarking on an orgy of murder.

I had to sing fourteen songs, including a duet between Jekyll and Hyde in which I switched from one character to another in alternate lines. My voice coach was Trish McCaffrey, who had coached many Metropolitan Opera artists. Trish told me I was a born singer who, had I been classically trained, would have made a great opera singer. She taught me a lot of the techniques that I had forgotten over the years of singing pop and rock.

Suddenly, the orchestra was playing the overture and the sound of voices was heard in the London fog. Dressed in top hat and cape, I was on stage. The voice of Dr Jekyll rises over the hubbub. He speaks of the duality of man and the struggle within him between his inherently good side and his evil nature. The play had started and I was speaking my lines.

Then I heard myself singing my first song, 'Lost in the Darkness.' I can't say I started to enjoy myself; I was in a daze for most of the performance. At one point, I was supposed to tear my shirt and forgot. At another point, I was supposed to ruffle my hair and forgot. When the final curtain came down, the relief was enormous. Anyone who has done the role would confirm that it's insane. It involves a lot of running through corridors and under the stage, and a lot of wig changes as I switched from Jekyll to Hyde and then back again.

For two weeks I'd walk off and say to the stage manager: 'Okay, who am I?'

'You're Hyde.'

'Okay, what scene is this?'

'You're in the Red Rat with Lucy.'

'Got it.'

'Okay . . . go, go, go!'

After a few performances, I got together with Frank Wildhorn, and found him supportive and gracious. He gave me his feedback and made several helpful suggestions. I found that the part of Hyde was easy, compared with trying to find my way into Jekyll. It was interesting to note that after each show the girls wanted to meet Hyde. There was a definite sexual attraction to him – they loved his wild long hair and his evil nature.

I was getting lonely, so Pam and my daughters unselfishly moved to New York to be with me, for which I will always be grateful. After dropping the girls off at their school each morning, I would go jogging in Central Park. We bought a new wiener puppy, Sir Henry von Hasselhoff. I took him back to the pet store to get his shots. Paul McCartney and his then girlfriend Heather Mills were having coffee in a sidewalk cafe. Paul called me over.

'Just so you know,' he said, 'she was looking at the dog.'

'Just so you know,' I said, 'I was looking at her.'

On my way to the theatre I bumped into John Ritter in the parking lot of the Marriott Hotel. John was appearing in Neil Simon's *The Dinner Party*.

'Can you believe it?' he said. 'This is Broadway.'

'Isn't it great?'

We were like a couple of little kids in a candy store.

I played *Jekyll and Hyde* for seventy-two performances, ending in January 2001. It was an emotional, wonderful, thrilling and terrifying ride, but worth of every drop of blood, sweat and tears. It was the hardest gig I had ever done and also the most rewarding. One night I overdid holding a high note and passed out on stage. Fortunately, it was the end of the scene and I awoke to find the scenery being changed around me. Next day, the notes for that performance said, 'David, could you get off stage quicker? We almost ran you over.'

Out of breath, I said, 'You'd better get some smelling salts for the next show.'

One of my performances, directed by Don Roy King, was taped for Pay-per-view on Home Box Office and was later released on DVD. I put my heart and soul into the Tuesday performance the week of taping. They told me after the curtain, 'That was only a rehearsal.' They taped every performance that week in case they had to strip bits in, but went with the entire Saturday night show.

Frank Wildhorn said, 'Honestly, I thought you all did a terrific job and David was wonderful. The whole thing was cool.' Overall, I was very pleased with the result. I had an amazing supporting cast in Coleen Sexton (Lucy), Andrea Rivette (Emma), George Merritt (John Utterson) and Barrie Ingham (Sir Danvers Carew). When you're on stage surrounded by a great team of actors, no other experience in show business is quite as fulfilling.

I'm so glad the show was taped – to this day, people stop me and say, 'I saw the DVD – you really can sing.'

While I had been occupied on Broadway, vultures had wheeled in from the sky over Oahu. A couple of weeks after the end of my run, Pearson Television, now part of the Luxembourg-based RTL group following a merger, had cancelled *Baywatch*. After a thirteen-year run during which it had made millions and entered the language, the show had earned a miserable 1.9 national household Nielsen rating for the week ending 28 January. It was all over. '*Baywatch* has been an incredible success story,' Brian Harris, North American chief executive of Pearson Television, told the press. 'The economics associated with bringing the programme back for another season could not be justified. This is a logical and natural end of the show.'

I was not surprised to hear the news. *Baywatch* had turned into a completely different show in its final season on Hawaii and I was relieved that I no longer had any responsibility for it. It had become an hour-long montage. In the words of *Baywatch* veteran Syd Vinnedge, 'It's no longer a water-cooler show.'

My career had taken a new direction with my Broadway run and I was looking forward to doing more live theatre. In the meantime, I had forgotten to take care of myself. When I was doing *Baywatch* and *Knight Rider*, my life had been planned, orderly. The hard times were between shows when I was often at a loose end. Things reached a head in the summer of 2002. I was living in a three-storey house in the San Fernando Valley with my wife, two beautiful daughters and six wiener dogs. There were platinum discs on the wall and a stack of TV awards on the mantel. I was discussing a couple of new musical projects, planning a Knight Rider movie and recording a new CD. Everything looked perfect.

I started drinking again – vodka. The end of the line was the Betty Ford Center, where I set the highest blood alcohol figure ever recorded there. Medically, I should have been dead. I chose Betty Ford because it had a strong family programme and I wanted my children to understand what was happening. I checked in, knowing that my reputation was going to be tarnished; knowing that everybody would know that I had a problem with alcohol and that the newspapers would cut me to bits. I remembered the old Hollywood joke, 'When your career is over, you check into Betty Ford to get press.'

That first night I went over the wall, with my male nurse pleading, 'Please don't go, please don't go.'

'I'll be right back – I just gotta take a little walk.'

I had been in rehab once before when my buddy Ron Armstrong had staged an intervention on behalf of my friends and family. I had seen all these cars pull up in the front driveway and thought, 'What's this? – it must be a party.' I went downstairs. Six people were there with Ron Armstrong. They sat around the room and told me how much they loved me and how my drinking had affected their lives. Every one of them cried and that made me cry.

Ron said, 'I've got a place for you. Your bags are packed. You're ready to go.'

'Where are we going?'

An hour later I was in a rehab in Pacific Palisades. I stayed for eight days before ordering a taxi and going over the wall.

The Betty Ford Center is on Bob Hope Drive, Rancho Mirage, in the desert near Palm Springs. It was dark when I took off down the street in sweatpants, tank top and tennis shoes but no wallet – I'd thrown that out of the window of my car the previous night. Even at night the temperature was over 100°F and the dry, suffocating heat was making me physically sick. A thought came into my head: 'Check into a Marriott hotel. Have a few drinks from the minibar and you'll feel better.'

After I had walked for about forty minutes, the welcoming neon lights of a Marriott came into view. Thanking God in his mercy, I opened the door and strolled casually across the lobby towards the desk. That's peculiar, I thought, all the guests seemed to be in walkers.

'You sure do have a lot of elderly customers here.'

'Yes, sir,' said the desk clerk. 'This is the Marriott Retirement Home.'

'Oh!'

I chuckled as I backed out of the lobby and hit the highway again. I walked and walked until I came upon a huge Marriott. There was no mistake this time – the Desert Springs Marriott Resort and Spa was the real thing. I fronted the desk.

'Here's the deal,' I said. 'I lost my wallet and my car, but I need a room for the night.'

'Mr Hasselhoff, of course you do,' said the clerk. 'I'm sorry you lost your wallet and your car but don't worry about a thing.'

I took a standard room for $135 a night. Once inside, I sat down at the desk, switched on the TV and proceeded to have a few drinks from the minibar. Pretty soon I was feeling well enough to watch a football game and eat a little dinner. I told myself I'd go back to Betty Ford in the morning, but first I needed another shot of tequila.

Next morning, I woke up and called Betty Ford and got hold of the lady who had checked me in.

'We'll come and get you,' she said. 'What room are you in?'

I went out and had a look.

'Room 7223.'

I put the phone down and that was the last thing I remember.

I woke up strapped to a gurney in the ER department of the Eisenhower Medical Centre at Rancho Mirage. The room was cold.

There was no light and the darkness deepened the chill. The only sound was the hum of an air-conditioner.

What had happened?

Had I been in an accident? A car crash? I couldn't remember. There was a black hole where the memories of that day should have been. Why was I tied down with leather straps on a gurney in this cold, dark room?

Some hours later I was transferred to the Betty Ford Center suffering from alcohol poisoning. After my phone call, the clinic's paramedics had combed every Marriott hotel in the Palm Springs area trying to locate me. The high room number saved my life – the Desert Springs Marriott was the only one with a Room 7223. When they'd got security to unlock the door, they had found me passed out on the bed.

I was now on the 'Most Watched' list at Betty Ford. Staff in white linen coats and rubber-soled shoes kept an eye on me in case I attempted another breakout.

'Promise me . . .'

The voices of Pamela, Taylor-Ann and Hayley came back into my head.

'Sure, I promise . . .'

Right now, however, it was imperative that I got back in control of my life and saved my marriage, and to do that I needed a telephone. My cellphone had been confiscated and I was banned from using the payphone for seventy-two hours in case I made arrangements for another escape bid.

Why did I need a phone? I had to get a new driver's licence so I could drive my car. With the help of a couple of patients, I got the number of the License Bureau and my new friends kept watch while I snuck into the phone booth with a handful of change.

A female voice answered, mid-forties, motherly.

'Hi, this is David Hasselhoff. I'm over here in Palm Springs on vacation.'

' Hi – oh my God! I know who you are.'

'Look, I lost my driver's licence and need to get another one real quick.'

'No problem, Mr Hasselhoff, we'll take care of it right away. Just so you know – I want to tell you my son looks just like you.'

'You're kidding me!'

'No, people used to stop him all the time and say, "Are you David Hasselhoff?"'

'Oh my God, I'm so flattered. What's his name? Can I send him an autographed picture because you've been so nice?'

'Aw, no – he died, Mr Hasselhoff. He was killed by a drunk driver.'

I dropped the receiver and began sobbing. After a few moments, I picked it up and said, 'Thank you very much.' I walked out of the booth and said to my two new buddies: 'They say there's a reason for everything, right? I just got mine.'

Next day, an eighteen-year-old girl came up to me.

'I broke your record.'

Betty Ford Center was like a college campus transplanted to the desert. After checking in at reception, you were admitted to one of the big halls of residence with thirty or forty other people. There were classrooms for lectures on the nature of addiction and relapse prevention. We were taught about dopamine, the feel-good neuro-transmitter in the brain, and serotonin, the one linked to anxiety and depression. My classmates included a judge, doctors, brain surgeons, ER nurses, stewardesses and airline pilots. I bumped into the president of a major television company. It was like a scene from *The Player*.

I told everyone to call me 'Michael Day' and settled into a healthy routine of regular meals, exercise and classes. I went jogging around the lake or bike riding, although I made sure I was back indoors by noon when the temperature hit 114°F.

After the first week, I started feeling better. 'We're going to move you to a house with four other people,' one of the counsellors said. 'You can go into town with a buddy.'

Doug, a wrestling coach, became my soul brother. We rode our bikes into town and went into a Walgreen's pharmacy. Doug said, 'No scissors, no vanilla essence, no aftershave – they're all banned.' In the pharmacy, the female assistants recognised me and asked for autographs on prescription pads.

'This would make a great picture for the *National Enquirer*,' I joked.

'Yeah – signing prescription pads at a pharmacy in Rancho Mirage would look really good,' Doug said.

At the front of the store, a young girl asked me for an autograph. I was signing it when I looked down and saw a headline on a stack of magazines: 'KNIGHT RIDER ESCAPES FROM REHAB'. I shuddered. I gave the girl her autograph and wondered what to do.

'Yeah, buy it,' Doug said, reading my mind, 'and put it on your wall so this shit doesn't happen again.'

At the checkout, a lady put her hand on mine. 'Don't believe everything you read,' she said. 'I got twelve years' sobriety.'

An older guy opened the door for me. 'You can do it,' he said. 'I got eight years.'

Angels were being sent to me.

My fiftieth birthday had fallen on 17 July. I received thousands of letters from fans all over the world, some of which said, 'You saved our lives – now let us help you. Keep positive.' As I was reading some of these letters, my counsellor said, 'Hey, walk outside – there's a present for you.'

I walked outside and looked up. A plane flew past trailing the message, 'HAPPY BIRTHDAY – LOVE YOUR GIRLS.'

After seven weeks, I left Betty Ford determined to stay away from the booze. I said a prayer, 'God, if I can't have what I want, please let me want what I have.' I was taking life too seriously and had forgotten what was important to me. In September 2002, Pamela and I flew to the Turtle Bay Resort on Oahu's North Shore for a vacation, while I returned to the role of Mitch Buchannon in a *Baywatch* reunion movie, *Hawaiian Wedding*.

Mitch? Wasn't he supposed to be dead? Apparently not. Unbeknown to any of the lifeguards, he survives the underwater explosion and swims to an island, where he has been suffering from amnesia for the past three years. It happens. *Hawaiian Wedding* was one of the most ridiculous scripts ever conceived in a long line of ridiculous scripts. However, it brought together fifteen *Baywatch* stars, many of whom had faced up to some personal trauma. Around the table, we called it 'the Curse of Baywatch'.

Pamela Anderson had been diagnosed with hepatitis C; Carmen Electra had been divorced from NBA star Dennis Rodman; Yasmine Bleeth was on honeymoon with husband Paul V. Cerrito Jr, whom she had met in rehab; Jeremy Jackson had been having problems with one of the LA gangs; while I was fresh out of Betty Ford after almost checking out permanently . . .

When anyone asked me, 'What's this show about?' I'd say, 'It's about an hour and a half long and you get paid.' No one took the film seriously. We spent most of those two weeks healing one another. The movie had given us a chance to share our personal lives rather than play our characters. It was a positive experience for all of us and we fell deeply in love with each other. We left Hawaii closer than ever before.

Just as *Hawaiian Wedding* was being shown in February 2003 there was more trouble in store. The first time I saw that big brute of a motorcycle I knew it was evil. Pamela had given me a black Harley-Davidson Road King Classic as a Christmas present. I delayed going out on it for several weeks but the day came when I had an appointment at the American Film Institute about a film I had just made. I asked Pamela to come with me on the bike. Everything went well and on the way home I said: 'Let's forget the freeway and drive along the small roads.' We hadn't been drinking and were wearing helmets and protective leather clothing.

With Pamela's arms wrapped around my waist, I was driving at 25 m.p.h. on Sepulveda Boulevard towards an underpass on the 405 Freeway. I heard Pamela say, 'Oh, it's got cold . . .' Then a powerful gust of wind hit the bike and the front wheel clipped the sidewalk curb. Pamela was thrown on to the hard shoulder of the road, breaking her wrist and crushing her ankle. I was thrown against a street sign and broke my elbow, two transverse vertebrae in my back and some bones in my hand.

One of the first things that went through my brain was that Princess Diana had suffered internal injuries. I was telling myself not to pass out when I looked over at Pamela. She was lying beside the road looking incredibly beautiful.

I called out, 'Hey, honey, are you okay?'

Both her eyes were open, but she groaned and didn't speak, and then there was panic. People came rushing over and said, 'Don't move.'

I said, 'I'm okay.'

Another driver stopped her car and called 911 on her cellphone. She stayed with us until an ambulance arrived. The paramedics started treating Pamela. There was a bone sticking out of her wrist, several ribs had been cracked, and every bone beneath her left knee had been broken.

I called my office and spoke to my assistant Heather Bogdanovich:

'We've just had an accident. Take care of the kids – I'm passing out.' I tossed my phone to a guy who was standing near me.

We were both admitted to UCLA Medical Centre. My blood pressure was very low and they were worried about me. The doctor who treated me had been at LAX picking up his parents when landings had been suspended owing to a wind sheer, a very severe wind gust. The wind had hit LAX at 4.30 p.m. and it had hit the bike at 4.31 p.m. The cop who tested me for alcohol and drugs – I was clean – said, 'I'm a motorcycle cop and I almost didn't make it over here. The wind almost blew me off the road. It's brutal out there.'

Next morning I remembered my telephone and had my office dial my number. A guy said, 'David has been taken to UCLA', and that was it. I never saw my phone again.

While I couldn't blame myself for the accident, it was painful for me to see the agony that Pamela was in. She received the best medical attention that money could buy but she still had to endure several operations and months of treatment. I was there for her physically and emotionally at every appointment, every operation. When we got her home, she was frustrated with the slowness of her recovery. I was frustrated with not working, and the situation had a damaging effect on our marriage. Instead of bringing us closer together, it drove us apart.

I breathed a sigh of relief when I got the third lead in the pilot episode of *News to Me* with Tom Hanks' son Collin Hanks, a sitcom about Joel Stein's journey as a young reporter on *Time* magazine. With one of the networks and *Time* behind us, we thought we couldn't miss. All the cast assembled for our first read-through and to meet Susan Lynne, president of ABC Entertainment.

After the reading, we laughed and said, 'What a cast! What a hit! What a great lady!' Next morning, with my wiener dogs in tow, I walked down the drive of my home in my underpants to get the newspapers. I picked up *Variety* magazine and read that Susan Lynne had been surprisingly fired after the read-through of *News to Me*. I looked down at my wiener dogs and said, 'This isn't a good sign.'

Nevertheless, the director and the cast worked hard on *News to Me*, although we knew that the first things to go under a new regime were the shows developed by the previous boss. And *News to Me* was Susan Lynne's show. It was no surprise when the new president, Stephen McPherson, decided not to pick it up.

I started drinking again and it caught up with me. One of my cardinal rules was never to drink and drive. Then late one Saturday evening in June 2004, I wanted a hamburger. It was past midnight, it was raining and I thought, 'I can make it to McDonald's.' I was arrested on suspicion of driving under the influence. The LAPD gave me a field sobriety test in the McDonald's parking lot on Ventura Boulevard. I was kept in the cells overnight and released in the morning after posting bail. At first, I was angry with the guy who arrested me but now I realise he was an angel. I was lucky that night – I could have hurt myself or, more importantly, I could have hurt someone else.

By the time I arrived back home from the police station, the story had gone all over the world. I got a call from Germany, 'Is the tour still on?' and one from Australia, 'G'day, mate – I've just been reading about you.' I was embarrassed, devastated and ashamed.

How bad did things have to get? When you look into the eyes of your children and they say they got abused in school because of bad publicity about their father, it breaks your heart. Yet the problem was as perplexing to me as it was to them.

With director John Waters and Johnny Knoxville
on the set of *A Dirty Shame*

On the beach with SpongeBob and Patrick in
The SpongeBob SquarePants Movie

21 Waving Not Drowning

'I was a counterculture icon – four-year-olds
wanted my autograph.'

The closest I had ever come to drowning was on a diving holiday with Alex Daniels at Cocos Island, 300 miles off the coast of Costa Rica. Marine life fascinated me and I was always looking for new places to explore the wonders of the deep. On the gentle sloping reef-tops off the island, we found beautiful butterfly and angel fish, while deeper down there were hammerhead sharks and giant manta rays.

For the first time, we were using facemasks incorporating a breathing apparatus and radio microphone. The masks enabled us to see clearly and we could also talk to each other underwater using the radio mikes. I knew from long experience of diving on *Baywatch* that my tank always ran out of air first, so when that happened I grabbed Alex's emergency air-hose, but in order to put the regulator into my mouth I had to take off my mask and once I had done that I was completely blind. We were eighty feet down in the Pacific Ocean and I couldn't see a thing.

While I was trying to get some air into my lungs, I had stopped swimming and my flotation vest tried to take me to the surface. Worried that I would go up too quickly from that great depth, Alex grabbed hold of me. I couldn't see him and nor could I communicate with him, so we struggled. Alex was doing his best to slow down the rate of our ascent, while I was desperate for air. We fought. Alex was holding me down and I was going to drown if I didn't get some air. We broke the surface just in time. It took me a while to appreciate the fact that Alex had actually saved me from the bends.

Marine life of a different kind came into my life when I was offered a part – the only human part – in *The SpongeBob SquarePants Movie*. It took me a while to catch on to SpongeBob, his buddy Patrick the starfish, Squidward, Mr Krabs, Plankton and all the other quirky residents of Bikini Bottom. *SpongeBob* was the most watched kids' show in television history with an audience of 60 million viewers, but it hadn't occurred to me to appear as myself in the movie. I thought: 'What's the big hoopla about SpongeBob? He lives in a pineapple under the sea. So what?' I told Taylor-Ann and Hayley I wasn't sure I wanted the part.

'Oh, my God, Dad,' they said, 'you *have* to do it.'

You can't turn down a chance to be a hero to your kids, so I turned up at the beach again in red trunks and holding a surfboard to meet SpongeBob, the eternally optimistic little yellow sponge with square cardboard pants, when he comes ashore at Malibu with his dim-witted sidekick, Patrick Star, on a journey to Shell City to retrieve King Neptune's stolen crown.

'Who are you?' SpongeBob asks.

'I'm David Hasselhoff.'

'Hooray!'

SpongeBob and Patrick climb on to my back and I jet across the ocean like a hydrofoil. They had constructed a huge mechanical clone of me to film this scene, an Animatronic replica twelve feet tall and weighing 750 pounds. The hair on my head and body was actually yak hair, so I called it Hasselyak. The film's director for Nickelodeon Movies was SpongeBob's creator, Stephen Hillenburg, a CalArts alum. He and the other six writers had worked hard to maintain the SpongeBob magic, especially the little flashes of humour, like: 'You can't fool me – I listen to National Public Radio.'

The movie gave me a whole new legion of fans. At the première at the Palladium, four-year-olds were queuing up for my autograph. Kenneth Turan in the *Los Angeles Times* commented: 'David Hasselhoff, rapidly becoming something of a counterculture icon after appearing in John Waters' *A Dirty Shame*, has a key cameo playing himself.' And John Keenan of the *World-Herald* said: 'The Hasselhoff cameo is almost diabolically effective. My five-year-old spent the day after seeing the movie running around the house screaming "Hasselhoff rules!"'

Then came *Dodgeball*, where I poked fun at myself as the Dodgeball coach who speaks only in German. I was suddenly King of the Cameos. At home, however, chaos ruled. Pamela was in immense and horrible pain and had surgery after surgery on her leg, wrist and ankle. She had been a tremendous dancer and was terrified of never being able to dance again, of always limping when she walked.

After the drink-driving incident, I checked into Cirque Lodge, a rehab at Mount Timpanogos in Utah, to sort myself out. Early one morning in July 2004 I hiked to the summit. At the top was a huge waterfall. I went as close to it as I could, sat down on a rock and meditated. I felt clean inside. I called out: 'How can you not believe in God? Who invented all of this?'

My voice echoed up to a lone hawk circling above in the crystal clear air. I jumped up on a huge rock and looked across the valley. I was high up in the Wasatch Range of the Rocky Mountains, and as far as I could see there were peaks, some snow-covered, some green, some covered in mist. I cried out: 'I get it. I get it.' I was looking at my destiny. There was my journey. I said to myself: 'I'm not going to die now. I have a way to go.' It was as clear as a bell.

As I was walking down the mountain, I chuckled: 'Okay, God, I got the message. Just tell me what to do.'

Back at the lodge, I got a call from Jan McCormack: 'You've been offered the lead in *Chicago* in London.'

I smiled and looked up at the ceiling and said, 'God, you're working really fast here. Do you want me to go?'

In the morning, there was no answer. I said: 'Okay, God, I hate to put you on the spot but I need an answer here. All right, I'll get down on my knees.' I got down on my knees which I rarely do – only because I spent too long on my knees with nuns hitting me with rulers – and I said: 'What do I do here God? Just let me know.'

As I got up off my knees, a sense of complete peace and serenity swept over me.

'Have no fear. *Chicago* is the right choice – have no fear.'

'Oh my God, are you kidding me?'

I flew to London and started rehearsals at the Adelphi Theatre. I was just getting over the jet lag when my father was rushed to hospital with a heart condition. I intended to take the next flight home, but Dad called and said: 'Don't you dare leave. Stay and do the show. It's important.'

Two weeks later I opened in *Chicago* with Rebecca Thornhill as Roxie and Anita Louise Combe as Velma. I said to myself, 'God, this is your will and I have no fear.'

Nevertheless, I was freaking out backstage on my opening night. The director told me to imagine that my father was in the audience.

I walked on to the stage as Billy Flynn.

'Is everybody here? Is everybody happy?'

And I thought, 'This one's for you, Dad.'

'Hit it!'

The *Daily Mail* commented the next day, 'There he stands among the mounds of ripe-stockinged female flesh, grinding his square jaw and perfect teeth and soft-shoe-shuffle-dancing like one great flirtatious eyebrow.' Not only that – I also had 'a handsome singing voice, a combination of Burl Ives, Tom Jones and David Essex'. The reviewer gave me four out of five stars – hey, things were looking up!

One night in my dressing-room I heard the sound of chanting in the street at the back of the theatre. I looked down from the fourth floor and found a dozen David Hasselhoffs looking up at me. The guys were wearing lookalike masks and chanting, 'We love the Hoff. We love the Hoff.' I thought, 'What the hell is this?' I guess it stemmed from an article in the *Sun* newspaper, which reported that I was going to change my name to 'the Hoff' and do a rap number with Ice-T, someone I'd never met.

A few days later I went to the MTV studios to do an interview and the kids in the audience were wearing 'Don't Hassle the Hoff' T-shirts. The Hoff craze grew from there until there was worldwide traffic in Hoff pictures and Hoff memorabilia on the Internet. Everybody started calling me 'the Hoff', so I went along with it. In Spain I was 'El Hoff', in Italy, 'Don Hoff' in Russia 'Hoffski'. There were endless puns: Bravehoff, Desperate Hoffwives, Harry Hoffer, Beef Stroganhoff, Some Like It Hoff. It was harmless and seemed to give a lot of people some pleasure.

I was invited to the Cartier International Polo tournament at Windsor Great Park, where I sat in the royal box to watch Prince Harry playing for the Prince of Wales team against Hurlingham. Harry threw himself into the game and scored a goal. Afterwards, he saw me and smiled. 'I wanted to tell you how proud I was to have known your mother,' I said. He thanked me and we had our picture taken together. All I could think of was the headline in the *National Enquirer*, 'FROM REHAB TO ROYALTY'.

Back in the States, I accepted an invitation from my buddies in the charity Wheels for Humanity to fly to Vietnam on the first commercial American airliner to visit that country since the Vietnam War ended in 1975. Wheels for Humanity was founded by David Richard, a former golf equipment salesman from Wisconsin, to provide wheelchairs for people in the developing world. David discovered that thousands of wheelchairs were being dumped in landfill sites in the USA every year. From a modest start with 150 wheelchairs in 1995, he had gradually built his charity to the point where he was sending 5,000 chairs to twenty countries in 2004.

I teamed up with three Paralympic athletes who had represented the USA at the Athens Paralympic Games to take United Airlines Flight 869 from San Francisco to Ho Chi Minh City. At a press conference, I said, 'Wheels for Humanity turns desperate dreams into reality by giving hope and freedom of mobility to people around the world.' At Tan Son Nhat International Airport, we were welcomed with lotus blossoms. We handed the chairs over to children suffering from cerebral palsy. It was a small thing for me to do, but it made a world of difference to the children. I loved making people happy. Life should be about love, about being happy.

The court had sentenced me to 250 hours of community service and I dedicated my time to helping others. At a fundraising luncheon for a cerebral palsy charity, I spoke about my experiences working with sick children. Then I was asked to draw a ticket from a barrel to raffle off a new car. One of the women in the audience called out, 'Hey, pick me!' Much to everyone's surprise, the ticket I pulled out of the barrel was indeed her's.

As the winner walked slowly and painfully up on stage to say thank you, everybody started crying. 'I developed cerebral palsy ten years ago,' she said. 'My marriage was over but this charity saved it and I now have four children.' One woman couldn't restrain herself; she walked up to me and said, 'I want to touch the person who has been touched by God.'

On the strength of *Dodgeball*, Adam Sandler offered me a part in his comedy *Click*, playing his libidinous boss, John Ammer. My secretary Stacy was played by Sophie Monk, a gorgeous Australian actress and former singer with the Popstars group Bardot. Working with Adam Sandler was one of the most enjoyable experiences of my career. *Click* is about time travel and it's Adam's answer to Jimmy Stewart's 1946 classic, *It's a Wonderful Life*. It has a great message about wanting the things you have and cherishing every moment of your life.

New prospects beckoned, both on TV and film. I was feeling very positive about life when I flew to Australia to shoot a commercial for Pepsi-Cola after the Pepsi marketing manager, Tony Thomas, had been inundated with Hoff images and had decided to spend $2 million on posters and billboards across the country, featuring the Hoff pulling a giant foaming bottle of Pepsi on the end of a rope.

While I was in Australia, Hoffmania really took off. As a guest on the *Rove* chat show in Melbourne, I was given a three-minute standing ovation. According to various publications, I was 'a retro stud', 'an icon', 'a hero of sorts' and 'a buffed beachside hero', but mostly I was 'the Hoff'. It was 'Hoff!' 'Hoff!' 'Hoff!' when I sang in front of 12,000 people at Randwick Racecourse to celebrate Foxtel's tenth anniversary, and it was the same when I appeared at the ARIA Awards at the Sydney Superdome and presented trophies to Missy Higgins and Ben Lee. There was even more Hoffology when I appeared on *Australian Idol* with Mark Holden, a good buddy whom I called 'the Song Doctor' because of his work on many of my albums.

Grudgingly, the press admitted they were witnessing something a bit special. Lucy Beaumont wrote in her 'Spy' column in the Melbourne *Age*, 'His tour Down Under has gone hoff without a hitch. Spy will even forgive the former *Baywatch* star for saying on *Rove* that America is the "lifeguard of the world", such is the fever that has gripped all those in David Hasselhoff's path.' At the Superdome, Noel Mengel of the *Courier-Mail* saw people checking out the huge video screens for my arrival.

And once the unmistakable figure of The Lord of the *Baywatch* arrives in the room, all thoughts of anything as unimportant as music seem to be forgotten. Young women well used to dealing with the demands of rock stars and sorting the brown ones out of the Smarties suddenly feel the urge to do the Hoff walk, innocently teetering past his table for a closer inspection.

Back in Los Angeles, Pamela and I joined the annual Hollywood Christmas Parade, driving through the streets with Taylor-Ann in a 1933 Duesenberg tourer and smiling and waving to well wishers and talking on TV about the great family Christmas we were going to have.

For me, it was a time of great loss. Eugen Joeckel died in December and Lou Rawls passed away a few days into the New Year, both taken by cancer. Hearing I was planning an Australian concert tour, Lou had said, 'Can I open for you in Australia?'

'Lou, you're too big to open for me. You open for me and no one is gonna want to stay. They'd come to see you. You can't open my show. Come on as a guest.'

But Lou didn't make it. My marriage had collapsed and I needed to stay close to my daughters.

Pamela and I separated after sixteen years of marriage. On 12 January 2006, I filed for divorce, citing irreconcilable differences. It was a difficult decision for me to make. I loved my wife, I worshipped my children and I believed in the sanctity of marriage, but I had realised I wasn't a husband any more; I was a puppet and I was playing a part. True marriage is based on trust and when there is no trust there is no foundation to build on.

It had taken a Driving Under the Influence charge, damage to my health, embarrassment to my children and placing my career in jeopardy to realise that I couldn't save my marriage. I had tried to make Pamela feel secure and had failed, so I had medicated myself with alcohol to the point where it had nearly killed me. Now I desperately needed to save myself and to do that I had to admit complete defeat. I had to surrender to win the war.

Writing this book has been a terrific form of therapy for me. It has restored my faith in myself. It has showed me who I am and it has proved to me that the tabloid smears are just more lies in the world of show business. Like they say, you put on a good show, you get good business; you put on a bad show, they give you the business.

I hope that the reader gets out of this book some of the adventure, the fun, the humour and the sense of wonder that have accompanied me on my path through life. I hope you have learned something from my mistakes – I certainly have. I know for a fact that people like Randy Armstrong, Michael Cuccione and little Darren are angels who make the world a better place. Randy, the boy who showed me that my true purpose in life wasn't fame or money but helping less fortunate people, is still my wingman to this day. He taught me that smiling at someone or taking time to speak to them is a spiritual experience that brings its own reward. The theme of *Knight Rider* was 'One man can make a difference'. *You* can be that person, you can make a difference in someone's life, but first you must make a difference in your own life. You must save yourself before you can save anyone else.

Sometimes walking away is the hardest decision you might have to make but it is the right one. If something is not working in your life, ask God for guidance about what to do and you might not get the answer you want, but you will get the right answer. I don't know what the future holds for me and my family; that book hasn't been written yet. However, I do know that I'll always be there for Pamela and my loving children. I don't blame anybody for my problems and I'm grateful for my life today.

There is no longer any need to dress up and pretend.

This Lost Boy has been found.

As the song goes, 'I've been looking for freedom, I've been looking so long . . .' Now I've finally found it. I'll see you around. The best is yet to come.

Acknowledgements

I want to write a special thank-you to all the people who have stood behind me: Mom and Dad and the other members of my family, my friends, Jan McCormack, but most of all to Taylor-Ann and Hayley. You are Daddy's true heroes. You are the prettiest, the most honest and the strongest of God's angels. It is my quest to make you proud.

A Letter from Paul Stuart Wichansky

New Jersey
January 2006

Dear Mr Hasselhoff,

It is with pleasure that I am writing to you! Happy New Year! It was twenty-four years ago when you first inspired me with your television character, Michael Knight. The theme of *Knight Rider*, where 'one man can make a difference,' is a theme I have consistently applied to my own life. After I watched the first few episodes of your television show in 1982, I became inspired to continue visiting schools to talk about the positive perspectives and realities of growing up with my cerebral palsy. You see, for the next two decades, I never lost the passion for educating young students to become the best they can possibly be, and to share their talents with others. Though Michael Knight was a fictional person who never asked me to believe in him, he was the first television character who taught me to believe in myself and try to always come out a winner.

Since I was ten years old in 1981, I have enjoyed visiting elementary, middle and high schools to discuss the importance of disability awareness and character education. By sharing personal experiences with humour, and encouraging students to ask questions that would help positively shape their understanding of people with disabilities, I try to instil the hope, energy, and inspiration that motivates them to realise their own goals and dreams. There is no better feeling in the world than to make students smile and feel good about themselves, so the future for all of us would then look so much brighter!

Since I was unable to walk unassisted for the first seven years of my life, you might be asking – what is my special dream? Simply being able to walk like everyone else, when I was a goalie in a soccer game at ten years old, which was the first time I was able to stand for two hours on my own two feet, and my heart surged with such pride and enthusiasm for reaching that simple goal! So with intense physical and occupational therapy over the years, my leg muscles have eventually gotten stronger to the point where I am now able to walk over three miles on the treadmill every other day! Presently, I am pursuing my academic dream too, since I am a meteorologist and PhD candidate at Rutgers University. (Meteorology is the only career where you can be wrong and still keep your job!) Despite earning two degrees in meteorology and pursuing a third one, my career goal is to continue challenging students to learn more about the world around them, enabling them to discover and share with others their own gifts and talents!

An experience that helped shape my own personality was a discovery that you must be your own best friend before you can discover and truly accept the meaning of having a disability. This occurred when I was fifteen years old, during a class trip to visit the beautiful St Joseph's Cathedral in Montreal, Canada, in 1986. The leg braces and crutches covering the walls and the entire ceiling of that cathedral were left there by thousands of people who believed that their visit to the shrine cured them of their challenges. So I took my leg braces off, left them on the floor, and was able to walk down the church steps with St Joseph guiding me. My mom took my braces home with her, and I still needed to wear them for another year. But, on the very same date one year later, my orthopedist finally decided to allow me to walk without my leg braces, and I have not needed them since. For the first time in my life, I understood that the question, 'Why me?' was an unusually selfish attitude; you should be asking 'Why not me?' In other words, your challenges are not supposed to paralyze you; they are supposed to help you discover that all life is yours – to conquer, to love, to live.

For the past five years, I have been especially proud to be a member of a unique speakers bureau called A Vision in Motion. This bureau specialises in experienced motivators who have each overcome tremendous adversity and inspire others through their workshops, programmes and keynotes! Thus, I am part of a team of speakers with various backgrounds, and we smoothly work together and address different topics such as disability awareness, self-esteem enhancement, peer pressure and violence prevention, anti-bullying strategies, and other topics that help enhance the intellectual growth of our audiences. A fellow speaker, Cornelius Barker, for example, is actually a former gang member who turned his life around and became a school teacher, principal and, in fact, a school administrator! Cornelius is a truly amazing guy who has become one of my role models for his attitude and outlook on life. You can see the amazing collection of speakers we have at the website www.avisioninmotion.com

Another speaker in our bureau, Tom Malloy, is a producer/actor who has actually inspired me to write to you! (Tom provided me with your agent's address.) In October, I spoke to students at a school in southern Virginia, and Tom and I took a seven-hour road-trip from New Jersey to get to the school. Tom was the one who was driving so that I would not be tired when it came time for me to speak to the students. During this time, we talked about television shows that had inspired both of us when we were kids, and *Knight Rider* was one of them. I discovered, to my amazement, that Tom took his grandmother out for dinner every New Year's Eve, which was exactly what I used to do every year when my own grandmother was alive. And even if she passed away five years ago, she is still living inside me. For when you are reading this very letter, Mr. Hasselhoff, you are not merely reading what I am writing. My grandmother is also talking to you as I type this, because she will always be a part of me. So isn't the heart a beautiful pen with which to write memories? It's an experience I pass along to students in my discussion of the importance of role models in life.

With the mention of *Knight Rider*, I cannot forget the impact that the prototype car, KITT, had on me! For eight years, I just did not realise that I had my own KITT but it wasn't a Pontiac at all! My aim was to make other drivers smile on the highways, so I transformed my white Mercury Topaz into a M-series BMW 330Ci. I removed all of the round Mercury emblems and replaced them with BMW hood emblems, on the grille and wheels! I even looked on eBay and purchased the chrome 330Ci logo and a M-series badge (to cover up the holes on the trunk lid!). It was an amazing transformation that looked very much factory-like, and the car was in excellent cosmetic and mechanical condition.

While I was driving to one of my school programmes early one morning last year, a driver cut me off so closely that it forced me off the highway and into a guardrail at 50 m.p.h. Fortunately, I was not hurt, and the car – though totalled – was still running! So I turned the car around when the traffic was clear, and drove a quarter-mile until the shoulder opened up, pulled on to the grass, and called the state police. As they took the report for the single-car accident, I was not worried about the car at all – I simply wanted to get to the school because I wanted to make the third-graders smile. I just didn't want to let the students down if I had to cancel the programme. The state police gave me permission to continue driving slowly to the school, though the car had virtually no front-end on it! I got to the school that morning and gave the programme, but I've got to tell you that this was among the most emotionally difficult programmes that I have ever done.

This experience made me realise that life itself is a fantastic dream. There are good times and bad times as you go through life. The good times are when the sun rises in the east, and when it's high in the sky, you feel good about yourself, and everything is going your way. But there come times when the sun sets, and you go through a period of nightfall – that's anger, frustration, depression coming to the forefront. But you cannot lose sight of the future – the sun must rise again, it has to, so good times are ahead. I am thus living a fantastic dream, having new experiences each day that help me re-evaluate myself and my purpose in life. And the good thing from this accident was the fact that I took care of that pseudo-BMW for eight years – but that morning the car finally took care of me: I wasn't hurt. So, in a way, my car has also been a KITT to me.

It is my dream to own, and take care of, a KITT replica. As I am continuing to pay for my education, and also help support the speakers bureau through my programmes, my dream of owning one would need to wait. That's okay with me – we are not given dreams without also being given the power to make them come true!

Mr Hasselhoff, it is also my dream to meet you one day and personally thank you for motivating me to succeed in my personal and academic life. Perhaps on your next visit to New Jersey or the New York City area, and if your schedule permits, you are certainly welcome to attend and audit one of my disability awareness programmes. If you know teachers in southern California who may be interested in my programmes, please do not hesitate to let them know that I am eager to visit California since my first and only vacation there during the summer of 1979! (At that time, I recall seeing a huge sign for Bakersfield on the highway, and since my mom was driving, I was actually pleading with her to stop by the California Highway Patrol office so that I could meet Jon and Ponch of *CHiPs*! That television show was then very real to an eight-year-old boy!)

I encourage you to visit my personal web site below, which I have designed myself to provide information (and hopefully inspiration!) to teachers, and that describes my school awareness programmes. I have an online photo album, a curriculum vitae, and even a five-minute online streaming video showing me in action in front of young audiences! I also hope that you can take a moment to autograph my *Yes! Magazine* article on Pages 8 and 9 of the enclosed magazine – I have also enclosed another copy, this one autographed by me for your collection! You can see that I truly enjoy positively shaping the lives of others so that they can become proud of themselves. I do hope that you support my passion for educating others about disabilities and how a positive attitude can affect anyone in their lives.

Though my family and friends cannot appreciate a television show like *Knight Rider* in the same way that I do, I believe that it inspired me to take the overall theme to heart and harness its power in a way that few people can understand, or even identify with. I now look back and realise those four years may have been the most critical in helping me to develop an appreciation that my own physical challenges might be among the greatest gifts that I have received. My parents and family certainly helped a great deal and deserve special thanks, yes, but I needed some sort of personal revelation that could only come outside of the family. Your show, along with others like the *Dukes of Hazzard* and *CHiPs*, made me understand that each of us can also be heroes – in other words, ordinary people facing extraordinary circumstances – like our favourite television characters did each week. I then began to understand that I have the power to share this positive perspective with others to effectively shatter negative stereotypes, because from what I have seen, it's a negative attitude that can very well become a disability. However, if you have learned to embrace a positive attitude and enjoy interacting with others, you have the power to dream about your future and also build upon that dream.

Best wishes for a successful and productive new year!

Sincerely yours,

Paul Stuart Wichansky
pstuart@eden.rutgers.edu
www.justthewayyouare.com

Appendix II

Knight Rider

The Cast
David Hasselhoff as Michael Knight and Garthe Knight
Richard Basehart as Wilton Knight
William Daniels as the voice of KITT
Rebecca Holden as April Curtis
Patricia McPherson as Bonnie Barstow
Edward Mulhare as Devon Miles
Peter Parros as Reginald Cornelius III

The First Season
1. Knight of the Phoenix (26 September 1982)
2. Deadly Maneuvers (1 October 1982)
3. Good Day at White Rock (8 October 1982)
4. Slammin' Sammy's Stunt Spectacular (22 October 1982)
5. Just My Bill (29 October 1982)
6. Not a Drop to Drink (5 November 1982)
7. No Big Thing (12 November 1982)
8. Trust Doesn't Rust (19 November 1982)
9. Inside Out (26 November 1982)
10. The Final Verdict (3 December1982)
11. A Plush Ride (10 December 1982)
12. Forget Me Not (17 December 1982)
13. Hearts Of Stone (14 January 1983)
14. Give Me Liberty . . . or Give Me Death (21 January 1983)
15. The Topaz Connection (28 January 1983)
16. A Nice, Indecent Little Town (18 February 1983)
17. Chariot of Gold (25 February 1983)
18. White Bird (4 March 1983)
19. Knight Rider Moves (11 March 1983)
20. Nobody Does It Better (29 April 1983)
21. Short Notice (6 May 1983)

The Second Season
22. Goliath (2 October 1983)
23. Brother's Keeper (9 October 1983)
24. Merchants Of Death (16 October 1983)
25. Blind Spot (23 October 1983)
26. Return to Cadiz (30 October 1983)
27. KITT the Cat (6 November 1983)

28. Custom KITT (13 November 1983)
29. Soul Survivor (27 November 1983)
30. Ring of Fire (4 December 1983)
31. Knightmares (11 December 1983)
32. Silent Knight Rider (18 December 1983)
33. A Knight in Shining Armour (8 January 1984)
34. Diamonds Aren't a Girl's Best Friend (15 January 1984)
35. White-Line Warriors (29 January 1984)
36. Race for Life (5 February 1984)
37. Speed Demons (12 February 1984)
38. Goliath Returns (19 February 1984)
39. A Good Knight's Work (4 March 1984)
40. Mouth Of The Snake (8 April 1984)
41. Let It Be Me (13 May 1984)
42. Big Iron (27 May 1984)

The Third Season
43. Knight Rider of the Drones (30 September 1984)
44. The Ice Bandits (7 October 1984)
45. Knights of the Fast Lane (14 October 1984)
46. Halloween Knight (28 October 1984)
47. KITT vs. KARR (4 November 1984)

48. The Rotten Apples (11 November 1984)
49. Knight Rider In Disgrace (11/18 November 1984)
50. Dead of Knight (2 December 1984)
51. Lost Knight (9 December 1984)
52. Knight of the Chameleon (30 December 1984)
53. Custom Made Killer (6 January 1985)
54. Knight By a Nose (13 January 1985)
55. Junk Yard Dog (3 February 1985)
56. Buy Out (10 February 1985)
57. Knightlines (3 March 1985)
58. The Nineteenth Hole (10 March 1985)
59. Knight and Knerd (17 March 1985)
60. Ten Wheel Trouble (24 March 1985)
61. Knight in Retreat (29 March 1985)
62. Knight Strike (5 April 1985)
63. Circus Knights (5 May 1985)

The Fourth Season
64. Knight of the Juggernaut (20 September 1985)
65. KITTnap (27 September 1985)
66. Sky Knight (18 October 1985)
67. Burial Ground (25 October 1985)
68. The Wrong Crowd (1 November 1985)

69. Knight Sting (8 November 1985)
70. Many Happy Returns (15 November 1985)
71. Knight Racer (29 November 1985)
72. Knight Behind Bars (6 December 1985)
73. Knight Song (13 December 1985)
74. The Scent of Roses (3 January 1986)
75. Killer KITT (10 January 1986)
76. Out of the Woods (17 January 1986)
77. Deadly Knightshade (24 January 1986)
78. Redemption of a Champion (31 January 1986)
79. Knight of a Thousand Devils (7 February 1986)
80. Hills of Fire (14 February 1986)
81. Knight Flight to Freedom (21 February 1986)
82. Fright Knight (7 March 1986)
83. Knight of the Rising Sun (14 March 1986)
84. Voo Doo Knight (21 March 1986)

Movie

Knight Rider 2000 (1991)

At a magazine photo session with my press agent Judy Katz, aka 'The Kat' . . . always wearing black. 'The Dog' loves ya!

Appendix III

Baywatch

The Cast

David Hasselhoff as Lt/Capt. Mitch Buchannon

Krista Allen as Jenna Avid [episode 10]

Jeff Altman as Ed Symes [episodes 8–9]

Pamela Anderson as Casey Jean 'C. J.' Parker [3–7]

Marliece Andrada as Skylar 'Sky' Bergman [8]

Vanessa Angel as Megan [2]

Susan Anton as Jackie Quinn [3–5]

Pamela Bach as Kaye Morgan [2–3, 5–8]

Gregory J. Barnett as Greg Barnett [1–8]

Buzz Belmondo as Guido Torzini [2–3]

Michael Bergin as Jack 'J. D.' Darius [8]

Traci Bingham as Jordan Tate [7–8]

Yasmine Bleeth as Caroline Holden [4–8]

Annalise Braakensiek as Jeri [8]

Angelica Bridges as Lt Taylor Walsh [8]

Jason Brooks as Sean Monroe [10]

Brooke Burns as Jessica 'Jessie' Owens [9]

Brandon Call as Hobie Buchannon #1 [1]

Jennifer Campbell as Neely Capshaw Buchannon #2 [9]

David Charvet as Matthew 'Matt' Brody [3–6]

David Chokachi as Cody Madison [6–9]

Donna D'Errico as Donna Marco [7–8]

Nicole Eggert as Roberta 'Summer' Quinn [3–4]

Carmen Electra as Leilani 'Lani' McKensie [8]

Erika Eleniak as Shauni McClain [1–3]

Holly Gagnier as Gina Pomeroy [1]

Ashley Gorrell as Joey Jennings [5–6]

Erin Gray as Chief Johnson [8–9]

Jeremy Jackson as Hobie Buchannon #2 [2–9]

Richard Jaeckel as Lt Ben Edwards [2–4]

Stacy Kamano as Kekoa Tanaka [10]

Mitzi Kapture as Capt. Alexis 'Alex' Ryker [9]

Bonnie-Jill Laflin as Tina [10]

Brandy Ledford as Dawn Masterton [10]

Simone Mackinnon as Allie Reese [10]

Michael McManus as Sid Wilson [1]

Tom McTigue as Harvey Miller [2]

Wendie Malick as Gayle
Buchannon [1–5]

Jason Mamoa as Jason [10]

Monte Markham as Capt. Don
Thorpe [1–2]

Kala'i Miller as Kai [10]

Pat Morita as Mr Tanaka [10]

John Allen Nelson as John D. Cort
[1–2, 4–5]

Michael Newman as Michael
'Newmie' Newman

Gena Lee Nolin as Neely Capshaw
[6–8]

Kelly Packard as April Giminski
[8–9]

Peter Phelps as Trevor Cole [1]

Alexandra Paul as Lt Stephanie
Holden [3–7]

Jandi Swanson as Jenny, Hobie's
friend [1]

Jaason Simmons as Logan Fowler
[5–7]

Kelly Slater as Jimmy Slade [3–4]

José Solano as Manuel 'Manny'
Gutierrez [7–9]

Parker Stevenson as Craig Pomeroy
[1, 8–9]

Nancy Valen as Capt. Samantha
'Sam' Thomas [7]

Vincent Van Patten as Tom, sky
surfer [6–7]

Billy Warlock as Eddie Kramer
[1–3]

Shawn Weatherly as Jill Riley [1]

Ingrid Walters as Sheryl Whalen
[8–9]

Gregory-Alan Williams as Sgt
Garner Ellerbee [1–5]

Sherilyn Wolter as Ms Amanda
Keller, Hobie's teacher [1]

The Episodes

Pilot 1989 (NBC)

	Episode # and Title	Original Prod #	Air Date
1	0- 1 Panic at Malibu Pier (1)	1001	23 Apr 89
2	0- 2 Panic at Malibu Pier (2)	1002	23 Apr 89

The First Season 1989 (NBC)

	Episode # and Title	Original Prod #	Air Date
3	1- 1 In Deep	1003	22 Sep 89
4	1- 2 Heat Wave	1004	29 Sep 89
5	1- 3 Second Wave	1005	13 Oct 89
6	1- 4 Message in a Bottle	1006	20 Oct 89
7	1- 5 The Sky is Falling	1007	27 Oct 89

	Episode # and Title		Original Prod #	Air Date
8	1- 6	The Drowning Pool	1008	3 Nov 89
9	1- 7	Rookie School	1009	10 Nov 89
10	1- 8	Cruise Ship	1011	24 Nov 89
11	1- 9	The Cretin of the Shallows	1010	1 Dec 89
12	1-10	Shelter Me	1012	8 Dec 89
13	1-11	The Reunion	1013	15 Dec 89
14	1-12	Armored Car	1014	5 Jan 90
15	1-13	Home Cort	1015	12 Jan 90
16	1-14	We Need a Vacation	1016	26 Jan 90
17	1-15	Muddy Waters	1017	2 Feb 90
18	1-16	Snake Eyes	1018	9 Feb 90
19	1-17	Eclipse	1019	23 Feb 90
20	1-18	Shark Derby	1020	2 Mar 90
21	1-19	The Big Race	1021	16 Mar 90
22	1-20	Old Friends	1022	30 Mar 90
23	1-21	The End?	1023	6 Apr 90

The Second Season 1991 (hereafter syndicated)

	Episode # and Title		Original Prod #	Air Date
24	2- 1	The One That Got Away	2008	5 Oct 91
25	2- 2	Money, Honey	2004	12 Oct 91
26	2- 3	The Fabulous Buchannon Boys	2006	19 Oct 91
27	2- 4	Point of Attack	2010	26 Oct 91
28	2- 5	Sandcastles	2012	2 Nov 91
29	2- 6	Thin or Die	2009	9 Nov 91
30	2- 7	The Trophy (1)	2003	16 Nov 91
31	2- 8	The Trophy (2)	2020	23 Nov 91
32	2- 9	If Looks Could Kill	2011	30 Nov 91
33	2-10	Nightmare Bay (1)	2001	7 Dec 91
34	2-11	Nightmare Bay (2)	2002	14 Dec 91
35	2-12	Reunion	2007	1 Feb 92
36	2-13	War of Nerves	2017	8 Feb 92
37	2-14	Big Monday	2016	15 Feb 92
38	2-15	Sea of Flames	2014	22 Feb 92

	Episode # and Title	Original Prod #	Air Date
39	2-16 Now Sit Right Back and You'll Hear a Tale	2019	29 Feb 92
40	2-17 The Chamber	2013	7 Mar 92
41	2-18 Shark's Cove	2021	25 Apr 92
42	2-19 The Lost Treasure of Tower 12	2022	2 May 92
43	2-20 The Big Spill	2018	9 May 92
44	2-21 Game of Chance	2015	16 May 92
45	2-22 Summer of '85	2023	23 May 92

Special Documentary

	Episode # and Title	Original Prod #	Air Date
	S- 1 Baywatch Summerfest Special		13 Sep 92

The Third Season 1992

	Episode # and Title	Original Prod #	Air Date
46	3- 1 River of No Return (1)	3001	20 Sep 92
47	3- 2 River of No Return (2)	3002	20 Sep 92
48	3- 3 Tequila Bay	3004	27 Sep 92
49	3- 4 Rookie of the Year	3003	4 Oct 92
50	3- 5 Pier Pressure	3005	11 Oct 92
51	3- 6 Showdown at Malibu Beach High	3012	18 Oct 92
52	3- 7 Point Doom	3009	25 Oct 92
53	3- 8 Princess of Tides	3008	1 Nov 92
54	3- 9 Masquerade	3011	8 Nov 92
55	3-10 Lifeguards Can't Jump	3010	15 Nov 92
56	3-11 Dead of Summer	3006	22 Nov 92
57	3-12 A Matter of Life and Death	3007	10 Jan 93
58	3-13 Island of Romance	3015	17 Jan 93
59	3-14 Strangers Among Us	3019	24 Jan 93
60	3-15 Vacation (1)	3013	31 Jan 93
61	3-16 Vacation (2)	3014	7 Feb 93
62	3-17 The Tower	3024	14 Feb 93

	Episode # and Title	Original Prod #	Air Date
63	3-18 Stakeout at Surfrider Beach	3018	21 Feb 93
64	3-19 Shattered (1)	3017	25 Apr 93
65	3-20 Shattered (2)	3023	2 May 93
66	3-21 Kicks	3020	9 May 93
67	3-22 Fatal Exchange	3021	16 May 93

The Fourth Season 1993

	Episode # and Title	Original Prod #	Air Date
68	4- 1 Race Against Time (1)	4001	25 Sep 93
69	4- 2 Race Against Time (2)	4002	25 Sep 93
70	4- 3 Lover's Cove	4004	2 Oct 93
71	4- 4 Blindside	4008	9 Oct 93
72	4- 5 Sky Rider	4010	16 Oct 93
73	4- 6 Tentacles (1)	4016	23 Oct 93
74	4- 7 Tentacles (2)	4023	30 Oct 93
75	4- 8 Submersion	4020	6 Nov 93
76	4- 9 Ironman Buchannon	4003	13 Nov 93
77	4-10 Tower of Power	4007	20 Nov 93
78	4-11 The Child Inside	4015	27 Nov 93
79	4-12 Second Time Around	4066	22 Jan 94
80	4-13 The Red Knights	4005	29 Jan 94
81	4-14 Coronado del Soul (1)	4011	5 Feb 94
82	4-15 Coronado del Soul (2)	4012	12 Feb 94
83	4-16 Mirror, Mirror	4018	19 Feb 94
84	4-17 The Falcon Manifesto	4025	26 Feb 94
85	4-18 Rescue Bay	4019	5 Mar 94
86	4-19 Western Exposure	4028	30 Apr 94
87	4-20 The Life You Save	4024	7 May 94
88	4-21 Trading Places	4017	14 May 94
89	4-22 Guys and Dolls	4021	21 May 94

The Fifth Season 1994

	Episode # and Title	Original Prod #	Air Date
90	5- 1 Living on the Fault Line (1)	5001	1 Oct 94
91	5- 2 Living on the Fault Line (2)	5002	8 Oct 94

	Episode # and Title		Original Prod #	Air Date
92	5- 3	Aftershock	5003	15 Oct 94
93	5- 4	Baja Run	5004	22 Oct 94
94	5- 5	Air Buchannon	5005	29 Oct 94
95	5- 6	Short-Sighted	5006	5 Nov 94
96	5- 7	Someone to Baywatch Over You	5007	12 Nov 94
97	5- 8	KGAS, The Groove-Yard of Solid Gold	5009	19 Nov 94
98	5- 9	Red Wind	5015	26 Nov 94
99	5-10	I Spike	5008	3 Dec 94
100	5-11	Silent Night, Baywatch Night (1)	5011	10 Dec 94
101	5-12	Silent Night, Baywatch Night (2)	5012	17 Dec 94
102	5-13	Rubber Ducky	5010	4 Feb 95
103	5-14	Homecoming [same title as episode 164]	5022	11 Feb 95
104	5-15	Seize the Day	5018	18 Feb 95
105	5-16	A Little Help	5019	25 Feb 95
106	5-17	Father's Day	5014	4 Mar 95
107	5-18	Fire with Fire	5021	29 Apr 95
108	5-19	Deep Trouble	5013	6 May 95
109	5-20	Promised Land	5017	13 May 95
110	5-21	The Runaways	5020	20 May 95
111	5-22	Wet and Wild	5016	27 May 95

The Sixth Season 1995

	Episode # and Title		Original Prod #	Air Date
112	6- 1	Trapped Beneath The Sea (1)	6003	30 Sep 95
113	6- 2	Trapped Beneath The Sea (2)	6004	7 Oct 95
114	6- 3	Hot Stuff	6008	14 Oct 95
115	6- 4	Surf's Up	6005	21 Oct 95
116	6- 5	To Everything There Is a Season	6007	28 Oct 95
117	6- 6	Leap of Faith	6002	4 Nov 95
118	6- 7	Face of Fear	6001	11 Nov 95

	Episode # and Title	Original Prod #	Air Date
119	6- 8 Hit and Run	6009	18 Nov 95
120	6- 9 Home Is Where the Heat Is	6020	25 Nov 95
121	6-10 Sweet Dreams	6017	2 Dec 95
122	6-11 The Incident	6014	20 Jan 96
123	6-12 Beauty and the Beast	6006	3 Feb 96
124	6-13 Desperate Encounter	6018	10 Feb 96
125	6-14 Baywatch Angels	6019	17 Feb 96
126	6-15 Bash at the Beach	6015	24 Feb 96
127	6-16 Free Fall	5023	2 Mar 96
128	6-17 Sail Away	6011	23 Mar 96
129	6-18 Lost and Found	6010	30 Mar 96
130	6-19 Forbidden Paradise (1)	5024	27 Apr 96
131	6-20 Forbidden Paradise (2)	5025	4 May 96
132	6-21 The Last Wave	6016	11 May 96
133	6-22 Go for the Gold	6012	18 May 96

The Seventh Season 1996

	Episode # and Title	Original Prod #	Air Date
134	7- 1 Shark Fever	7004	28 Sep 96
135	7- 2 The Contest	7011	5 Oct 96
136	7- 3 Liquid Assets	7001	12 Oct 96
137	7- 4 Windswept	7010	19 Oct 96
138	7- 5 Scorcher	7012	26 Oct 96
139	7- 6 Beach Blast	7019	2 Nov 96
140	7- 7 Guess Who's Coming to Dinner	7021	9 Nov 96
141	7- 8 Let the Games Begin	7013	16 Nov 96
142	7- 9 Buried	7006	23 Nov 96
143	7-10 Search and Rescue	7024	18 Jan 97
144	7-11 Heal the Bay	7017	1 Feb 97
145	7-12 Bachelor of the Month	7002	8 Feb 97
146	7-13 Chance of a Lifetime	7005	15 Feb 97
147	7-14 Talk Show	7007	22 Feb 97
148	7-15 Life-Guardian	7022	1 Mar 97
149	7-16 Matters of the Heart	7023	8 Mar 97
150	7-17 Rendezvous	7014	12 Apr 97
151	7-18 Hot Water	7008	19 Apr 97

	Episode # and Title		Original Prod #	Air Date
152	7-19	Trial by Fire	7015	26 Apr 97
153	7-20	Golden Girls	7020	3 May 97
154	7-21	Nevermore	7018	10 May 97
155	7-22	Leo's Last Chance [aka Baywatch at Sea World]	7016	17 May 97

The Eighth Season 1997

	Episode # and Title		Original Prod #	Air Date
156	8- 1	Rookie Summer (1)	8001	27 Sep 97
157	8- 2	Next Generation (2)	8015	4 Oct 97
158	8- 3	The Choice	8002	11 Oct 97
159	8- 4	Memorial Day	8003	18 Oct 97
160	8- 5	Charlie	8005	25 Oct 97
161	8- 6	Lifeguard Confidential	8004	1 Nov 97
162	8- 7	Out of the Blue	8007	8 Nov 97
163	8- 8	Eel Nino	8008	15 Nov 97
164	8- 9	Homecoming [same title as episode 103]	8009	22 Nov 97
165	8-10	Missing	8021	29 Nov 97
166	8-11	Hijacked	8011	6 Dec 97
167	8-12	No Way Out	8019	31 Jan 98
168	8-13	Countdown	8016	7 Feb 98
169	8-14	Surf City	8024	14 Feb 98
170	8-15	To the Max (1)	8006	21 Feb 98
171	8-16	Night of the Dolphin (2)	8014	28 Feb 98
172	8-17	Full Throttle	8010	7 Mar 98
173	8-18	Quarantine	8018	25 Apr 98
174	8-19	Diabolique	8022	2 May 98
175	8-20	The Wedding: Bon Voyage (1)	8023	9 May 98
176	8-21	The Wedding: White Thunder at Glacier Bay (2)	8012	16 May 98
177	8-22	The Wedding: White Thunder at Glacier Bay (3)	8013	23 May 98

The Ninth Season 1998

	Episode # and Title	Original Prod #	Air Date
178	9- 1 Crash (1)	9001	26 Sep 98
179	9- 2 Crash (2)	9004	3 Oct 98
180	9- 3 Sharks, Lies & Video- tape	9005	10 Oct 98
181	9- 4 Dolphin Quest	9009	17 Oct 98
182	9- 5 The Natural	9010	24 Oct 98
183	9- 6 Drop Zone	9008	31 Oct 98
184	9- 7 Hot Summer Night	9002	7 Nov 98
185	9- 8 Swept Away	9011	14 Nov 98
186	9- 9 The Swimmer	9014	21 Nov 98
187	9-10 Friends Forever	9015	28 Nov 98
188	9-11 The Edge	9013	19 Dec 98
189	9-12 The Big Blue	9003	16 Jan 99
190	9-13 Come Fly with Me	9016	23 Jan 99
191	9-14 Boys Will Be Boys	9012	6 Feb 99
192	9-15 Grand Prix	9017	13 Feb 99
193	9-16 Baywatch Down Under (1)	9021	20 Feb 99
194	9-17 Baywatch Down Under (2)	9022	27 Feb 99
195	9-18 Waterdance	9007	27 Mar 99
196	9-19 Double Jeopardy	9006	1 May 99
197	9-20 Wave Rage	9018	8 May 99
198	9-21 Galaxy Girls	9019	15 May 99
199	9-22 Castles in the Sand	9020	22 May 99

The Tenth Season 1999 (hereafter Baywatch Hawaii)

	Episode # and Title	Original Prod #	Air Date
200	10- 1 Aloha Baywatch (1)	2101	25 Sep 99
201	10- 2 Mahalo, Hawaii (2)	2119	2 Oct 99
202	10- 3 Weak Link	2107	9 Oct 99
203	10- 4 Shark Island	2109	16 Oct 99
204	10- 5 Strike Team	2106	23 Oct 99
205	10- 6 Sunday in Kauai	2114	30 Oct 99
206	10- 7 Risk to Death	2121	6 Nov 99
207	10- 8 Father of the Groom	2113	13 Nov 99
208	10- 9 The Hunt	2115	20 Nov 99

	Episode # and Title	Original Prod #	Air Date
209	10-10 Gold from the Deep	2104	27 Nov 99
210	10-11 Bent	2122	11 Dec 99
211	10-12 Path of Least Resistance [aka Fire Up Above]	2103	18 Dec 99
212	10-13 Liquid Visions	2124	22 Jan 00
213	10-14 Lines in the Sand	2123	5 Feb 00
214	10-15 The Hero	2105	12 Feb 00
215	10-16 Thunder Tide	2102	19 Feb 00
216	10-17 Breath of Life	2118	26 Feb 00
217	10-18 Big Island Heat	2120	18 Mar 00
218	10-19 Maui Xterra	2117	29 Apr 00
219	10-20 Baywatch O'Hana	2116	6 May 00
220	10-21 Last Rescue	2112	13 May 00
221	10-22 Killing Machine	2111	20 May 00

The Eleventh Season 2000

	Episode # and Title	Original Prod #	Air Date
222	11- 1 Soul Survivor	3101	7 Oct 00
223	11- 2 A Knife in the Heart	3102	14 Oct 00
224	11- 3 Bad Boyz	3103	21 Oct 00
225	11- 4 Dangerous Games	3104	28 Oct 00
226	11- 5 Stone Cold	3105	4 Nov 00
227	11- 6 Broken Promises	3106	11 Nov 00
228	11- 7 Dream Girl	3107	18 Nov 00
229	11- 8 The Cage	3108	25 Nov 00
230	11- 9 Ben	3109	2 Dec 00
231	11-10 Ties That Bind	3110	9 Dec 00
232	11-11 Black Widow	3111	16 Dec 00
233	11-12 Ex Files	3112	3 Feb 01
234	11-13 The Stalker	3114	10 Feb 01
235	11-14 Father Faust	3116	17 Feb 01
236	11-15 A Good Man in a Storm	3117	24 Feb 01
237	11-16 My Father the Hero	3118	3 Mar 01
238	11-17 Boiling Point	3113	7 Apr 01
239	11-18 The Return of Jessie	3115	21 Apr 01
240	11-19 Trapped	3119	28 Apr 01
241	11-20 Dead Reckoning	3120	5 May 01
242	11-21 Makapu'u Lighthouse	3121	12 May 01
243	11-22 Rescue Me	3122	19 May 01

Reunion Movie 2003

	Episode # and Title	Original Prod #	Air Date
R-1	Hawaiian Wedding (2 hours)		28 Feb 03

NOTE: The *Baywatch* pilot and all two-hour specials count as two episodes in this list.

My thanks to Danny McBride for his friendship over the years and for his artistic contributions to this book. Check out his paintings on www.whiterockgallery.com

Appendix IV

Filmography, with role

Click! (2006) . . . John Ammer

Dodgeball (2004) . . . German coach

A Crying Shame (2003) . . . Himself

Don't Call Me Tonto (2003) . . . Clint Northern

Baywatch: Hawaiian Wedding (2003) TV . . . Mitch Buchannon

Shaka Zulu: The Citadel (2001) TV mini-series . . . Mungo Prentice

Layover (2001) . . . Dan Morrison

Jekyll and Hyde: The Musical (2001) DVD of Broadway stage show . . . Dr Henry Jekyll/Mr Edward Hyde

One True Love (2000) TV . . . Mike Grant

Legacy (1999) DVD . . . Jack Scott

Nick Fury: Agent of S.H.I.E.L.D. (1998) TV . . . Colonel Nicholas 'Nick' Joseph Fury

Baywatch: White Thunder at Glacier Bay (1998) Video . . . Mitch Buchannon

Gridlock (1996) TV . . . Jake Gorski

Baywatch Nights (1995) TV series . . . Mitch Buchannon

Baywatch: Forbidden Paradise (1995) Video . . . Mitch Buchannon

Avalanche (1994) (TV) . . . Duncan Snyder

The Bulkin Trail (1992) TV . . . Michael Bulkin

Ring of the Musketeers (1992) TV . . . John Smith D'Artagnan

Baywatch: River of No Return (1992) TV . . . Mitch Buchannon

Baywatch Summerfest Special (1992) TV . . . Mitch Buchannon

Knight Rider 2000 (1991) TV . . . Michael Knight

The Final Alliance (1990) Video . . . Will Colton

Bail Out aka *W.B., Blue and the Bean* (1989) Video . . . White Bread

Baywatch (1989) TV series . . . Lt/Capt. Mitch Buchannon

Fire and Rain (1989) TV . . . Dr Dan Meyer

Baywatch: Panic at Malibu Pier (1989) TV . . . Mitch Buchannon

Zärtliche Chaoten II (1988) . . . Alexander Trutz von Rhein

Witchery (1988) . . . Gary

Perry Mason: The Case of the Lady in the Lake (1988) TV . . . Billy Travis

Starke Zeiten (1988)

Bridge Across Time (1985) TV . . . Don Gregory

The Cartier Affair (1984) TV . . . Curt Taylor

Knight Rider (1982) TV . . . Michael Knight

Knight Rider (1982) TV series . . . Michael Knight (alias of Police Detective Michael Arthur Long)

Semi-Tough (1980) TV series . . . Shake Tiller

Star Crash (1979) . . . Prince Simon

Pleasure Cove (1979) TV . . . Scott

Revenge of the Cheerleaders (1976) . . . Boner (first movie appearance)

Griffin and Phoenix: A Love Story (1976) . . . Walk-on role (first TV movie appearance)

The Young and the Restless (1976–1982) TV series . . . William 'Snapper' Foster

Appendix V

Discography

Singles

I Get The Message / Piece of Cake

Our First Night Together (Remix)

Les Kids De K.I.T.T. / Stay (with Julie)

Looking for Freedom

Lonely Is the Night

Torero – Te Quiero

Is Everybody Happy?

Flying on the Wings of Tenderness

Song of the Night

Je t'aime Means I Love You

Crazy for You

Are You Still in Love with Me?

Freedom for the World

Let's Dance Tonight

Do the Limbo Dance

Gypsy Girl

Casablanca

Hands Up for Rock 'n' Roll

Everybody Sunshine

The Girl Forever

Darling I Love You

Dance Dance d'Amoure

If I Could Only Say Goodbye

Wir zwei allein (with Gwen)

Au Ciel, Une Étoile (with Nadége Trapon)

The Best Is Yet to Come / Hot Shot City

Summer of Love

Pingu Dance

Du

I Believe (with Laura Branigan)

Looking for Freedom – The Oliver Lieb Remix

Hooked on a Feeling

More Than Words Can Say (with Egine Velasquez)

Looking for Freedom (Remixes 2000)

Promotional singles

Night Rocker

Do You Love Me?

Life Is Mostly Beautiful With You

Looking for Freedom (Picture Disc)

Rockin' the Night Away

Fallin' in Love (Picture Disc)

Albums

Night Rocker

Night Rocker (incl. Medley and Remix)

Lovin' Feelings

Knight Lover – 18 Greatest Hits

Looking for Freedom

Crazy for You

David

Everybody Sunshine

You Are Everything (incl. A Star Looks Down Tonight)

You Are Everything (incl. Wir zwei allein)

Miracle of Love

Du

David Hasselhoff

Looking for . . .THE BEST!

Hooked on a Feeling

Hooked on a Feeling (incl. Heyla-Heyla)

Hooked on a Feeling (Swiss version with intro)

Hooked on a Feeling (gold edition with Helena Vondrácková)

More Than Words Can Say (Asian version / Asiatische Version)

Looking For Freedom (incl. Looking for Freedom, remix 2000)

David Hasselhoff Sings America

Other longplay releases

Baywatch-Soundtrack 1993

Baywatch-Soundtrack 1994

Patricia Payee: Time Of My Life (incl. duet: If I Had the Time of My Life)

Videos

David Hasselhoff and the Night Rockers Live in Concert

Best of . . . David Hasselhoff

David Hasselhoff Live – Freedom Tour

Behind the Scenes (documentary)

Backstage Baywatch (documentary)

Jekyll and Hyde (Broadway musical)

Live and Forever